LEAVES FROM THE
AFRICAN JUNGLE

LEAVES FROM THE AFRICAN JUNGLE

The Life Story of Robert Crawford Allison

with Lois Fleming

JOHN RITCHIE LTD
CHRISTIAN PUBLICATIONS

40 Beansburn, Kilmarnock, Scotland

ISBN 0 946351 87 2

Copyright © 1999 by John Ritchie Ltd.
40 Beansburn, Kilmarnock, Scotland

Illustrations:
Cover, frontispiece, scenes on pp.12, 96, 99, 129, 140, 162, 204, 219, 229, 262; also cameos on pp.45, 112, 121: from original paintings by African artists supplied by courtesy of Medical Missionary News.
    Other photographs throughout by R.C. Allison (supplied by courtesy of Mr. David Allison.)

Typeset by John Ritchie Ltd., Kilmarnock
Printed by Bell & Bain Ltd., Glasgow

Contents

Prologue

The following story is about a man who was uniquely qualified by the Lord Jesus Christ to carry the gospel to various tribes in central southern Africa. Having left high school at the age of fourteen, most observers would pronounce Bobby Allison as uneducated and unfit for the mission field. However, never was the adage "whomsoever God calls He equips" more true and meaningful than it was in this case.

My father's focus on the mission field was evident by the time he reached his early teens. This burning desire made him leave the 'Needed Truth' assemblies to fellowship with the believers at the Evangelistic Hall in Galston, Ayrshire, Scotland. He never forgot his roots. Although he was so long in Africa, Scotland was always referred to as "home". I can recall the emotional time when in August 1954 he and mother were leaving to go back "home" on furlough. Many of the believers in the Chokwe and Afrikaans assemblies literally wept as they said good-bye and sang in Chokwe, "God be with you till we meet again". Although I was only thirteen years old, I came to appreciate the deep mutual love between Mum and Dad and those whom they had won for Christ.

Sometimes Dad was larger than life. But how could such a wee man accomplish so much? Where did he get his energy even when plagued with severe illness for many years? Indeed, in retrospect I cannot recall a father who was physically well. In 1960 my older brother, Kenneth, got married in Ayr and the family sent me a photograph of the wedding party. I searched in vain to recognise my Dad. Where was he? Yes, he was there, but his illness had so changed his appearance during my two years absence to finish high school that I did not recognise him in the photograph. Yet, the Lord was still able to use him for another nineteen years and through him opened the door of the gospel in many parts of Southern

Rhodesia (modern Zimbabwe), Malawi, Mozambique and Botswana.

Although Mother did not develop the linguistic skills of my father, she had her unique role to support her husband and bring up her family under the Word of God. Her quiet disposition betrayed a rugged determination to stick to the truths of Scripture and not give up when faced with unbelievable difficulties and dangers. Only the Lord knows the loneliness of those days in Angola living with a husband so often on the verge of death and having no one to talk to. Then, when he was well enough to travel, she experienced the loneliness of being left behind at the mission station. Yet, through it all, the Lord used that unconquerable Scottish spirit to pull her through and be the perfect help meet for her husband. Scotland doesn't produce any braver women. After Dad's passing, Mum retired to Scotland with a deep desire to see her own brother baptised and in fellowship in the Galston assembly. The Lord fulfilled her wish and then took her to her eternal home on May 22, 1996.

There are many folk who need to be thanked for their unfailing support of Mum and Dad over more than forty-four years of service for the Master. It is not possible to mention them all. Dad has paid tribute to some. But I would mention his dearest colleague, George Wiseman, who must surely be the unsung hero of assembly missionary work in Angola. Now in his ninety second year, "Uncle George" as I affectionately know him, was mightily used of the Lord to pioneer the gospel in north-eastern Angola. His gracious spirit coupled with his knowledge of New Testament church principles have left an indelible impression on African believers.

This book is essentially a collection of Dad's writings. If they are a little incohesive, that is due to their being written after a severe illness in 1969 that left him speechless for a week. My sister, Helen, typed the first manuscripts which Dad had written in the third person because he really didn't like autobiographies. Then I gave the manuscripts to Mrs. Fay Smart who at that time was serving the Lord with her husband, John, at Emmaus Bible School, in Oak Park, Illinois, USA. Mrs. Smart was able to "clean them up", and later Lois Fleming did a great job of rewriting the entire manuscript as an autobiography. Her father, Kenneth C. Fleming, who himself served the Lord with his wife, Helena, in South Africa, was able to do further extensive revision and editing. Finally, I am indebted to Dr. Bert Cargill of Scotland for the final revision and to John Ritchie, Ltd. for publishing what you are about to read.

This book is designed to record the faithfulness of our great God and Saviour to a missionary couple and their family through difficult days of pioneering the gospel in Africa. It is also my hope and prayer that some young believer, after having read this book, will dedicate his or her life to serve the Lord as Bobby and Meg did in the "train of His triumph".

David M. Allison
Dubuque, Iowa, USA
November, 1998

Perspective

Historical Context of the Ministry of Crawford Allison

Many of our readers will be surprised to learn that the entrance of the gospel to north eastern Angola in west-central Africa occurred little more than one lifetime ago. Crawford Allison joined the first generation of missionaries in that part of the world, yet he is also our contemporary.

The 'Light' first dawned on Central Africa after the exploratory trips of David Livingstone in the nineteenth century. When he was presumed lost, an American journalist, Henry Stanley, mounted an expedition to search for him. In November 1871, he found him at Ujiji on the shores of Lake Tanganyika and greeted him with the now famous line, "Dr. Livingstone, I presume!" When the impact of Stanley's book *Through the Dark Continent* was added to the powerful appeals of Livingstone himself, literally hundreds of new missionaries gave themselves to bring the light of the gospel to Africa.

Livingstone crossed Angola from east to west in 1855 along the infamous slave route. Home in Scotland a little later, his appeal to a school in Hamilton, near his native Blantyre, fired the imagination of at least one schoolboy, Fred Stanley Arnot. F S Arnot became the pioneer missionary in that area from the assemblies. After his first furlough in 1889, he took with him a group of missionary recruits which included Dan Crawford (another Scot) and Fred Lane. Both of these men touched the career of Crawford Allison. Of Dan Crawford's influence you will read later. As for Fred Lane, through him Ernest Wilson from Belfast was called to serve in Angola, and in turn in 1930 God used him to interest Crawford Allison in the unreached areas to the north-east.

Crawford Allison arrived in Angola in 1935 and two years later was joined by Margaret Haggerty who became his wife. They served God there until 1960 when they moved to a new field of service in Zimbabwe. Crawford proved to be a capable teacher of the Word of God, an excellent linguist, and a perceptive student of African culture. With his colleague George Wiseman, he pioneered with the gospel among several tribes in north-eastern Angola where literally tens of thousands of Africans have since come to Christ, forming hundreds of assemblies which exist there today. He played an important part in bringing the Light to an area where darkness had reigned until very recently. He was called home to glory in 1979 at the age of sixty eight. From him we have much to learn.

Ken Fleming
July 1998

CHAPTER 1

Terror in the Night

"Thou shalt not be afraid for the terror by night ... nor for the
pestilence that walketh in darkness"
(Psalm 91.5a,6a)

"Shoo! Shoo! Shoo!" Margaret yelled at the pigs rooting and snorting and causing havoc in our garden. They happened to be the chief's pigs, but three times already they had invaded the garden, destroying the vegetables she was raising as the mainstay of our diet in the wilds of Angola. Now here were those pigs yet again!

The chief's village lay only a few miles from the mission compound. This man was not only chief, but the local witchdoctor, which gave him immense power over all the people in the district. He had despised and rejected the gospel, and he made these feelings very clear each time any believers visited his village. I had warned the chief that if he didn't keep his pigs out of our garden I would have to shoot them because of the damage they were doing! My usual tolerance of such hazards and the acceptability of the local rights and privileges of pigs and their chief were becoming very strained in this instance!

A few days had passed, and the chief showed no sign of controlling his wandering and destructive animals. There they were again rooting up our vegetables! So, true to my word, I got my gun and shot one as I had told him I would. And off I went to let him know that he now had a pig's carcass with a .303 bullet lodged in it, ready for him to prepare into a feast for his household!

"*Moyo, Mwane* (good day, sir)" I said, and sat down to talk, since it is very impolite to stand while others are seated, thus making oneself higher than they are. The chief listened to me with growing anger, glared at me, then he flew into a great rage.

"My pigs can roam wherever they like!" he shouted. "And I will have my revenge on you! My witchcraft cannot touch you, but I will get revenge. I will call the lions to kill your cattle. I say, my pigs can go where they like!"

Immediately a verse of Scripture came to mind, "He that is begotten of God...that wicked one toucheth him not."(1 John 5.18) This verse was to become a real comfort to Margaret and me. We did keep a few cows at the mission for milk, and they were important to us, but for the present we laughed at the chief's threats, forgetting the terrible power of Satan. Life on a mission station is hectic, and we soon forgot the incident.

* * *

Late one Saturday evening we returned home from a prayer meeting, uplifted in spirit from communion with the Lord and His people but exhausted in body and mind, and we went right to bed. It was the hot season just before the rains came. The humidity was uncomfortably high so we left the bedroom doors wide open. At midnight we both suddenly awoke at the same time, sensing danger in the blackness of the bedroom. I fumbled under my pillow for my torch only to discover that the batteries were dead. My rifle stood in the opposite corner of the room, well out of reach. Slowly we sat up, hardly daring to breathe. When our eyes became accustomed to the darkness we made out the shapes of two fully grown lions standing with their noses poking the gauze curtain that hung in the open door, only a few feet away.

"Don't move," I whispered to Margaret. Move? she thought! We were both well and truly bed-fast and unmoveable! I knew it would be sheer folly to shoot even if I could reach my rifle, for at best I would probably wound only one of the lions and then we'd be in worse danger. The lions stared at us a moment longer - but it seemed a long moment - then each gave a great yawn and a grunt, then they turned and vanished into the darkness. I got up and hastily closed the door, and shoved heavy boxes against it, but neither of us slept again that night.

Early in the morning I went outside to find all eight of our cows dead. Seven had only marks on them where the lions had jumped on their backs and broken their necks. The eighth had been dragged about five hundred yards into the thick jungle where the lions had eaten half of it. As I stood and stared at my dead cows, who should saunter by but the witchdoctor chief. He said with a smirk on his broad face, "*Ngana* (my African name meaning Mr.), did I not tell you that my witchcraft would never reach you, but I would call the lions and they would kill your cattle?" I had to hang my head and pray to my God at that moment of seeming defeat. Looking up again at this fine but arrogant African chief I said, "Chief, our God has not yet had the last word. This is only the beginning."

The male lion returned the following night and again feasted on the cow which the pair had dragged into the jungle. The Africans in the area were aghast at the apparent power of the witchdoctor, and fear gripped all in the neighbourhood. For days an awful pall of spiritual darkness and evil seemed to hang over us in our mission station. We had never experienced anything like this before. Here we were, deep in the Angolan jungle all alone. We had come with the sole purpose of bringing the gospel of Jesus Christ to animistic tribespeople, far from civilisation. Was this going to ruin everything that had been accomplished up till now? In the eyes of the Africans the Evil One had conquered. The gospel must mean nothing to them now. Margaret and I ourselves could not shake off the horrible feeling of being surrounded by evil spirits. We recalled again the verse in 1 John 5.18 "...that wicked one toucheth him not." Had he touched? Surely not! The story had not yet ended. We were "cast down, but not destroyed" (2 Corinthians 4.9).

* * *

Some time before all this, I had started a work preaching the gospel among Boer gamehunters, white, Afrikaans-speaking men of Dutch descent. Eighteen of them had turned to Christ, were baptised and received into assembly fellowship. When they got to hear what had happened, they set off right away and trekked through the forest to the mission compound to protect us. Since they faced lions in the forest continually, these men were virtually fearless. Using their hunter's skill and ingenuity they secured a loaded rifle in a trap baited with a dead cow, tying a string to the trigger. When the lion returned the next night, unsuspectingly he pulled the string and tripped the trigger. A bullet ripped into his heart, he stumbled several hundred yards, and fell over, dead.

Not knowing how really successful the trap had been, in the morning I set off with the hunters and a group of local people to track the lion, thinking it might still be alive. Several Africans climbed trees to see the narrow path ahead, as the grass was ten feet tall and could easily hide a lion. After we had gone part of the way the Africans turned to me and said, "Look, Ngana, you are our father; you brought us to the Saviour. We do not want any harm to come to you. It's so dangerous tracking a lion in this jungle; please go home and wait for us." I had no choice but to return home as they asked, and wait.

Of course there was great joy when the hunters discovered that their clever trap had worked perfectly, and it took eight strong men to carry the great beast back to the compound, where they arrived on a Sunday. Villagers soon converged on the mission from miles around, bearing clubs. With great gusto they beat the dead lion shouting, "Take that, and that, and that!"

For a few days we enjoyed peace, but then the lioness returned with another husband! She prowled round and round the compound, always just out of range of my rifle. In one week she killed and ate five women as they were on their way down to the river to draw water. For a whole year lions threatened and attacked the mission, and all meetings at night had to be cancelled. Only daytime meetings were possible under such dangerous circumstances. We took precautions and we prayed and we waited.

* * *

One day at the end of that long year I was out on the veranda of the house I'd built, working steadily with my hands but feeling sad at heart. Suddenly I saw a shadow and looked up to see none other than the witchdoctor chief standing there! Had he come again to make more threats to try to drive us from this land to which God had called us?

But soon I saw that the chief bore a different demeanour. A bundle lay at his feet and his once arrogant and haughty eyes were downcast. We exchanged greetings as normal and then he said slowly, "Ngana, I have come today to get forgiveness from your God for what I have done." I stared at him without saying a word.

"Yes," he said, "I want forgiveness. You came to my village and told us about Jesus the Saviour of all people, but I hated you and your message. I often tried the power of my witchcraft against you. But God has spoken to me. Now I see and know that He is the true God, and now I want to get rid of all my witchcraft. I have finished with it."

He stooped down, picked up his bundle and held it out to me. Here was his divining basket, his idols, and all the other paraphernalia used in witchcraft, so essential to him before for his power and prestige among his people. I put my hands behind my back and said, "No, Chief, I cannot accept these things from you. You must burn them yourself!"

What a moment of crisis! Would he do that? Could he? Calling together a group of Christians, he kindled a fire on the ground in the mission compound. Then the Christians joined hands and sang in their own tongue the words of that lovely hymn,

My chains are snapped, the bonds of sin are broken,
And I am free!
Now let the triumph of His grace be spoken,
Who died for me.

As they sang, the chief stepped forward and resolutely threw his bundle into the consuming fire. What a victory! What sweet revenge God took on that man by saving his soul and making him a new creature in Christ Jesus! (2 Corinthians 5.17).

Did that chief really have power to summon the lions on that Saturday evening? Never! It had been the work of Satan through him, as that enemy of God and man sought to undermine the work of the gospel and oppose the power of God. It was Satan's effort to try to chase us from this land of darkness to which God had called us, where five huge tribes were living in this heart of Central Africa, as yet untouched by the gracious gospel of Christ. How we thanked God that we went through even this agonising experience for the sake of this one man's soul.

Often during this trial of our faith we recalled the words of a poem written by a man from my home town of Galston in Ayrshire, Scotland:

Kept by His power!
Whatever changes lower,
The strength of God's almighty arm
Secures my soul from every harm,
Kept by His power.

But however did Margaret and I find ourselves in such a primitive place, surrounded by the powers of witchcraft, the deep darkness of heathendom, and the tremendous pressures of evil spirits? Were we out in that lonely jungle for the thrill of adventure and discovery? Who sent us here? Why did we decide to leave home with all of its comforts, our loved family and friends, to live among five different tribes who knew nothing of the gospel? The answer traces back through three generations in the west country of Scotland.

CHAPTER 2

Consecrated to the Master's Service

My grandmother possessed two open things - an open door to her home, and an open Bible which lay on the kitchen table, easily seen by all who looked into that humble cottage in Galston, Ayrshire. In the mid-nineteenth century relatively few people were literate, so Granny would take up the old Bible and read to them. Granny Houston's soul was enriched by a love for Christ, and she loved to read to others about the Saviour who had won her own heart. Through this witness some of the townsfolk came themselves to a personal knowledge of Christ as their Saviour. Most of all, Granny Houston desired that her precious little girl, Barbara, would grow up to follow in the footsteps of the Lord Jesus.

Towards the end of that century, missionary interest reached a zenith and focused particularly on China and Africa. The names of Fred Stanley Arnot, David Livingstone, and Dan Crawford became household words in Granny Houston's abode. Little wonder that the child Barbara became deeply impressed with the needs of the foreign mission field. As she grew into her teens this desire became a burning flame in her heart. Above all she wanted to carry the message of Life to the women of Old Calabar, West Africa, a place forever linked with the name of Mary Slessor, the mill girl from Dundee on the other side of Scotland.

Though she had accepted Christ as her Saviour, Barbara was not yet baptised. This was a step of obedience to the Lord Jesus that she had been taught from the open Bible by Granny Houston at the fireside. She asked the elders in the local church for baptism, but to her immense disappointment they said she was too young. Returning home in tears she cried out, "Mother, if they will not baptise me then I'll go down to the river Irvine and baptise myself!"

When the elders heard of this cry from one so anxious to please her Lord, they immediately decided to meet her request.

The burning desire to go to Old Calabar did not flicker in Barbara's heart. She longed to go and tell the women and girls there of their need of the Saviour. But when she applied to the mission, to her great disappointment, she was refused because of a chest complaint which may have been tuberculosis, a fairly common disease in those days. To her, this was the breaking point of all she hoped for. Her whole life had been focused on reaching West Africa with the gospel. Why had she been set aside? Her experience is summarised in the following poem:

Did He set you aside when the fields were ripe
And the labourers seemed too few?
Did He set you aside and give someone else
The task that you longed to do?
Did He set you aside when the purple grapes
Hung low in the autumn sun,
While hands, not yours, just gathered them in–
The trophies you'd almost won?

Did He set you aside on a couch of pain
Where all you could do was pray,
And when you whispered, "Please let me go,"
The answer was always "stay"?
Did He set you aside with no reason at all,
No reason that you could see -
And your heart cried out, "In this limited space,
Lord, how can I work for Thee?"

Did He set you aside with a heavy cross,
And were you filled with despair,
Thinking He'd gone and left you alone -
Till you suddenly found Him there?
There in the shadows, the world shut out,
Kneeling alone at His feet,
Did you learn the answers? Not all just yet!
But wasn't it - wasn't it sweet?

(Author unknown)

This was the lesson that my mother, Barbara, had to learn.

In the course of time Barbara married, and I was born into the family. My young mother determined to do what Hannah had done so long ago - to offer her baby boy to the Master, so that He might send him to take her place in West Africa, if it was in His good pleasure to do so. This consecration of her little lad was a momentous occasion in her life. Now she had found a new goal. She was learning that "God moves in a mysterious way His wonders to perform".

And so I was reared just like the other lads in that village in the west of Scotland. I had, sometimes against my will, to attend regularly Sunday School, gospel meetings and even the Breaking of Bread service. I had no thought of my own need for the Saviour until one night when I was thirteen years old I heard the gospel preached from John 5.24, "Verily, verily, I say unto you, he that heareth My word and believeth on Him that sent Me, hath everlasting life, and shall not come into condemnation; but is passed from death unto life." I sat on in my seat till nearly everyone had left the hall.

"Wee laddie, what are you waiting for?" asked a Christian lady as she touched me on the shoulder.

"I want to be saved," I said.

Unfeelingly she replied, "Run away home. You're too young to be saved!"

Too young to be saved! Was that true? But I never mentioned the incident to my mother. The following year I was troubled by a deep conviction of sin. Too young to be saved! The words haunted me yet. But whilst the words often seared my thoughts I gave myself to every kind of boyish mischief I could think of. The policemen were often at my school asking uncomfortable questions!

Life became almost unbearable. Night after night I crept up to my parents' bedroom door and listened. Were they there? When I heard them breathing I felt a great relief that the Lord had not returned as I knew He was going to, and raptured them, leaving me, the only one unsaved in the family, all alone.

Two incidents were finally used by God to impress me indelibly with my need to accept the Saviour. Early one morning my friends and I went to a cross-roads where there were clearly marked signposts. One showed the way straight on to Glasgow, and the other to Edinburgh, via Newmilns and Darvel. My chums and I had brought spades along, and we dug up the signposts and turned them round the other way! Then we climbed into nearby trees to watch motorists slow down, scratch their heads, and travel in the wrong direction. It was a sheer delight to us to watch the effects of the deceiving signposts! On the way home, however, the Lord convicted me of how the devil had deceived me in the same way. I thought I ought to be on the way to heaven, but the path on which I was travelling was clearly the wrong one.

Later that year I was with the same two friends one dark night when we heard a noise in the graveyard nearby, and decided to investigate. We climbed over the wall into the graveyard and crept forward slowly in the darkness. As we stood under a tree listening for the noise, we were about to give up and leave when one of my friends looked up to see a tall white apparition walking slowly toward us! I tried to bolt, but was immobilised with fear. When we finally were able to move, we made for the wall at race-horse speed and cleared it like steeple-chasers! Looking back, to our horror we saw the apparition clear the wall effortlessly too. I ran without glancing round until I reached home and dived under my bed. In spite of my mother's pleadings to come out I stayed there, trembling, for hours. Conviction of sin reached its climax that night, and soon after, on June 6, 1925, as I heard the gospel message once again, I gave my heart to the Saviour, and my sins were gone.

My parents and sister were so overjoyed about this that my mother called all the neighbours together and made a feast, much as the father of the prodigal son of Luke 15 must have done. When everyone had left, Mother took me aside to tell me something important. She told me that when I was born she wanted to name me Crawford after the great pioneer missionary to Africa, Dan Crawford, but my father wanted me to be given his own name, Robert. And Robert I was, often changed into Bobby, but that day my mother made me promise that when I was older I would take the name of Crawford.

All her life my mother was a great soul-winner. The butcher, the baker, the vegetable-seller and the milkman always heard the gospel when they spoke to her. She asked the elders of the assembly if they would arrange gospel meetings in our cottage, and she would supply the audience. I remember the living-room being filled with unsaved friends, and the preacher standing in front of the coal fire, sweating from the heat. God blessed those efforts, and a number of people traced their salvation and subsequent reception into the fellowship of the local church in Galston to those meetings.

One Saturday afternoon in the dead of winter I was baptised in the nearby river. It was so cold that the ice had to be broken before we could go down into the water. Several young people were baptised that day, but none of us noticed the fierce cold! It was to us such a thrill to be able to obey the Lord's command and be baptised.

In the neighbouring village of Newmilns a missionary conference was held near an old missionary home. On this particular occasion one of the speakers was Mr. Andrew Borland from Irvine, who was the editor of the "Believer's Magazine" for many years. He chose as his text John 10.16, "And other sheep I have which are not of this fold: them also I must bring, and they shall hear My voice." As I sat there on the grass with two other friends who also sensed God's call to the mission field, I heard the unmistakable voice of the Good Shepherd calling me to seek some of those other sheep for whom He died. Bowing my head as Mr. Borland continued his God-given message, I gave myself to God for this task. This moment was one of the highlights of my life.

When I was seventeen, I told my parents that the Lord had called me to service on the foreign mission field. My mother wept, telling me for the first time that at my birth she had consecrated me to the service of the Master. It was a long time before she could compose herself sufficiently to explain to me her own deep exercise concerning missionary work in Africa and then her tremendous disappointment at not being able to go. She quoted to me 2 Timothy 1.5, concerning "the unfeigned faith that is in thee, which dwelt first in thy grandmother.. and thy mother... and I am persuaded that in thee also." And she rejoiced. All of this was a great surprise to me. I had never suspected her desire to serve the Lord overseas since she served her Master so well at home where she was.

Next came the difficult matter of attempting to equip myself for the arduous task of reaching unevangelised tribes. My thoughts and longings turned toward the Amazonian Indians who had never been reached with the gospel message. Consequently I began the study of Portuguese and also linguistics under the masterly teaching of Mr. George Borland, also of the Galston assembly. This godly man, convinced of my missionary call, spent much time with me teaching me what he could. Although these were hard days of study, in later years my knowledge of linguistics was of tremendous help in translating the Bible into various African languages.

I knew that in the wilds I would have to build my own house, starting with making the bricks, and also build my own furniture. I spent several years learning these skills. Simultaneously I commenced a study of dentistry with a dentist in the nearby village of Newmilns. This man, though not a Christian, was exceptionally kind and co-operative. I had only to provide my own patients for the teaching sessions, and these gracious folks deserved the free treatments! While on furlough many years after this, I was saddened to learn that my dentist friend had died. But he had left me a message specially for me. "Please tell Bobby Allison that the Saviour of whom he so often spoke I have accepted into my own heart." What a joy that was to me.

During these busy days I rose at four o'clock in the morning to spend time with my Master over His sacred Word. This, in addition to the Bible teaching I received at the assembly in Galston, was the most important component of my equipment for foreign missionary service.

By this time I had a girlfriend, Margaret, who was also burdened for the salvation of unreached tribes. Because of my commitment to missionary training, our courtship could not be like that of other young couples. Margaret accepted this gladly for the gospel's sake. She was to learn later on in an even greater degree what real sacrifice there would be in loneliness and separation from each other. As our friendship deepened, Margaret asked the Lord for a sign confirming His will as to her own service on a foreign mission field. The sign was that she would be able to lead her own sister to the Saviour. When this took place, Margaret had the calm assurance that her calling was indeed sure.

One afternoon I attended a conference in Ayr where several

experienced missionaries were speaking. One of them was Mr. T. Ernest Wilson from Angola who described the pressing need to take the gospel to the unreached Mbangala, Shinji, Minungu, Ruunda, and Northern Chokwe people of that vast land. My heart was stirred with this, but I was confused. Why had I devoted so many years to the study of Portuguese, which is the official language of Brazil, if the Master now seemed to be pointing me toward the tribal peoples of Northern Angola? Why the waste of time and energy? To my great surprise and sheer delight I learned that Portuguese was also the official language of Angola! How wise God is, far wiser than His young servant! No time or effort had been lost at all.

I am eternally indebted to the two men from Galston, George Borland and Andrew Borland, who taught me so much in my younger days and faithfully followed my missionary career for many years. Looking back over half a century of pioneer work among many different tribes in Northern Angola, Rhodesia (Zimbabwe), Malawi, Mozambique and Botswana, they rejoiced in a special way to hear of thousands brought to the Saviour, of many assemblies formed, and of the Word of God translated for the first time into several African languages.

Believers in Angola with new Bibles

25

CHAPTER 3

The Initiation of a Missionary's Wife

In 1934 I was commended by the assembly in Galston to the grace of God for the work I had been called to (Acts 14.26), and travelled to Portugal for further studies in the Portuguese language. The following year I set sail for Angola alone, and arrived with only five shillings in my pocket. But it was five shillings *plus God.*

All the time I studied Songo and Chokwe at Peso mission station I never forgot my goal of going further north, some five hundred miles, to reach those large tribes of people who had never heard the gospel. During these months of constant study, interspersed with visits to African villages secluded deep in the bush, I began to understand the importance of studying more than language. If I was to communicate effectively I had to understand the peoples' folklore, customs, etiquette and traditions. I had to become culturally literate as well. Without this understanding, effectual teaching of the gospel would be impossible. As the prophet Ezekiel said (3.15), "I sat where they sat."

I was privileged to spend much time with an older, experienced missionary, Mr. William Maitland, commended from what is now Woodside Bible Chapel in Maywood, Illinois, USA. A colleague of the late Fred Stanley Arnot, Mr. Maitland initiated me into understanding the world from a specifically African point of view, a process which Dan Crawford first called "Thinking Black". This apprenticeship convinced me that a new missionary should always learn from one who is more experienced, and my months of training with Mr. Maitland served me well in later years.

Until Margaret joined me and we were married, I lived with Mr. Donald McLeod on the Peso mission station, many miles away from the railhead. Letters took far too long to reach us for my liking. Since a carrier had to be sent on foot to the railhead, I didn't receive Margaret's letters until a month and a half after she'd written. The two and a half years we were separated seemed to pass very, very slowly as I waited for my bride.

Finally Margaret sailed to Angola and we were married in 1937 at Mboma mission station where Dr. and Mrs. Leslie Bier developed a splendid medical work. We had to be married twice, once by Mr. Maitland and again by the Administrator at Luso. I'm glad to say that the second ceremony took only a few minutes, and then came the honeymoon! But there was no seaside resort for us, although you could say it was abroad! The time was spent packing up our belongings into bundles to be transported on African carriers' heads to the as yet unknown north of Angola.

Though our wedding ceremony was doubled, our celebrations were simple. But we did have a wedding cake which Margaret made herself with sugar borrowed from Mrs. Persis Bier, promising that we would send home as soon as we could for a replacement of the precious sugar. After some months the sugar arrived, and we dispatched a carrier to take it back to the Biers at Mboma. His route was across a wild part of the country where there were few villages, no roads, and only a narrow path which was in places very poorly defined. Where the tall grass had overgrown the path, the man had to proceed very slowly. Like all African carriers, he had his pole to help him push away the grass, to be ready to kill ever present poisonous snakes, and to help him manage his heavy load. He often carried our provisions from the railhead to our mission compound away up north. On this journey, after many days of walking he reached a large and dangerous river and he found it was in flood. So he laid down his bundle while he explored for a safe way to cross.

He employed the fairly common African bridge-making process of felling a tree right across the water. Cautiously he started to cross over. But alas, the tree was slippery, and the carrier, together with the valued sack of sugar and all the mail from overseas he had carried so far along that lonely jungle trail, toppled into the raging river. He managed to retrieve the letters, but of course the sugar was lost - sweetening these waters at least for a little while! In later years my African co-worker, Little Bird, used this incident as an illustration of how so many people, when faced with tests in life, neglect their pole (the Word of God) and fail miserably, whereas they could have stood their ground firmly by using it to help them through. At the time I jokingly reflected that in reality the icing was off the wedding cake in no time! But the marriage lasted!

On the first night out we camped in the forest. Carriers built several fires in a circle, each man sleeping between two fires for safety from wild animals. When Margaret opened our suitcases she discovered to her great consternation that I had inadvertently left my clothes back at the mission station and brought along a trunk of books instead! But there was no turning back, and those books somehow had to take the place of a change of safari clothing! George and Emma Wiseman accompanied us part of the way and then they turned back to their mission station. It was a difficult and sad farewell there in the heart of the jungle, particularly for Margaret, as a new bride from bonnie Scotland without any experience of the rigours and demands of the primitive African jungle trail.

Day after day and week after week we followed the narrow trail, crossing many rivers and deep muddy swamps. The malarial swamps were particularly difficult for Margaret to navigate, up to the waist in the slime where mosquitoes breed so well. Often we helped her across by tying a strong rope around her waist and pulling her to the opposite side. At other times she had to be carried across on the back of one of the men. When it rained she walked on until the sun dried her dress. This was a honeymoon minus the honey! If there was a large tree growing near a river's edge I would make a bridge by felling it so that it lay across the stream, and over it we would venture - always having to be on the lookout for crocodiles. Some larger rivers had to be crossed in a dugout canoe with the help of an African ferryman who usually haggled about the price, which was a length of cloth. The carriers were also paid with cloth and salt.

One day we arrived at a village deep in the jungle at about ten o'clock in the morning. The chief in that village would not allow us to go any further, warning us that lions were marauding in the villages ahead, and that the trail was too dangerous. So we heeded his warning and erected our small tent and stayed the night. The following morning two of our carriers rose up early and went off into the bush to hunt for antelope to feed us all. Spotting a small buck ambling slowly by itself, they trailed it until it stopped to feed in the rich grass in the valley. Unfortunately for the carriers, a lion was already stalking this buck, and they had come between the two animals. This, of course, was too much for the lion, which crept up silently and sprang on the first carrier, killing him with one swift blow of its paw. The other man leapt up into a tree and had to sit there in sheer terror watching while his friend was eaten by the lion. Placing his hand to his mouth, he made the danger call which Africans living in the bush all recognise. The men of the village grabbed bows and arrows and ran to the valley where this grisly sight met them. This was Margaret's indoctrination to the dangers of the pathway she had chosen to follow with me for the sake of the gospel.

Suddenly one evening a tropical storm arose and it blew so hard that our sleeping-tent was blown away. The side was ripped completely open, and we were left exposed to the full blast of the storm. Certainly this was no honeymoon! During my bachelor days I would hollow out a comfortable spot in the sand, spread my blanket over it and call it home sweet home, but I couldn't ask this of my bride! I thought the tent was better - but not always!

Margaret had to retrace the five hundred mile journey to the hospital at Mboma when our first child, Kenneth, was to be born in August 1938. I made a hammock for her to be carried, with side flaps to keep out the rain, but that proved futile as the wind blew rain into the hammock anyway. She was more comfortable walking the trail for the rest of the six week journey. The last river to be forded was the worst obstacle as it was in flood, but she bravely strode across, up to the waist in water. Our God protected her so that she arrived safely without even a head cold. For her the Scripture was literal, "When thou passest through the waters, I will be with thee" (Isaiah 43.2).

Another part of the great price a pioneer missionary wife has to pay is loneliness and isolation. Many times I left her all alone on the mission station while I trekked further north, with the only means of communication a hand-carried letter. Night after night, week after week would go by without any letters. She had to struggle with the attendant dangers of jungle living all alone, including the possibility of sickness with no medical help nearby. One day a snake slithered into the baby's bedroom and took up residence in one of the bricks which had been laid for a floor with mud between them. What could she do, since I was four or five hundred miles away? She quickly boiled a kettle of water and poured it into the hole. The moment the snake showed its head she clobbered it with a thick stick!

Since there were no locks on the doors, suitcases or packing boxes had to be pushed against them every night because of the raiding lions which always seemed to appear about five o'clock in the morning. Then there were the rats which scampered all over the place once the oil lamps had been extinguished. Margaret used to line up all the shoes alongside her bed as ammunition, quickly reach from beneath the mosquito net and take a flying shot. Yes, her aim was good, nailing some of the big "game" night after night!

Teaching school, caring for the sick, and helping the local women with the Word of God consumed Margaret's hours, along with the non-stop job of caring for the family. Only a woman truly called of the Lord, and who had a consuming desire to stay with and stand by her husband, could endure the rigours which jungle life demanded of her. In due time, the verse, "and she that tarried at home divided the spoil" (Psalm 68.12) became a reality for Margaret as she was able to accompany me on treks into Shinjiland to see the fruit of her sacrifice.

After one particular trek when lions had been particularly troublesome around the compound, I arranged for four men to stand guard at the four corners of the station. When one heard a lion coming he was to beat loudly on his tin can and everyone would be warned. One night one of the men was confronted by a lion only a few feet away. In terror he dropped his can and bolted for home! It was only about ten o'clock, and so although I heard the noise I had no thought of it being a lion. I shoved the cases away from the door and went out to investigate, calling an African lad to join me. A few hundred yards further on I stumbled across an ox which had been killed by the powerful lion. Then we heard the frightening growl of the lion! Away ran the lad, leaving me alone - but not for long. I too got off my mark like an Olympic athlete and ran, and threw myself inside the house, barricading the doorway. Night after night the same two lions prowled about. Wearied of the tension this caused, we wished that the king of the jungle could be as easily disposed of as a rat with a good whack of a shoe!

Another time Margaret complained that eggs were being stolen from her henhouse, so I dutifully set out to discover the thief. Africans recognise a person by his footprints, just as the police can recognise a person by his fingerprint. But there were no footprints by the henhouse and no other clues. As I rested at midday a man rushed to the house shouting, "Come quickly! I have found the thief, but bring your gun!"

With muddled thoughts about the Africans' response to my shooting one of their people for stealing eggs, I nevertheless grabbed my gun and ran to the coop to catch the thief in the very act. A very large Egyptian cobra had been coming every day, taking the eggs and eating them. It was a spitting snake, one which aims at its victim's eyes causing blindness for a few moments. I threw my arm over my eyes and the snake's venom spattered on my forearm. I then quickly shot the snake and so ended the mystery of the vanishing eggs!

One day as I was going along the trail I saw a spitting cobra on one side and a small frog on the other. The snake spat and blinded the frog, and immediately swallowed it. I took a stick and killed the snake, then slit it open and extracted the live frog! I rubbed the little creature's eyes until it could see, then released it to hop off into the forest. I hope it lived a while after this. The effect of the venom lasts only a few moments, but it can be painful.

I had not been in tropical Africa for more than a few months and was still struggling to master my first African language when I encountered the perils of the crocodile. The young men of the village where I lived were a great help in my language study, and I spent as much time as possible with them, engaging in their various activities to learn new vocabulary and to practise my slowly developing skills.

On Saturday afternoons these young men liked to cool off in the nearby river, splashing and jumping about in the water. The village elders warned them of the danger of crocodiles, but they replied that this was a small, insignificant stream.

"Yes," replied the elders, "small streams lead to a big river." But the young men would not listen. One Saturday afternoon it was unbearably hot under the tropical sun, and the slowly moving stream appeared particularly enticing as the sunlight danced on its rippled surface. I longed for a refreshing swim, but knew to venture in was utterly foolish. 'It is in the silent stream that the crocodile lives', runs the proverb. That day I was to learn more of the African proverbs through tragedy.

The fun started right away with the older lads diving from the bank into the middle of the stream. At that point the river bank was covered with thick vegetation, but here and there were sandy spots from which they could dive and play. They began to think that their elders had just been envious of them having such fun in the water.

"Let go!" called one lad, thinking that one of his friends was holding his leg. "Ha! Ha!" laughed the others. Who was pulling legs under the water? But when the lad disappeared, everyone realised that this was no joke. A red stain soon surfaced, and the other boys dashed for the bank. Suddenly the stricken lad surfaced too, gasping for air. By a miracle he had pulled his leg free from the crocodile's horrible jaws, something which is unheard of. He lunged for the bank where willing hands hauled him from the water.

"My mother, what shall we do now?" the young men cried as they laid him on the bank. They put their fingers into their mouths and gave the tribal call of danger as loudly as they could. I heard this troubled call, and set off with the men who quickly grabbed their spears and started off at a brisk trot. When they saw what had happened, they stripped a tree and strung together a barkrope hammock on which to carry the lad back to the village.

The poor boy groaned in extreme pain. The crocodile had grabbed his leg about three inches above the knee, and the razor-sharp teeth had stripped it entirely of its flesh, and also shattered the bone. I knew that the lad would soon die of blood poisoning, yet I still had a difficult decision to make. Should I amputate or not? I had never been faced with such a decision before. The mission hospital was a good five days' march through the bush, and the lad would never survive the journey. So I prepared some disinfectant and amputated the leg just above the knee.

Late that afternoon the boy sank into unconsciousness. I held him in my arms and whispered in his ears the words of John 3.16, "For God so loved the world, that He gave His only begotten Son, that whosoever believeth in Him should not perish but have everlasting life". Over and over again I repeated these words to the dying boy.

"*Unevuko nyi*? (do you understand?)" I whispered. He responded with a faint nod of assent and slipped away. He had left a mud house to take his eternal abode in the King's Palace. What a change for any lad!

The Africans found it very difficult to understand why I didn't have to pay a "dowry" or bride price for my wife. That her parents would accept all the expense of the wedding was to them unthinkable. "How many cows, Ngana, did you pay for Ndona?" they would ask. When I said that I had paid nothing, they shook their heads, amazed at my "good luck". Little by little they came to understand the principles of a Christian home, and how much better such a home was than those founded on the principles of dark heathendom.

One more thing that puzzled the Africans greatly was that I had only one wife. To them this was the characteristic of a slave. The more wives a man had, the greater was his esteem among his fellowmen. It was quite common to find a man with six to ten wives, especially among the chiefs. Was I, then, merely a slave? Before attempting to impress them with Biblical principles of monogamy, I showed them Philippians 2.7 concerning the Master from heaven who became a slave in order to serve freely all mankind. This, I explained, was my example: to serve others that they might have eternal life. Yes, I had become a slave in order to serve them in the gospel of Christ. When men involved in polygamous marriages requested baptism, we often wrestled with tremendous problems. Were they willing to make themselves like a slave because of the One called Jesus? And if they kept only the first wife, what about the welfare of the other wives and children who would then be abandoned? Such difficult questions plague and perplex the missionary working among remote heathen peoples.

*Tribes and Assembly Mission Stations
in Northeastern Angola*

CHAPTER 4

Early Trekking

Jungle Leaf:
Relish pots cannot take each other off the fire.

By the time we reached the beginning of our second year of marriage we had established what was to become our lifestyle for many years. It involved us in much separation, with Margaret usually remaining on the mission station while I trekked from village to village preaching the gospel to tribal groups who had never before heard this life-giving message. Many had never seen a white person before I came. Only when all our three children had gone off to boarding school in later years could Margaret accompany me on these extensive travels.

Trekking among the bush villages of Central Africa was hard but it was a constant joy to me. Preparation for a trek always created plenty of hard work and excitement. Men had to be hired to carry the needed supplies through the tall grass of the bush country. The hiring process was no easy task, as the Africans always delighted to barter over how much cloth they would receive for carrying the loads. Such business could take days before a proper understanding had been reached, yet it was all done in good humour. It was good sport for them to see if I would lose my temper! Indeed great grace and patience was needed for all of life in Africa. Sometimes the Africans quoted their proverb, *Kasumbi keshi kulemana mu chihunda* (a chicken does not weigh heavily carried inside the village). They meant that when they carried a load, even though it did not weigh much at the beginning, it soon became a heavy burden when it was carried for many days and weeks on a long trek.

Margaret prepared food for the first days of the trek. Also, she usually dried bananas and vegetables which could be used to make a good pot of soup. But I had to rely mostly on African food for which I could barter in the villages along the way.

I walked many miles along those narrow paths through the long grass each day, stopping now and then with my fellow travellers to tell different village people the message of God's love for them. One African known as the forerunner always walks ahead, at times with a stick in hand, prepared to deal with whatever might appear on the jungle path. The African does not walk along the jungle paths, but trots, clicking his bare heels together. When I tried to imitate their rhythmic gait I landed flat on the path, affording them all a good laugh.

As the men trot along the trail they banter quite freely, but it is difficult to keep a serious conversation going when it is necessary to move in single file. More than once I got a sore neck trying to talk to the person behind me. I also discovered to my cost the constant danger of tripping over tree roots! As the African's life is circumscribed by nature, so I, too, learned to notice the varieties and subtleties of the jungle flora and fauna.

Soon the sun burns high and hot overhead and the drenching of the early morning dew is forgotten. On and on we'd press toward the next village. If we meet a hunter along the path, courtesy demands that we stop to greet him. A common question would be to ask how far it was to the next village. He would stand with his legs apart, stroking his stubbly beard a while and say, as he pointed with his chin, never breaching etiquette by pointing with his hand, "Ngana, it is quite near."

"Oh, quite near, eh?"

"*Ewa* (yes), quite near."

"How far is 'quite near'," I'd ask.

"Well, you cross over this part of the forest, you cross the river, turn toward the sunset and keep going, and it is quite near." To me 'near' means no more than five or six miles, but through experience I learned that 'quite near' to an African meant at least ten miles!

Usually I was able to visit three villages in a day's trek, and I would sleep that night within the perimeter of the last one. Often the villages had high stockades built around them to afford protection from hungry lions.

Upon reaching a village I always spoke first to the chief to ask permission to hold a meeting. In keeping with African custom, the visit must begin with gift-giving. I would offer the chief a gift which he would have to (and want to) accept, then he would reciprocate with something such as a live chicken for my evening meal.

Around the campfire at night it was my greatest thrill to speak to these people in the villages, living and dying without a knowledge of the Saviour. These were men and women to win for the Master who had sent me to them, among whom I could live for Him, and whom I could help in their sicknesses and sorrows. My earthly home is there with these jungle dwellers, whose language I learned, and whose ways and customs surrounded Margaret and me for so many years that they became our own.

It was getting dark one night when I approached a certain village, only to find that the wooden gates were already barred, and the people bedded down for the night. After a good deal of shouting I managed to arouse a few folks from their grass huts, and they allowed my carriers and me inside. There was no gospel service that night, however, and we lay down under the stars to sleep after our twenty five mile walk through the thick forest without doing what I loved best - telling the message of the Saviour.

After a night's sleep I would leave the village right at daybreak, because when the sun is high in the sky the mid-day heat overcomes the traveller in the dense bush. Early morning dew clings to the tall grass on either side of the narrow trail, showering the carriers as they pass by with their loads on their heads. They sing as they move, until a heavy shower of dew annoys them into effusive exclamations of discontent. At such a time I would quote to them their own proverb, *ungeti mume* (a journey means dew), and they would laugh, delighted at the white man turning their own saying on them.

The carriers usually slept in huts in the villages, but lice in the thatch made the open air, with the campfire for protection, preferable to me. Every night as the villagers relaxed around their campfire I told them the good news of the Saviour of the world. In the far north country none had ever heard the message before. I continually strove to find ways to explain it simply and clearly in a relevant manner for them to grasp the great truth that God has a real Son whom He sent to earth to die for them. Just as Mr. Maitland had trained me to "think black", very early in my itinerant preaching experience I proved that the most effective means of communication was to use local customs, folklore and proverbs to illustrate and explain the gospel.

Real challenges emerged when I tried to explain Biblical concepts which were quite foreign to African cultural experience. One example is the parable Jesus told of the two builders, in Matthew 7. When I was trying to describe the folly of the man who built his house on the sand they said, "Hi! Was not this the wiser man?" After all, they built their houses of mud, supported by poles stuck in the ground! To hear of a man trying to stick a pole into a piece of rock was sheer folly, and the one who chose the sandy place must be the wiser of the two! The Minungu knew nothing of "foundations", for they had never seen a house constructed of stone or brick. The real support for their houses is the centre pole propping up the entire roof, and so I learned to adapt my theological interpretations in terms of their cultural understanding.

Similarly, I learned another lesson when I wanted to explain Revelation 3.20, "Behold, I stand at the door and knock". In Minunguland the doors of the houses are made of grass. The cultural equivalent to knocking at a person's door is to clap hands respectfully at the entrance, thereby alerting someone within to one's presence at the door. If a person tried to knock on the wooden bar of the grass door, the owner would say crossly, "Do you want to knock my house down, doing such a disgraceful thing?"! And so for the Minungu, Revelation 3.20 should read, "Behold, I stand at the door and clap my hands".

The Honey and the Honeybird

Jungle Leaf:
What has horns cannot be wrapped up in a parcel.

For those who enjoy seeing and studying exotic flora and fauna, the trek through the African jungle is a fascinating journey which provides a rich display of both. You will nearly always see the little, brownish coloured honey guide, a bird not much bigger than a British sparrow, as it twitters in the trees inviting the unwary traveller to follow it. I never succumbed to my curiosity to do so, however, as I well remembered the stories about the honey guide I had heard around the evening campfires.

One such story concerned two hunters who had gone off into the forest to track game. After a long and tiring hunt they finally shot two duikers, and sat down to rest. Right there above them was a honey guide twittering on a branch overhead.

"I say, I hear the honey guide!" said one. "It is calling us to go after it!"

"Friend, do not allow that bird to get you away from these animals that *Mulungu* (God) has given us," the other replied.

"Yet if it takes us to the honey we could have a good feast when we get back to the village, would we not?"

"No, I don't think we should go after that bird. Let it twitter away," the second man insisted. And so they continued to argue. Finally one jumped to his feet, laid his gun on the ground and said, "Well,

I'm going after it!"

"Look my friend," the other cautioned, "this bird may guide you to a wild animal like a lion or a leopard. It would be better not to follow it. Let us go back right now to our wives and children with the meat Mulungu has given us in the chase today." But the man would not listen.

The small bird flew from branch to branch, leading the man deeper and deeper into the jungle, and far from the path. The man was soon panting for breath. The many small thorns on the bushes he brushed against stuck into his legs and arms, and eventually worked themselves under his skin, causing great irritation. The only cure is to strip off all clothes and remove the burrs one by one. When he stopped, he had to do battle with the ants which crawled up his legs. But he continued to follow the honey guide deeper into the jungle.

After some time the man who had stayed on the path guarding the game decided to follow his friend in the quest for honey. He followed the tracks the first man had made through the bush, and soon caught up with him. They were in a very dense part of the jungle where they could not see well for the darkness. And there at the foot of the tree where the honey guide stopped waited a lion. With one leap the powerful king of the jungle killed one of the men. The other escaped, as the Africans say, "through the eye of the needle", but he, fearing that the lion might come after him, made straight for the village. He left his hard-earned game on the path. Yes, the Africans say, "Honey is sweet but it draws bitter things." The Bible speaks of the man who refused the pleasures of sin for a season (Hebrews 11.25), knowing that they would have brought death in the end. As Romans 6.23 says, "For the wages of sin is death."

* * *

Early one morning on trek I was startled to see a huge snake lying under a mahogany tree. It was the fear-inspiring python, fast asleep after eating a good meal. Judging by the snake's distended shape, I guessed the meal must have consisted of an African antelope about the size of a goat or a small sheep. On finding such prey, the muscles of the python's mouth relax and a sort of saliva oozes over the body, allowing it to be swallowed slowly. Then the

41

snake curls up and goes to sleep until it has digested its meal. With one swift blow on the head I killed that python and ripped it open to extract the antelope, but I was too late. The antelope had already died and had been partially eaten by the snake.

Some tribes eat snake meat because of what they call "meat hunger", but other tribes despise such meat. I once arrived at a village some time before the carrier who had my food box. Since it was past noon and I had trekked from early morning I was particularly hungry. I sat on the ground and leaned against a hut to wait, and watched as a woman prepared her family's meal. Out of respect and sympathy she offered me a piece of the meat and a plate of her manioc mush, which I eagerly accepted. Then I noticed that the meat came from a well-known snake, a puff adder, and I immediately felt sick! I vowed that day that I would never eat snake.

The African jungle equivalent of a trip to the butcher's shop to obtain meat is much more exciting - a game hunt. The African man becomes skilled at this task early in life. The hunter has to be a patient fellow, skilled in the chase, and with sufficient stamina to follow the animal for days if necessary, without becoming tired. The white man comes to the jungle with a gun that barks, but the

Hippo from George Wiseman's shot

skilled African with his bows and arrows knows the forest trails as no white man will ever know, and the African has no real rival in the hunt. Very often when we left the mission station for a hunt down in the plains the whole village accompanied us as the people were almost always meat-hungry. Another very effective means of hunting game used by the African is to dig a large pit across a game trail, camouflaging the trap with dry sticks overlaid with grass. As they dig, the hunters shape the trap like an hourglass, narrowing it halfway down, so that as an animal falls, the weight of its body forces it through the narrow part into a wider pit beneath. One day our mail carrier had started on his long, wearying walk to the railhead to collect our mail from overseas. Since it had taken him several days to reach the depot, on his return he decided to take a shortcut so that he would reach the mission station in time for the Saturday evening prayer meeting. The trail was new to him, and trotting along he fell into a game pit, mailbag and all hurtling to the bottom. Mercifully the pit had no spears in it, and a search party found the man alive and uninjured.

Another time, an African living near the mission station dug a game pit into which fell a large antelope. Unfortunately for the hunter, he had not positioned spears at the bottom to kill the animal as it fell. In the morning when the hunter went to check his pit, he was delighted to see such a lovely, large animal which would provide many days' meat for his family. He leaned over, spear in hand, to make a powerful thrust and kill the antelope. But as he did so he lost his balance, and toppled into the pit beside the animal. Now their roles were reversed and the hunter became the hunted. The antelope impaled the man against the side of the pit on its large, vicious horns, and the man met with a violent death in the pit he had made.

Mbangalaland

The large territory in Angola where the Mbangala tribe lived and roamed was a treeless country. There they built houses of grass, towering to fifteen feet and divided into three compartments. T. Ernest Wilson, a tireless pioneer, first contacted the Mbangala before going on to work in Songoland. It was he who encouraged me to "go north, young man", and to whom I owe a great debt of gratitude. One day Mr. Wilson reached an Mbangala village, very tired and much in need of a drink of water. A villager brought it to him - in the skull of a person who had recently been killed! Naturally Mr. Wilson took one look and lost all desire to drink.

George Wiseman and I trekked up into this country, crossing sixteen rivers to reach the Portuguese Chefe de Posto at his administrative post. We camped near the fort and were welcomed and entertained by the chefe, whose wife cooked dinner. But while cooking it, it became a burnt offering! We were completely starved before the lady called us to partake of a second meal at midnight!

This chefe owned a Bible which his grandfather, who had been "Protestant" had given to him. He was sympathetic to us as missionaries and set guard over our encampment lest dangerous men should attempt a raid. But this was unnecessary.

One of the advantages of those early treks was that when George or I had finished preaching the gospel, the chief would beckon to one of his counsellors and tell him to get up and go over the message to the crowd, word by word. Thus they got a double dose, and it meant that the chief's counsellors had to listen carefully to the message. During his reiteration of the talk, he would be interrupted many times with the chief's exclamation, "*Momo, momo* (that is the very thing)."

At the close of one of these sessions, a tall young man walked into the light of the campfires. After a short time he stood up and said, "I was away at the river fishing when I heard that missionaries had come to our land telling of Yesu. I left my fishing and have hurried over the bushland to hear the story for myself. Will you repeat it to me?"

He listened, his heart was opened, and a man who had been spiritually lost in witchcraft sought the Saviour. Through ensuing years he became a burning torch, carrying the news of the gospel far and wide to his own people. Said he, "I've found Him, I've found Him!"

All of the experiences I had during those very early years proved of great value in the years ahead when I presented the gospel among the Shinji, and Ruunda tribes which live even further north, when the time was ripe in the plan of God. And always this was the grand vision I looked forward to - that of reaching those who sat in darkness and in the shadow of death with the glorious, life-giving message of the Saviour.

Give thanks, O heart, for the high souls
That point us to the deathless goals -
Brave souls that took the perilous trail
And felt the vision that could not fail.

(Author unknown)

CHAPTER 5

Little Bird

Jungle Leaf:
A big bird is not trapped with chaff.

Little Bird, or *'Muido Katola'* in Chokwe, was a young African who lived in a village three days trek to the south-east from our mission station. This young fellow was very skilled in bushcraft and in the ways of his tribal culture but he had never heard the name of Jesus.

He was a hard worker, labouring diligently in the fields which he had cleared for himself out of the jungle. Little Bird had a peanut patch, and grew a rich crop of tobacco which he planned to sell in the diamond fields far away to the north, where he could get a good price for it.

Little Bird's day began soon after dawn was breaking over the eastern horizon. He ate some stiff porridge that was left over from the evening before, took a drink of water and set off for his fields. For his midday meal he roasted a piece of manioc in a small fire which he kindled at the edge of his field. In these parts of Africa the people have only one main meal a day, taken in the evening when their work in the fields is finished and the sun has dipped low in the western sky. Then they sit back and take their rest around the campfire.

In the evening Little Bird joined the older men at the palaver place to listen as they recounted their hunting experiences and repeated the local folklore. The young man eagerly absorbed the exciting stories, some of which were linked to his people's spirit worship, for they were all steeped in animistic beliefs. Their tribal customs had been practised for centuries. Little Bird smoked tobacco in the evening, but not too much, for he was yet a teenager. The greater portion of his crop he hoarded carefully, having dried it as he saw the older men doing, to sell at the diamond mines so far away.

As Little Bird prepared to make the long journey north, he had no idea that his plan was going to fit into that of One of whose existence he scarcely knew. At last one day in the dry season he was ready to march. He struggled with his sixty-pound load until it rested comfortably on his head, then he passed a stick over his shoulder and under the load to help him balance it as he made his way along the path. Little Bird secured his knife and axe in a skin belt around his waist and tied his bow and arrows on top of his load, as is the custom.

He soon became hot as he marched along all by himself. He rested at each river to have a long, cool drink before crossing. Then he disappeared once more onto the forest trails. Someone was waiting for Little Bird along that jungle path, unaware as Little Bird was of it. He was not a lion or a leopard, but someone of whom Little Bird had never heard.

One of the days of his journey, as he entered a village and slid his load to the ground he saw a group of people gathered around listening to a white man speaking to them. Now what had his elders said to him? Ah yes! The proverb said, "Curiosity finished the goats

of our ancestors." Little Bird was very curious, but he thought, "I don't want my curiosity to finish my father's goats; I don't want to become involved in a crime for which I will have to pay with my father's goats." Little Bird understood the proverb well. Nevertheless he approached and sat down at the outer edge of the group. The white man sat on a small wooden stool, talking to the people.

"Why, that white man is speaking my own tongue!" Little Bird said loudly. "Forgive me, my elder, what is this?" he asked the man nearest him.

"Be quiet, you young fellow," the man responded.

"What is he saying?" Little Bird asked again.

"I told you to be quiet! Do you want the white man to beat you?" So Little Bird sat still and listened.

"*Mumu Chocho Zambi Wazangile akwa hashi,*" said the white man.

"*Zambi...zambi...*I do not know that word," thought Little Bird.

"Hi, neighbour who is *Zambi*?" he asked.

"*Kanuke,* look at your nose, be quiet!" his neighbour replied. Then Little Bird heard the rest of the verse...... "*Iye wechele Mwanenyi wa wika......*"

"*Hoho, chitaka chinene!* (What a great puzzle!)" thought Little Bird. "Hi, neighbour," he called again, "Forgive me, who is *Mwanenyi*?"

"*Kwiji* (I don't know)" the man said. "Ask the white man when he is finished, will you not?"

For the first time, Little Bird was hearing, "For God so loved the world that He gave His only begotten Son... " As Little Bird reflected on the words he said to himself, "Yes, I have heard of *Zambi* (God), although I don't know Him. He made the trees and the grass and the forest and the rivers. But this *Mwanenyi* (His son).....who can He be?"

Then the white man asked the people to memorise the verse so that the words would stay with them. Little Bird repeated the words over and over with the rest of the villagers. He wondered what this white man was doing all alone in the wild bush country. He looked to see if the white man had brought a load of cloth for barter, but there was none. Oh dear! what did this mean! Little Bird had heard of white men who stole black men and forced them to work for them as slaves. Was this white man such a person? *Zambi...Mwanenyi...* now *Mahamba* (spirits), yes, he knew of such matters. There were *Mahamba* in his village. The *Mahamba* never showed the people *zango* (love), yet *Zambi* talks of love! Little Bird was intrigued but oh so puzzled!

When the heavens thundered and Little Bird was afraid the elders said, "God is speaking." Now this white man was trying to tell the people that God loves them. "Well," thought Little Bird, "this matter is very difficult to understand. God roars like thunder and flashes like lightening. Strange that our ancestors never spoke to us of Him as if He shows love. We have no idol of the name *Zambi*, but I recall what an old man in my tribe once said, 'In ancient days we worshipped one called *Kamwili*. He was God'."

Little Bird became more deeply perplexed by the presence of the white stranger in the village as he watched him move about. He seemed to have nothing to sell, but here he was, living in this jungle village! Was he inciting rebellion? Hi! Little Bird must be wary of him! But he could not stop thinking of the matters of which the white man spoke. Whoever heard that God had a son? And what was the short name the strange white man gave him?

Yesu. Yesu. Little Bird sighed. He had never heard of him. "I wonder where He lives," thought Little Bird. "What a pity that I cannot get near to ask this one Yesu why He died."

Puzzle upon puzzle for Little Bird. And still he could not stop thinking of the words he had learned by heart. Since he, like the rest of his tribespeople, could not read, he did not want to lose those words. Before he left the village he learned a song the white man taught the people, "*Kachi unevu liji, sako ku mbunge* (if you have heard the Word, place it in your heart)".

After resting longer than usual, Little Bird again loaded his tobacco on his head and set off through the forest. His people say that a word is a plant which grows. And so the seed of the Word of God had taken root in Little Bird's mind. Trekking day after day in the hot sun he had plenty of time to reflect on the word he had heard. He thought of another proverb, "Man, don't swallow what you have not chewed." Unhappily Little Bird just could not chew the message he had heard sufficiently to swallow it. Eventually he reached the diamond fields and sold his tobacco at a good profit. Relieved of his burden and with money in his pocket, he returned home.

A year passed, and one Sunday Little Bird came upon our mission compound. He was amazed to see a building larger than any he had seen before. He went inside and sat on a bench at the back. To his greater surprise, there was the same white man he had seen before in the village on the way to the diamond mines! And he was again teaching the people a verse. What was it? Yes! It was the very same one he had learned in the village so far away. *Zambi*, again? *Mwanenyi*, again? Death, again? *Yesu* again? Maybe this time he would understand. Little Bird waited at the back of the large building until someone came to him and asked what he wanted. That day that young African boy knelt by the bench and gave his life to the Saviour. What a thrill that was - Little Bird and the Saviour together!

Now Little Bird knew something that his fathers had never heard. *Zambi* was so different from their conception of Him. And he was told *Zambi* wanted to be a father to him. What? *Zambi* a father - to him?

Never! How could anyone approach God without the mediation of the *Mahamba*? Yet now Little Bird knew that he could dispense with all of the *Mahamba* since he had a personal relationship with his Father in heaven.

Soon Little Bird realised that if Zambi's Spirit lived inside him he could not smoke tobacco and defile his body which had become the home of the Holy Spirit. And so he stopped growing tobacco as well.

Little Bird stayed on at the mission station for three months. He was baptised in the stream nearby, with the villagers, believers and unbelievers alike, watching. One morning he came to my office, the office of the strange white man who camped in remote villages to tell the message of Zambi's love. Little Bird clapped his hands, the sign that he wanted to come inside and talk. I invited him in.

"Forgive me, I want to talk to you Ngana; may I?"

"Sit down, my brother, and let me know what is in your heart," I said.

"Ngana, I want to go away to my old village in the jungle."

"What, you want to go away back to where they worship the

spirits and do all the other things connected with witchcraft?" I asked.

"*Ewa* (yes), Ngana. I want to go back. Ngana, do you not know our wise saying, 'When you have eaten, don't forget to vomit up for the sake of others'."

"What?" I said.

"Yes," he continued, "you must share with others what you have enjoyed yourself. And I have a mother," said Little Bird. "She does not know John 3.16. She has never heard of *Zambi*, or of *Mwanenyi*. I want to go and tell her of the love of the Saviour who came to die for us."

"Go, Little Bird," I said, "and God be with you." We knelt together in prayer on the reed mat and I commended Little Bird to the Master who cares for all His messengers.

Off went Little Bird, walking three days back home to his old village to tell one dear soul of the Saviour's love. What excitement when he appeared in the forest clearing where the village stood. His friends crowded around, asking questions and yelling with delight to see him again. They wanted to know what he had seen in the world beyond their village. "Perhaps," they thought, "Little Bird will now stay with us again, and hunt as before and cultivate his tobacco. Did he not fetch a good price for it at the diamond mines?"

"Let's start a dance!" cried one. "Man, bring out the drums from where they are hanging in the trees! In the middle of the clearing grew a sacred tree called the *Muyombo*. Little Bird stayed clear of it. He also knew where the idols lay outside of the village, at the edge of the bush. When his friends couldn't find him in the morning they assumed he had gone to the idols to anoint them with fine meal and with the blood of a sacrifice to the ancestral spirits. After all, no young man in his right senses would risk grieving the ancestral spirits! But Little Bird was not there.

"Hi, Little Bird!" they called. But there was no answer. Then the young men looked inside the grass hut where he had spent the night. They gasped. Little Bird was kneeling by his bamboo bed. He was praying, but there was no idol there! They heard him as he was praying aloud. What, a man calling God 'Father'!

"He's gone off his head," they whispered. "What will the village men think of him now?" The elders questioned Little Bird about this strange report they heard of him. His answers were clear, and he used familiar proverbs to illustrate his points to them. Little Bird's mother listened carefully, but he saw that she was not impressed. Her old ideas concerning her idols still gripped her heart. She avoided making fun of her son, yet she clung to her beliefs in the ancestral spirits.

"Son, I am an old woman," she said. "I worship the way our fathers worshipped. I cannot forsake those ways; leave me alone."

"But Mother, I have found something better! I have found God - *Zambi* - who has a Son!" Little Bird said.

"What? God had a son, eh? Don't laugh at us! God lives away in the thunder clouds. Have you ever seen the lightening, my son? That is what God is. You say he had a son? Never!" Day after day Little Bird pleaded with his mother to convince her to receive the new message which he had received. At last, when she could endure his pleadings no longer, she agreed to go with him to the mission station to hear more of this unusual story.

They started out early in the morning when the dew hung heavily on the long grass alongside the jungle path. Little Bird walked first so that the dew would fall on him, and his mother could remain dry. All along the winding path Little Bird talked of Zambi's love, so far as he understood it. They finally arrived at the last river before climbing the hill to the mission station. Little Bird crossed over first with a thick stick in his hand to chase away any crocodiles lurking in the muddy water. He crossed safely and started climbing, when he heard a splash in the river.

"Mother, what is wrong?" he called. His mother stood in the middle of the river, her hands at her waist, and she was laughing. He jumped into the water again and waded over to her.

"Mother, what is it?" he panted.

"Well, my son, you know when we left our village I brought something with me, tied around my waist. It was the old ancestral idols, because I could not leave them," she said. "I have listened to you talking all along the bush path, and now, in the middle of the river I have decided that the Saviour you have been speaking of will be my Saviour too."

"But the splash in the river, Mother, what was it?"

"Ah, my son, that was the splash of my idols being thrown into the river. Since I do not need them any longer down they went, into the river!"

What a prayer meeting in the middle of the muddy jungle river there was that day! Little Bird, have you forgotten the crocodiles, man! So Little Bird returned to the mission compound with a mother quite changed from the old lady who had left the heathen village. Now she was washed by the blood of the Lamb. Some time later she was baptised, and joined with the other African believers to remember the Lord in the breaking of the bread each week.

Again I was busy in my office doing translation work, when Little Bird appeared once more. "What can he want today," I thought, "he has his mother here, and she is being looked after?"

"Ngana, I'm going away," he announced.

"Going away where, Little Bird?"

"Ngana, I have a brother, and my brother knows nothing of John 3.16," he said.

And so away went Little Bird along another jungle trail to reach his younger brother with the Good News of God's love. His brother gladly responded to Little Bird's urging, and they returned to the mission station together. There was the same twisted path, the same rivers to ford, the danger of crocodiles, the sleeping outside with all the attendant hazards of a night in the jungle. But it was all worth it to Little Bird, who had brought another lost sheep to the Good Shepherd.

But before Little Bird's brother could be baptised he crossed over his last earthly river and appeared in the clearing of the King Himself. The old mother lived on at the mission station, cared for by Margaret, until she, too, passed into the presence of her Saviour. Little Bird became my constant companion and my right hand man for many years after on my treks north into Shinjiland, teaching the people of *Zambi* and His Son.

The Africans say, "A wilting flower attracts no bee." Little Bird was a flower of God's grace who never allowed himself to wilt. He kept fresh for the service of the Master in the land of Angola, a land where blood would soon flow, and a new group of martyrs from the Shinji would enter into the presence of the Saviour, having gladly laid down their lives for Him.

CHAPTER 6

God's Faithfulness

*"...Under His wings shalt thou trust: His truth shalt be thy shield
and buckler... He shall call upon Me, and I will answer him: I
will be with him in trouble; I will deliver him and honour him"*
(Psalm 91.4b,15).

During the Second World War our communications with Britain
became difficult, and after the fall of Dunkirk were completely
severed so that we received no supplies and no funds. These proved
to be days of real testing. Eventually we had to sell most of our
clothes to obtain food for ourselves and our young child, Kenneth.
Margaret was left with only one dress and I had only one pair of
shorts and a shirt. We had come to what seemed to be the end.

Right then a letter arrived from the British Consulate in Luanda,
the capital of Angola, offering to repatriate us safely back home to
Scotland. We spread out the letter before the Lord and sought His
guidance and wisdom. In the quiet of His presence we decided to
stay, and that we would have to decline this kind offer of help. God
had sent us to Angola and He had not told us to leave. We would
stay. And so we waited to see how our God would provide for us.

One of the missionaries who was retiring from the field very
kindly sent overland to us a herd of milk cattle, which was a
tremendous help in providing milk for Kenneth. God had come in
to meet our need. Then came the dry season when no rain fell for
several months. The entire bush country became like an oven,
and the long grass became dry and dangerous. Some of the young
African boys were playing in the grass near where our eight cows
were foraging for feed. Without any thought of doing wrong, they
set fire to the grass. Immediately, the flames roared over a vast

area, trapping the cows and burning all of them to death.

When we came out of the house to see what had happened, we were speechless with the enormity of this loss at such a time of need. The African Christians gathered around to see what our reaction would be to this crucial loss. They stood with tears running down their cheeks, too overcome with emotion to speak. We returned to the house and fell on our knees in prayer to our sovereign Master who had sent us to this land. No words would come as we knelt on the reed mat. My Bible lay between us, and I did something I had never done before. In deep anguish of soul I just opened it at random to see what would happen. Like a flash from heaven we read the words from 1 Kings 19.12, "After the fire, a still small voice." Yes, we were to prove that God is faithful to His servants, and was keeping account of each circumstance of our lives. We rose from our knees refreshed in our spirits and confident that we were safe in the Lord's care. Little did we know that we were also about to face another test.

Senhor Horacio de Sa, a Portuguese trader whom I'd known well for some time, and who had come to me for dental work at various times, sent a message to the mission station for me to come down to his store to talk to him. I was ushered into a small office at the back of the store where the trader kept a large safe. He took a key and opened the safe which was literally bulging with money. He had in it thousands of pounds in Portuguese currency.

"Senhor, I know that you have been cut off from your homeland these many months and nothing has been coming through to you," he said. "You have helped me in the past. Please take whatever you need and pay me back when you can." I was immobile, seeing so much money within my grasp yet knowing that I could take none of it. This was the severity of the test. The Scripture says, "Owe no one anything" (Romans 13.8). How could I promise to pay anything back? When the trader saw my hesitancy he stooped down, filled his hands with money and tried to force me to take it. I moved away and clasped my hands behind my back. (What a temptation for a Scot!)

I tried as best I could to express my gratitude to my friend for his kindness. When words failed me I simply turned and headed back to the mission compound. As I climbed the hill I wondered if I had done the right thing by refusing such a kind and sincere offer. Was I being fair to my wife and child? It was a great relief to reach home and unburden my heart to Margaret and to find that she fully understood why I had responded as I did. We still had little to eat and experienced weeks of gnawing hunger. In fact the hunger pangs seemed to grow more severe after that test with the trader. Still we believed that God had promised to meet our needs and we waited for his answer. His promissory note was Psalm 91.15, "He shall call upon Me, and I will answer him."

One Saturday afternoon the weather was fine and we decided to take a walk down the hill from the station. Half way down we looked up to see two white people approaching. Margaret cried out, "Oh, my dress!" I, too, suddenly became painfully aware of my shabby attire, but there was no chance to turn back, and we went on to meet these people.

As we met, the man asked, "Are you Mr. Allison?" He introduced himself, and I recognised the name of a well known African explorer. We invited them back to our home - but with sinking hearts. How could we possibly entertain this American couple when we had not even one spoonful of tea to offer them? We sat down, and to save further embarrassment I said, "I'm sorry, folks, but we have nothing to offer you except a cup of water."

They laughed heartily. "We haven't come to take, but rather to give to you!" Then they opened their boxes and began pulling out every kind of tinned food, tinned milk and cream, and Roses tea bags. We had never even seen tea bags before. What a feast! This was the answer, the "still, small voice" for which we had been waiting. We recognised it without any doubt; our Father had spoken at last. I drank six cups of tea without stopping! The visitors had also brought clothes for Kenneth, his proper size, of course, for God makes no mistakes. We had been without quinine for many months, and here before us in a heap lay *one million* life-saving tablets of mepacrine, a gift from the American government. We had been going about with body temperatures of 101-102 F, not ill enough to be in bed, and not fit enough to be on our feet.

We learned that the British Consul in Luanda had told these kind folks about us, and they had made their way into the interior without delay. What touched us most was that they had enquired as to

Kenneth's age and had brought him new baby clothes they paid for themselves.

The following week, on the strength of the feast, I started out on trek to visit some of the African villages. When I returned home, I spotted Margaret out on the veranda, waving excitedly to me. She pushed into my hands a cablegram that had come from New York, addressed "Allison, Angola," yet it reached us. What was this? We knew no one there. But there it was - a cablegram for the royal sum of sixty four pounds sterling. Our God had not just given us the cake, but the icing too! We never found out who sent the money, but we were convinced that it too was part of "the still, small voice". God had promised to meet our needs and He had done it in two ways. First, He had given us the grace to do without, then He had sent the food and the money in His own chosen time. We richly experienced the truth of Isaiah 25.9, "Lo, this is our God; we have waited for Him, and He will save us: this is the Lord; we have waited for Him, we will be glad and rejoice in His salvation."

Then and in later years too Margaret had to learn to improvise many things in the food line, not having a supermarket round the corner. Since peanuts were plentiful she made gourmet peanut butter! She also learned the art of cooking in a hole in the ground when we were out on trek. Dried grass and sticks were thrown into a hole about four feet long by two feet wide and about three feet deep, and kindled. This is a bush oven! On top of this Margaret placed a piece of tin which soon became hot and served as a baking tray on which our home-made bread rose to bush perfection.

We soon learned that salt was a rare commodity and deeply appreciated by the Africans, so, whenever we could, we took a supply of it on trek to use as gifts for chiefs and for barter when we needed to purchase chickens and other kinds of food. There were salt blocks on the River Quango, but most villagers had to make a five-day trek to reach the river to procure the salt, and then make another five day walk home.

The story is told of Dan Crawford who instructed his servant to spread the table, to put out knife, fork and plates, and to wait for heaven's dinner bell to ring. Sure enough, in came a woman with a plate of mush and meat. God's dinner bell had sounded in heaven and Dan's needs were met.

> *O Thou in whose Presence my soul takes delight,*
> *On Whom in affliction I call,*
> *My comfort by day and my song in the night,*
> *My hope, my salvation, my all.*

(Author unknown)

"Thou shalt not be afraid...for the arrow that flieth by day..."
(Psalm 91.5b).

In the same way, many times George Wiseman and I relied on the lovingkindness of the Lord to meet our needs when out on trek, sometimes as far as four or five hundred miles from the mission station.

Before leaving our camp very early one morning we committed our problem of lack of food into the hands of our heavenly Father who had promised to take care of us while we were taking care of the spread of the gospel. We had camped under the stars on the edge of a vast plain, until the first rays of light in the east awoke us to the coming day. On such a morning the men rise and go about their tasks silently, preparing their weapons. As the lovely antelope are timid creatures which are easily disturbed, the hunters must be quiet, and test the wind. They must remain downwind of the animals so that the creatures do not catch their scent and run away. A hunt is not recreation for these people, but a survival search for food.

We moved out of camp in single file, still as silent as snakes slithering through the bush. I took care to watch for twigs and branches on the path. One snap and an animal will be alerted. Off he runs, ears standing erect. As the Africans say, "It is the rabbit whose ears are lying down who is caught, but the one with the ears alert escapes." My legs soon become tired, and the rifle on my shoulder a heavy burden.

"Oh, Ngana," said the guide walking behind me, "an elephant never feels the weight of his own tusks."

"Ha, ha!" laughed other hunters nearby. "The Ngana has fallen behind. He's feeling the weight of his tusks! Let's wait for him." They were very amused. Such banter is common as hunters follow the trail to the place where the hunt will begin.

On this particular day I suggested to George, "You go that way with a group of the hunters, and I'll go round the far clump of trees to get the animals between us." One of the hunters served as a decoy, gently waving a stick with an old rag tied to it. We watched his every step. Up went the heads of the animals grazing quietly in the early morning, and they too watched him as he moved slowly along the plain.

"Little Bird," I whispered to my friend, "we'll go down here and circle." Little Bird hunched down and moved slowly to keep out of sight and smell. Suddenly a loud P-i-n-g —— p-i-n-g —— p-i-n-g ripped overhead, and Little Bird straightened into a speedy gallop. I dived for his legs in my best rugby tackle, slamming him to the ground, my arm thrown over him. George's bullets continued to whiz overhead. Once more Little Bird tried to jump up and run. Pi-n-g! again a bullet cratered into the earth right by his head.

"Lie down, Little Bird," I whispered hoarsely, "death is riding the air. Get down, man, get down, stay down!" I realised that my foolish strategy of separating from my colleague had nearly cost Little Bird and me our lives. "Death does not spread a mat," says the African proverb. No, it comes unexpectedly, and it had never come so near as at that moment. Another proverb says, "Death, like an eagle, takes the chicks and the big ones." Lying still on the ground in the bush I reflected how swiftly the eagle of death had swooped to the African plain that morning.

"Shall we get up now, Ngana?" said Little Bird.

"Wait to hear if any more 'pings' come," I said. A few moments later George ran over the ridge toward us, white-faced. He knelt on the ground by us in great relief. Never again would we separate in such a way during a hunt. God's faithfulness and care in preserving our lives that day was yet another gift of His unfailing goodness to us.

Perhaps the material privations which we suffered for the sake of Christ were less severe than the emotional strain Margaret bore when we had to send Kenneth, David, and Helen far away to boarding school. Starting at the age of six, they had to go to Sakeji school in what was then Northern Rhodesia for their education. Only a mother can fully realise what those partings meant, but the path had been chosen long before, and the Master always gave the grace necessary for that time when it came. This verse of a hymn was a great comfort to her:

> *Lead, kindly light, amid the encircling gloom,*
> *Lead Thou me on.*
> *The night is dark and I am far from home -*
> *Lead Thou me on.*
> *Keep Thou my feet; I do not ask to see*
> *The distant scene; one step's enough for me.*

(John Henry Newman)

Great creativity came into play when preparing the children for the long, long road to school in a different country. Often we did not have the school fees available, and often Margaret sold clothes to obtain cash to help meet the fees.

The service of the Lord demanded our all, and was worth all that it cost. Could we have seen the thousands who would come to know the Saviour in later days, how light those trials would have seemed! But of course that was all hidden from us during the early days of ploughing and sowing the Good Seed. These were not fields "white unto harvest" but fields on which much labour had to be expended before the harvest could be gathered in. The ploughing, sowing, and scattering of the Seed is not easy work, but "He that goeth forth and weepeth, bearing precious seed, shall doubtless come again with rejoicing, bringing his sheaves with him" (Psalm 126:6).

Family Group 1950

CHAPTER 7

Fire in Shinjiland

George and Emma Wiseman lived on a station about sixty miles away, which was many days' journey by foot. Despite the distance, George and I developed a mutual burden for the Shinji tribe of the beautiful far north country. One day the loved physician Dr. L B Bier had spread a map of Angola on his floor and, pointing a prophetic finger on the Shinji, Ruunda and Mbangala lands, said, "Look, fellows, there is this vast region, the neediest in Angola." George and I were kneeling together there on the floor, and the desire kindled within us to reach northward with the good news of 'Yesu'.

Between the strong Mbangala and the fierce Chokwe, the Shinji lived as mere slaves, always at the mercy of invaders from either side. The Shinji had two nicknames, one of which they took themselves, signifying 'The Ants', and another given to them by the surrounding tribes meaning 'Firebrands', mere sticks that have been left over after the larger burning.

When George and I first trekked into this northern region of Angola in April 1948, we estimated, by making an unscientific linguistic survey, that there were about 40,000 Shinji, many of whom lived a semi-nomadic life. They spoke Chokwe with some variations, so we were able to communicate with them relatively easily. I was struck by the fact that Shinji grass or bamboo huts, contrary to any other African huts I had ever seen, had two doors. The tiny, two feet high by one and a half feet wide rear door was usually well camouflaged, and when a stranger clapped his hands at the front opening, the whole household disappeared out the back to hide in the jungle until they could determine the identity of

the visitor to make sure it wasn't someone who would carry them off as slaves.

We later learned that they built only grass or bamboo huts because in their fear they dared not make stronger ones of wattle and mud that reminded them of graves, where only the dead lie. In fact the land the Shinji live in was often called Bambooland because of the widespread use of bamboo for everything from houses to chairs, beds, and boats, and it was a common sight to encounter a person carrying his lightweight bamboo bed from one place to another.

As George and I trekked through this country to explore the possibility of developing a gospel work among the Shinji, inevitably we found the villages deserted. In each village someone had seen us approaching along the twisted forest path and had alerted the entire population, so that everyone had vanished to hide in the surrounding undergrowth by the time we entered the clearing. We were left with an audience of goats, sheep, chickens, and sometimes pigs! This was discouraging to say the least, until we discovered a strategy that worked while we gained the confidence of the villagers.

Since a literal reading of the Scriptures mandates that the gospel be preached "to every creature", we sat on low village stools and began to teach the gospel to the village livestock as listed above! What we had realised was that the people were actually within earshot though we could not see them, and even though we must have appeared ridiculous they were hearing the Good News of salvation.

It was a most difficult task to make contact with these people who always lived in terror. We were, after all, merely two more unknown men who, for all they knew, might have been sent as decoys by either the Chokwe or the Mbangala to trap them into enslavement. In addition to their fear of strangers, the Shinji were spiritually bound by the power of witchcraft, a power which is tangible and not imaginary. While most tribal people keep their idols in the bush near the edge of their village, the Shinji kept theirs in their huts.

David Livingstone was the first white person to visit Shinjiland, and since then the only others to do so were Portuguese traders, and a few officials who maintained lonely forts. No missionary had yet brought the Good News of God's salvation. The following extract from Livingstone's diaries document his impressions of the Shinji.

"Fashions of the BaShinji"

"10th March, 1855. The physical development of the negroes of Angola seems to have deteriorated. They are not so strongly formed as the independent tribes. The slave system acts injuriously on their physiognomy [facial features] as well. They are much addicted to lying and thieving, and have many immoral practices besides.

"The BaShinji, too, just over the border, seem to possess the same characteristics. Their colour is dirty black; foreheads in general low and compressed above the eyes, the noses flat and much extended laterally, the alae spread over the cheeks. This arises from their custom of inserting bits of stick and reed in the septum; these expand the alae. Their teeth are deformed, being filed to points. The covering is a loose skin hung in front and equally loose behind. They cultivate pretty largely and rely on their agricultural products for the supply of salt, flesh, tobacco and cloths.

"No sooner does a [travelling] party arrive at the usual resting places than numbers of women are seen wending their way to them with meal, manioc roots, pumpkin, etc. on their heads for sale. The wants of the travellers are soon supplied, and the more expeditiously if they happen to have slaughtered an ox. This draws forth all the resources of both old and young. The haggling is sufficiently noisy but all is conducted with good temper and civil banter. The villages present groups of conical, irregularly planted brown huts with some trees (bananas) in their midst and stands for drying manioc meal and roots near...

"They plait their hair fantastically. A woman passed this morning with hers in the form of a man's hat, and except on near inspection, it was impossible to perceive that it was really her own hair and not a hat. Others have the whole arranged in tufts, a cord of hair being plaited along the ridge of each. Some preserve the fashion seen in ancient Egyptian paintings. All live in comparative ease and independence. When they cut themselves, they do it daintily, making incisions which form ornamental cicatrices afterwards. Many of the women tattoo their bellies all over with these raised cicatrices.

"The men show different tastes. Some are dandies; everything about them is ornamented. Others drill a musical instrument all the livelong day, and those who cannot afford one with iron bars make one of wood and reeds. Others never go anywhere without a canary in a cage, and others carefully tend a little dog which is to be eaten.

"The scenery of their country is generally green with a tint of yellow, the grass long, the paths about a foot wide most worn in the middle, and the tall grass overhanging and brushing against the feet and legs. Lizards are often disturbed by the passing traveller; they rustle among the grass. A serpent occasionally lies across the path. There are not many birds. Everything animal is trapped and eaten. Mice are dug up, and the half of the labour required to follow them in their burrows would cultivate food for many swine."

(David Livingstone's Diary)

George and I found Livingstone's descriptions still applicable to a large degree. The women were so poorly dressed that they were almost naked, and they still decorated themselves by boring a hole in the bridge of their noses and inserting a stick about four inches long. While amused at their appearance, I was intrigued to know how they wiped their noses wearing such an apparatus! Curiosity overcame me one day and I asked a Shinji woman how she coped with such an emergency. To my surprise she swiftly and expertly extracted the stick, blew her nose with two fingers and popped the stick back in again! Needless to say I never asked to see a repeat of that performance! The women also wore large copper bangles on their legs, from the ankle to the knee, and on their arms. As they walked along the bush paths the bangles made such a noise that the women could be heard long before they could be seen.

We were amazed at the widespread sickness in Shinjiland. We saw many young children with two sets of teeth, the first ones having never come out. They presented rather a curious spectacle when they opened their mouths. We offered to extract the teeth, but the adults were adamant in their refusal of our help. We saw cripples in almost every village, some with pieces of wood strapped to their hands to protect them as they crawled about. Nowhere else in Angola had we seen so many women with goitres, and not just one, but many had three or four around their necks. What a paradise for a surgeon! During a later trip we witnessed a moving scene as an old blind man came up to the front to confess faith in Christ, and I thought if I were a Shinji I would certainly have an extra reason to trust Christ and make right sure of getting a new body one day!

The Shinji appeared to us to be poor traders, evidently content with their mush, and tobacco which grows prolifically throughout their country. While the Shinji cultivated some manioc, peanuts, pumpkins and sweet potatoes for food, tobacco was their favourite crop. Although most westerners think of these as indigenous African crops, most in this region were imported by the Portuguese. Manioc came from Brazil in two varieties, poisonous and non-poisonous, and the banana plant and rice from other countries. Among the tobacco fields, the Shinji also cultivated a kind of *cannabis sativa*, which caused a drug-like sensation. This they called *leamba*. They seemed to have no desire to work or to tidy their villages.

Appalled as we were by the conditions these folks lived in, their bodies covered with filth and their huts overrun with rats and lice, we knew they were loved by the Saviour and we considered it an immense privilege to be the first to tell these precious tribespeople of the Lord Jesus Christ who had died for them. Their villages had been established long before either of us was born, and through all the intervening years God had been at work. He had prepared us, through discipline and trial, for this greatest of all tasks. We had to learn not only the language, but the customs, the etiquette and modes of thinking which were unique to the Shinji. And at the same time God had been preparing them to receive His message. In the language of the proverb, "A small rabbit does not cut down tall grass", yet here were we, God's messengers, small in ourselves, sent to cut down the "tall grass" in Shinjiland. Yes, there were many dangers, much loneliness and sickness; and for years, a lot of sowing to be done ere the harvest would be reaped.

During a second trip north in 1948, between Camaxilo and the Congo border we met two Africans who had been taught to read by missionaries from the Unevangelised Tribes Mission, and we left copies of 'God's Way of Salvation' in their own language. We were warmly received by all the Portuguese Chefes and traders we encountered, and gave them copies of the Scriptures. Most encouraging of all, several Shinji professed faith in Christ during this trip. When we returned the following year we found that some had continued to pray by themselves, though in much ignorance.

In this same village the chief's wife had erected a brewing still and was making a real alcoholic intoxicant. I found her busy with it just before the gospel meeting one evening. I was interested to see how well designed and constructed it was. We poured some of the liquid on the ground and found when we lit a match to it that it was real fire water. Whoof! It ignited and burned. We spoke to the chief and begged him for his own good and that of the people to destroy the still and to pour out the vicious liquid. It makes people mad while under its influence, and they often became extremely dangerous. One time only the grace of God and George's long arm saved me from having my head split open with an axe by a man who was drunk with the stuff. By the end of the third trip we realised that whilst there was great need for pioneer treks such as we were making, the only way in which something permanent would be accomplished was by slogging on at the various places where we had already reached people.

On the fourth trip, in late 1949, we found that several Roman Catholic priests had followed in our wake and planted their catechists in the three strategic centres in which we had been working. A less discouraging surprise awaited us when we entered the Kwilo district and found a large population composed of Luunda, Shinji, Marapa, Songo, Lwona and Chokwe. We'd never encountered such a tribal conglomeration. We spent most of our time among the Luunda and found them to be quite different from the others. Their villages were bigger and much cleaner, and it was such a welcome change from the constant filth of the others. The Luunda also seemed more sympathetic toward us, and more attentive and respectful toward the teaching.

The Lord gave us large audiences among these people three times a day. Often they gathered in the morning before we had risen from our beds. In the evenings the women hurried to prepare their mush so they wouldn't be late for the gospel service. At each meeting several hundred sat on the ground and heard the Great Evangel for the first time in their lives. After we'd been with them a short time, fear concerning their idols gripped them, and it was pathetic to see them groping in their spiritual darkness for the Light. They crowded to our tent door with their idols, begging us to take them. Others plead with us to burn theirs. We had to sit down again and quietly explain that God first of all wanted them to repent. Their cry was, "Don't go and leave us with these idols!" Many made a profession of faith, including one man who confessed that he had murdered quite a few people.

The last Sunday evening before we left this village, an African appeared from an adjacent river where he'd been fishing. He said that he was a believer! He entered his hut and returned with a New Testament, a hymnbook and a copy of 'God's Way of Salvation', all in his own language. Apparently he had been brought to the Lord at the diamond mines, but on returning home he had not followed on in his faith. For us, meeting a believer in the land who could also read and write was like finding a gold reef in a wilderness. At the evening meeting he professed restoration to the Lord.

The Francisco Story

At the Camaxilo Fort, an African approached us and introduced himself as a believer in Christ. His name was Francisco. He led us to a hut where we saw something we'll never forget. There sat six young men on logs, reading Portuguese Bibles! These men had just arrived the day before from an island off the west coast of Angola, where they'd been brought to the Lord by a Portuguese Christian. Sitting down with them we marvelled at the Spirit's leading us to them as they had been seeking someone to help them. And we learned the story of Fransisco.

The island of San Tome has been infamous in history because of the slave trade that was carried on from the interior of Africa. Having been forced from their homes on the mainland, some slaves remained on that island to work the rich plantations for the benefit of their owners, while others were shipped to the American colonies. The history of the great work which the Spirit of God accomplished in Shinjiland is intimately connected with San Tome.

Many years before George and I trekked into Shinji country to start our pioneer work, a man and his wife, along with their family were harshly uprooted from their home village in the Camaxilo district of Shinjiland and taken as slaves to San Tome. What agonising thoughts must have been theirs as they were driven like beasts of burden to the coast, and what bitterness lingered against the Europeans who perpetrated such cruelty upon innocent people.

Dr. David Livingstone was the first to do something to heal what he called the "open sore of Africa". Charles Swan, one of the early brethren pioneers in Central Africa, also did much to lay this "open sore" before the supposedly civilised world. Swan published a book entitled *The Slavery of Today*, which aroused tremendous interest and had great repercussions even in England where certain commercial firms had vested interests in San Tome.

While these poor people were prisoners on the island, God in His mercy sent one of His servants from Portugal to work among the slaves, bringing to them the liberating power of the gospel. One of those who responded was the son of the slave couple from Shinjiland. Seeing that the boy had potential, but was completely illiterate, the missionary decided to teach him the rudiments of reading and writing. Progress was slow, as the lessons had to be learned after the day's hard toil was completed. By the light of a flickering fire, the missionary and the lad got down to work, and eventually the boy was able to read the New Testament in Portuguese. When the missionary left San Tome, he gave the Testament to the boy, and since it was the only book available, the young man continued to read and study it in the evenings.

After more than twenty years of hard labour the parents were freed to return to their former home in Shinjiland, a place where no one among their semi-nomadic tribespeople would know them. Although it was a relief for them to leave the plantations, the bitter years of forced labour had sapped their strength and left them without much hope for the future. The son, Fransisco, began to inquire about Christians and missionaries, but to no avail. And then one afternoon Fransisco was sitting on a small stool at the front of his mud hut reading his Portuguese Bible when he heard a cry, "*Alongeshi heza, Alongeshi heza*! (the missionaries have arrived!)"

Jumping up from his stool he ran down the hill and met George and me face to face. Grasping our hands, he praised God for sending us to his home. We climbed the hill together and sat down to hear the story of what happened in San Tome and of his conversion to Christ. He introduced us to his six friends. What a meeting was held that day on top of the hill, when hundreds of men and women thronged to hear the message of the gospel.

More Opportunities

During 1950, George and I made two more trips to Shinjiland. The second of these, to the Camaxilo area and way beyond to the Luunda tribe, was most heart-warming. At Maha-Chikoka we found a group of believers progressing very well with their daily meetings. We stayed with them ten days, and many more professed faith in the Lord Jesus. Each day we held three meetings, one for believers and then two gospel meetings. Afterward we pushed on down the Kwilo valley to the Luunda villages and were encouraged to find two more villages where the people were holding meetings daily. There, too, we had meetings that were splendidly attended.

Some of the local traditions we encountered paralleled Scriptural truth in appearance, but they did not mean the same thing at all.

So we had to be very careful to explain the Word of God as fully and as accurately as possible to avoid any confusion in the African's minds. But despite our earnest efforts to communicate, there were misunderstandings galore in those early days of pioneer work!

The Song of the Suffering One

One night George and I were sitting around the campfire as we usually did with a group of Shinji in a previously unreached district, when the young men brought out their drums and started dancing. The dancers formed two lines facing each other, about three feet apart. Africans across the subcontinent love to sing in this antiphonal manner, chanting the same words over and over in turn. Singing is sometimes a way of communication, and a song can also serve as a warning. Knowing this, I listened to catch the words as the men danced before me. Suddenly George and I startled at the same moment. What were these words they were singing?

"*Mumwese lamba, ngwe amwesele lamba, Mwana wa Kalunga* (Make him to suffer just as they made the son of the infinite one to suffer; make him to suffer just as they made the son of the infinite one to suffer... !)" Where did such words come from, and what could they possibly mean?! Plenty of noise as they continued to dance, but no explanation was forthcoming. The meaning had been lost in the mist of the centuries, though it had been passed down faithfully from generation to generation.

In the early morning I called the old men of the village and enquired about *Mwana Kalunga*.

"Oh," they replied, shaking their wise heads, "this song was handed down to us from our elder men who learned it from their ancients, but we don't know who this *Mwana Kalunga* was," they said. "Do you?"

"Yes, Fathers, we know," I replied. "His name is Yesu and He was made to suffer for our sins." So starting from this jungle song, I revealed to them from the Scriptures the message of this Son of the Infinite One, who was Jesus, the One who suffered on the cross for their sins. The meaning of it all swept over these young men that night and many turned to this Son of the Infinite One who suffered for their sakes. A few years later, in terrible situations of conflict, some of those very young men would in turn lay down their lives for the sake of the name of this Son of the Infinite One whom they had come to know and serve.

The Tribal Custom of Baptism

Roosters woke me early one fine morning in one of the bush villages, and as I sat at the entrance of my tent fully rousing myself from sleep with a cup of coffee, a group of Shinji came out of the village walking toward the river. Hoping they weren't leaving for the day before I had a chance to hold a gospel service, I called out greetings and asked where they were going so early.

"We're just going to the river - we'll be back in a little while," they called. Now I knew that a "little while" could mean all morning in remote bush country where the only clock is the sun moving across the sky, but as the river was close by I watched from a distance. Two men entered the water and were followed by a woman who stood between them in the water. After a few moments, they dipped her in the water and then they all returned to the river bank. I could hardly believe my eyes! What! A Christian baptism! I thought. Why, I was sure that the gospel had never reached this remote district! Eagerly I ran down to meet them.

"I thought you had never heard the gospel before!" I said.

"No, we have never heard the word that you are bringing to our village," one replied.

"Well then, who told you about baptism?" I asked.

"Baptism?" They looked at one another, puzzled. "No, we have never heard of baptism."

"Then what was that you did with that woman in the river just now?" I asked.

"Oh, Oh! That? That is a custom of our tribe!" they laughed quietly. "Our forefathers told us about this and their forefathers told them too. We do this all the time," they said.

"You elder men, please tell me what this means to you?" I then said.

"Well you see, that woman whom we dipped in the water is a widow. Her husband died a short time ago and she is going to be remarried, and this is our custom for all widows who are going to be remarried. We take them down to the river and immerse them." Now I was really puzzled. I invited some of the elder men to sit in my camp, and they continued.

"Because the woman is a widow she has to go through tribal rites before she can be given to another man. You see, Ngana, when we immerse her in the water we are breaking the past life with her 'old man'." Her old man! Could I be hearing properly?

"Yes, we break the ties with her old man by immersing her in the water and then she is free to be joined to her new husband."

How I was amazed at yet another custom, hidden in the mist of many centuries and handed down from one generation to another, which helped me to explain Biblical truth to these tribespeople. Romans 6, with its teaching about believers' baptism and the concept of the 'old man' and the 'new man' presented no problem to the new Christians of this tribe. Wherever I went among the Shinji after this, I used this picturesque illustration, and the smile of identification and understanding lit up their faces.

Meanings of other tribal customs, however, had to be carefully disassociated from Biblical practices. One group performs a ceremony in which teenaged youths are taken down to the river and completely immersed, "baptised" by two of the village elders while the witchdoctor watches from the bank. As soon as the youths emerge from the water he calls out, "Now you are born again, and you are getting a new name!" And so we came to realise that while great dangers lurked in the forest in the forms of lions and other wild beasts, greater dangers to the spread of the gospel hid in such rites that blinded the minds of the people to the Truth. Such discoveries spurred us on to get an ever greater knowledge and understanding of as much tribal rite, ceremony and superstition as we could learn.

Blood In The Eyes

There were no books and no schools in Shinjiland. The people were completely illiterate. When they saw George and me sitting at the entrance to our tent, often reading our Bibles, they were amazed at this strange behaviour, and it gave opportunity for one of the witchdoctors to invent and disseminate a strange rumour.

The witchdoctor was very displeased by our presence because he saw that should people accept the story of the gospel and follow Christ, he would lose trade and ultimately his power over his people. Inspired by his evil master, Satan himself, the witchdoctor called together the young men in the village.

"Youths, listen to me," he said. "Do you know why these missionaries are able to read a book and you cannot?"

"No, *Mwata* (Sir), we do not know."

"Well listen and I'll tell you," he said. "These folks caught a slave, killed him and then took his blood and anointed their eyes with the blood of the slave; so that blood opened their eyes and gave them the gift of being able to read a book."

The young men gasped. "*Mwata*, can that be true?" they asked. "*Ni Zambi*! (Before God!)". And they began to look sideways at George and me as if we really were the evil ones.

"Watch out, fellows!" the witchdoctor concluded, "If you follow their teachings you will be forced to capture a slave too, and kill him and anoint each other's eyes with his blood!"

Within a few days this fantastic story had gripped the imaginations of all the timid young Shinji men, already in that district. People stopped attending meetings through fear of the witchdoctor's tale. It seemed that the Evil One had gained a victory, and George and I were hard pressed to know what to do, for it was almost impossible to try to convince the people of the witchdoctor's lies.

As we struggled with the answer I thought of how this tale of "blood in the eyes" in some small way illustrates the gospel story.

In Ephesians I.18, Paul prays that they might have "the eyes of your understanding enlightened", which, of course, has been accomplished through the blood of the Son of God, our Saviour, shed on the cross for our sins.

These people lived daily in the fear of the *Mahamba* (spirits). They resisted looking closely into another person's eyes, saying, "Why, we cannot, we dare not look into the eyes of another in case that one is wicked, and the evil spirit might jump out of their eyes and enter ours!" With a superstitious background like this, it was not difficult to understand how these tribespeople believed the witchdoctor's story. The real struggle was not between the missionaries and the people, but rather between God and Satan. The powers of darkness knew that the liberating power of the gospel was now at hand, and the Shinji, who had lived in gross heathendom for centuries, would not easily be let go by Satan and his emissaries.

The solution which George and I arrived at was to gather all the young folk together and to teach them the rudiments of reading and writing. What a job! Not only had we to teach the gospel message but to run a bush school as well! So the idea of "each one teach one" emerged, and the Shinji learned that there is no magic in being able to read.

Yet we were able to use the story of "Blood in the Eyes" as a bridge to explain the gospel to the Shinji. We praise God for each one of the thousands who have had their eyes opened and who have received the precious gift of eternal life paid for by the blood of Christ. Their blindness has gone forever. Like another of long ago they can say, "One thing I know, that, whereas I was blind, now I see" (John 9.25).

Cultural Understanding

Another hindrance to the work came about in a very innocent manner. Some years later Margaret was with me one time and we made our camp outside one of the villages overlooking a vast plain. Early in the morning I went around the village urging the people to come and sit down while I told them of Jesus. Jesus? Who was He? They knew and spoke of God, and believed that He created the heaven and the earth. Did He not speak when thunder rolled over their land? Yes, that was God! But how strange to hear that this unknown One had a Son called Jesus. Now who could believe this? And who was the mother of this Son? Finally that morning some of the most curious Shinji came trembling to the tent and sat down outside, and I began to teach them slowly and carefully.

Now Margaret had false teeth which she removed at night and popped into a glass of water. While I was talking, she came out of the tent carrying the glass, removed the teeth from it and put them into her mouth.

"Ngana! Ngana! Your wife is a witch! She can take out her teeth and put them back!" yelled the Shinji as they jumped up in sheer terror, and fled. It was impossible for me to coax them from their huts to listen to the gospel that day. With sad hearts we trekked away to another village having learned yet another lesson in cultural sensitivity. Not only had we to watch our tongues, but our teeth as well!

We might have been somewhat prepared for this by an earlier experience in Mbangalaland. George and I had taken along an old wind-up gramophone and played records of gospel singing by the campfire at night. The Mbangala squatted around the machine, their eyes wide with amazement, trying desperately to understand this mystery. Where did the voice come from? Who spoke? An almost naked people sat in the jungle clearing listening spellbound as the music echoed through the silent forest.

One by one the people crept forward, knelt down, and said, "Oh God, you who are in this black box... "

Startled, I suddenly realised that these people thought George and I travelled with our 'god' in this small black box! Never again did we bring out the gramophone until we were sure the people understood how it worked.

We also had to learn to be more than just teachers of the gospel, and to become sincere friends of the people. The African word for "friend" actually means "blood friend". True friendship involved a certain ritual. Two friends, wishing to seal their relationship, kill a chicken, drain its blood in a bowl, make manioc mush and sit down facing each other. Each takes a lump of the mush and dips it in the blood before eating it. And so their friendship is established by the shedding of blood. Another way to seal friendship is to cut one another on the chest, just enough to draw blood, then dip mush in each other's blood and eat that.

Opposition also came from traders who were not doing the brisk trade in strong drink and images they had done in previous years. Some of the images were used by many of the diviners, who mixed them in their divining baskets with bones and other articles which they "threw" to identify a guilty person.

Those first years, laying the foundation for the work, were really hard. The late Dr. Laws of Malawi once remarked, "Foundations don't usually show; they are hidden underground." But, praise God, the superstructure of His church would appear in Shinjiland, growing steadily for all to see and admire the true grace of God, until the whole of Northern Angola from the Quango River in the west, to the Congo border in the east, would be fully occupied for Christ.

> Saviour, sprinkle many nations;
> Fruitful let Thy sorrows be;
> By Thy pains and consolations
> Draw the Shinji unto Thee:
> Of Thy cross and wondrous story,
> Be it to the Shinji told
> Let them see Thee in Thy glory
> And Thy mercy manifold.
>
> Saviour, Shinji still are waiting;
> Stretched the hand and strained the sight
> For Thy Spirit, new creating,
> Love's pure flame, and wisdom's light.
> Give the word, and of the preacher
> Speed the foot and touch the tongue,
> Till on earth by every creature
> Glory to the Lamb be sung.
>
> (R. Crawford Allison)

> Go, labour on, spend and be spent,
> Thy joy to do the father's will;
> It is the way the Master went -
> Should not the servant tread it still?
>
> (Horatius Bonar)

CHAPTER 8

Shinjiland Ablaze

Jungle Leaf:
Water never sleeps; God made it ever flowing.

Chipi-Kweswe

A certain Shinji village was almost completely hidden during the wet season because of the tall tobacco plants that encircled it, taller than the houses. In this village lived Chipi-Kweswe, the first person George and I saw converted among the Shinji tribes after our treks up into their far north country several times. We were thrilled the evening she stood up at the meeting and said, "Yes, I'm a sinner, but may God and Yesu forgive me all my sins!" Could words be sweeter to our ears and to the ears of the Saviour? This gallant lady stood firm in her profession of faith in her Saviour against much opposition from her tribespeople who had never before heard the gospel, and who were gripped in rigid beliefs venerating their ancestral spirits, and in idol worship.

Real persecution for Chipi-Kweswe began when the issue of baptism was raised. She had to face the challenge of being rejected by her own people, few of whom had as yet received the gospel as she had.

The root of Chipi-Kweswe's problem with being baptised lay in the fact that she was the younger wife in a polygamous marriage. When the older wife heard of her request for baptism, she objected, countering that she, due to superiority in age, should be the first to be baptised.

"What!" she exclaimed, "you want to despise me! I'm the older and I have to be the first to be baptised by the white Ngana!"

"Fine, Mother," answered Chipi-Kweswe, "but how can you request baptism when you have not yet trusted in Yesu the Saviour?

"Be quiet! Look at your eyes! I demand to be first. Don't you dare go ahead of me... remember your place!" said the elder wife.

Now here was a strange thing - a heathen woman wanting to be baptised! The elder wife argued with Chipi-Kweswe day after day, but the new Christian would not be shaken in her resolve to obey her Master. George and I knew that the threats were not hollow. After being consulted by the elder wife, the local witchdoctor threatened Chipi-Kweswe with death. Now what would she do?

It was a sacred Saturday afternoon during a seventh trip to Shinjiland in 1951 when we made our way to the river where seven new Christians were to be baptised. George and I had scouted around until we found a most impressive baptismal site. A large pool had formed at that point in the river, and we cleared away undergrowth so that the people on the river bank could see what was taking place. It seemed like everyone in the district had turned out to witness the event and there was great excitement and a sense of expectation. "A Christian baptism to Yesu!" was the shout that passed from village to village. Even the children were caught up in the excitement of the day. But among them stood the elder wife of Chipi-Kweswe's husband, watching with evil eyes, and the witchdoctor himself.

Chipi-Kweswe walked into the river first, and I asked her if she was prepared to be baptised. "Look, Chipi-Kweswe," I said, "the witchdoctor is here and this may cost you your life."

"Ngana, please baptise me now!" she replied. The very angels of heaven must have been bending down to watch that great event in Shinjiland, which in itself proclaimed the gospel. She was dipped under the water in obedience to the command of her Saviour, and was raised up to proclaim her new life in Him. She faced death for it, but obedience to the Lord remained her choice at any cost.

The next day, the Lord's Day, we met under the shade of a mango tree near her village for the first Lord's Supper among the Shinji converts, and there Chipi-Kweswe, suitably attired with a piece of cloth wound around her body in contrast to her former lack of clothing, broke bread with the other six believers who had been baptised, and George and me. She also had a small piece of cloth

on her head to show her obedience to her Lord in this matter too. Who taught her to cover her body? Not the missionaries, but the inner conviction of the Holy Spirit. And what of the witchdoctor who threatened her life? Ah, the Lord later saved him!

There, too, one of the seven, sat a tall young man in his thirties who was a chief designate. I remembered the night in the young man's home village when he stood up and confessed Christ publicly. He had a great cost to count: by his open confession of Christ he was deliberately setting aside any claim to the chieftainship, choosing rather, like Moses, to suffer with the small company of baptised believers than to enjoy the earthly privileges of chieftainship. He knew that a chief is appointed, not merely by the elders of the tribe, but by a special spirit. Since Christianity and animistic beliefs could not coexist, he would have to choose one or the other.

"Yes, Ngana," he said to me, "my name is now Paul, which comes from our word *Kupaula*, meaning "to barter". Now I must go among my own tribe and trade with them. I'll be a trader for Christ."

"Paul, do you know what the apostle Paul's name was before he met Christ?" I asked.

"No, Ngana, please tell me," he said.

"It was Saul."

"Saul, Ngana! Do you know what that means in our language?" He looked at me incredulously. "It means to insult, to deride, and that is what I did before I knew Yesu as my Saviour." And so Saul the scoffer became Paul the trader, and what things had been gain to him he now counted loss for the sake of Christ. What a change, and at what a cost!

Another woman sat with us at the Lord's Supper that morning, a woman George and I had met not long before. We'd trekked into her village one morning, sat down on small stools and greeted the people. In no time a large group had gathered to hear what the strange white men had to say. Carefully we talked to the people concerning Yesu and the good news of salvation. This woman sat at my side, listening to something that shattered her own concept of *Zambi* (God). What? she thought. Speak to God directly and not through ancestral spirits? Listen to that white man calling God, "Our Father in Heaven!" Slowly she rose and stood with her right hand covering her face, then she bravely confessed this Yesu as her Saviour who died for her. She was the only one who had the courage to face up to the opposition from the spirit world which circumscribed the lives of her people.

During the week leading up to the Saturday which we had arranged for the baptisms, she made her way through the long grass to the campsite under the mango trees, requesting to be baptised. She had been a Christian for only three weeks.

"Listen, Mother, we cannot baptise you this Saturday," we said, "but when we return next time we'll talk to you, all right?" But she wanted nothing of our suggestion. Instant obedience was her motto, and nothing else would do. The following day she left her village at the hour when the elephant washes and returned to make the same plea.

"Ngana, please baptise me on Saturday!"

"No, Mother, you must wait. Have a long heart (patience) till we come back again," I said.

"*Ewa* (yes), Ngana, but you may never come again, and you also said that Yesu may return any day!" she replied poignantly, and went away disappointed.

George and I thought that we had given her the final answer. The sun set like a fireball in the golden west as she retraced her steps over the winding trail. But on the afternoon of the baptism as we made our way down to the river we heard her voice again.

"Ngana, please!" came the voice from behind me. After George and I conferred once more we told her to have patience and that we would return - she could be baptised then!

I waded into the pool in its beautiful tropical surroundings, and

received the six new Christians one by one as George helped them into the water and out again. After the last one, just as I turned to climb out of the water, I heard a splash, and there standing waist deep next to me was the same woman. She simply touched my arm and quietly said, "Ngana, please baptise me! Now!" Hundreds of people surrounded the pool in silence, waiting to see what I would do. I could not resist her single minded desire for instant obedience to her Master any longer, and I lowered her into the semi-warm water and baptised her in the name of the Father, the Son, and the Holy Spirit. She had justly won the day against the reluctance of the missionaries! And her future walk proved that she was a genuine child of God.

There, too, at that first commemorative sacred supper was a man who was a self-confessed murderer. He had viciously hacked to death not just one person, but several. Could this man be forgiven and cleansed from his horrible crimes? Ah, yes, the blood of Jesus Christ washes away all sin (1 John 1.7). The ground at the cross is level for all.

And then there was an old man, the oldest of the seven baptised, one of God's true gentlemen. The day he heard in his jungle village the story of Calvary's love, he took his water pipe of tobacco, crossed to the nearest tree and smashed the pipe to pieces. At the dull thud his neighbours shouted in amazement. Away with the remnants of his old life! Then he went to his house, uprooted his wooden idols and smashed those made of mud, which symbolised the tribal spirits. This dear man grew in grace and became a wise and humble counsellor in the local fellowship. At this first Lord's Supper he poured out his heart in verbal praise for the Saviour who had died for him.

How did that first small company manage to conduct and participate in such a sacred service held for the first time there in the open? After these believers confessed their faith, George and I had spent long hours teaching them to memorise key portions of Scripture like Psalms 22 and 23, Isaiah 53, John 19, and 1 Corinthians 11, since they could not read. They also memorised suitable hymns, of which their favourite at the Lord's Supper was a translation of:

> *"See from His head, His hands, His feet,*
> *Sorrow and love flow mingled down;*
> *Did e'er such love and sorrow meet,*
> *Or thorns compose so rich a crown?"*
>
> (Isaac Watts)

Margaret had sent a small white tablecloth along with me on the journey - a great act of faith on her part! We placed a small loaf of bread on the bamboo table along with a glass of Portuguese table wine, and the believers sat around the table on logs. As the Lord Jesus Himself promised (Matthew 18.20), He was there too, "in the midst" of His gathered people.

Those seven with us at the "table in the wilderness" were a harbinger of the many thousands who would follow their triumphal trail from among the Shinji, Ruunda, Minungu, Northern Chokwe, Shona, Chewa, Afrikaans big-game hunters, Lomwe, Portuguese and the Sena tribe. This polyglot character stamped the pioneer work which the Lord gave us to do in several African countries. These believers were only seven torches lit, but soon the fire spread over the valleys and hills until it reached the uttermost parts of Shinjiland. Years later George remarked to my son David one day, "There's not one village in Shinjiland which has not been reached by the gospel, and which does not have a company of redeemed men and women gathered together in a local church fellowship."

One Sunday during a visit to this first assembly of Shinji, George and I noticed a woman at the Lord's Supper who had a stick tied on to her curly hair. At the close of the service I greeted her and asked, "Mother, why do you have this stick in your hair?"

"Ah, Ngana," she said, "I gave birth to a son who has gone away east to the diamond mines. Before he left me, he took a stick and tied it to my hair and said, 'Mother, I'm going away from you and will be gone for a long time. I want you to keep this stick in your hair, so that every time you touch it you will remember me, so far away from you.' Ngana, I cannot forget my son, and he also told me that he is coming back again to stay with us in our village."

I glanced across at the small bamboo table on which were the bread and the cup of wine, of which the little group had partaken in remembrance of their Saviour. Had He not left these "sticks" with us before He left to go to a far country? Did these same "sticks" not remind us that the One who left us is coming back again? The Greater Son had left a remembrance for us all. I never knew if the woman's son eventually came back, but the Greater Son, I assured the believers in Bambooland, is certainly coming back to take His own to be with Him for ever.

One day I said to Chipi-Kweswe, "Now that you are a Christian you must change your name. This one means 'Evil Everywhere.' Now you must be known as *Chipema-Kweswe*, 'Good Everywhere'."

"No, Ngana, I do not wish to change my name," she said.

"Why, Mother?" I asked.

"Because my name, Chipi-Kweswe, will always remind me of what I was before Yesu came into my heart," she answered. And Chipi-Kweswe she remained. This brave woman began to witness to the women and young girls in her village, and the persecution increased against her. Eventually her husband divorced her, and she decided to give her life full-time to the service of her Lord. Such a decision increased the ridicule, as no young woman ever remained single. If one man didn't want her, she would be married off to another. But for Chipi-Kweswe there was no turning back. She was advised to leave that district and move to another where, it was hoped, she could live and witness to the power of the Lord in peace.

The rough itinerant life Chipi-Kweswe led for several years in her missionary work made her vulnerable to the ravages of tuberculosis. As she lay dying, she expressed no regrets, for she had gladly given her life to make known the gospel which meant everything to her. What a triumph was hers as she went into the presence of the Saviour whom she had served during her brief life!

Chipi-Kweswe

> *Afraid? Of what?*
> *Afraid to see the Saviour's face,*
> *To hear His welcome, and to trace*
> *The glory gleam from wounds of grace?*
> *Afraid - of that?*

(E.H. Hamilton)

Throughout Shinjiland it became known that Chipi-Kweswe was the first Christian to die and to receive a Christian burial. Some Christian young men made a bamboo coffin for her body and laid her to rest. Many lamented and said, "*Mukuyu munene waholokela hashi, kuliki mutuswama* (the large fig tree has fallen; where will we find shelter)?" Did her spirit hover over the villages as the Shinji believed? Ah, no! Her spirit was with her Saviour in heaven, though the heathen Shinji had great difficulty in accepting this new concept which was so foreign to their tribal beliefs. For Chipi-Kweswe and the other Christians to follow her, there would be no traditional anointing of the corpse with fat, no pouring of milk and fat into the mouth, no more ceremonial tying of a hide around the body.

And so Chipi-Kweswe taught her tribespeople how a person should live and how a person should die. She became a pioneer for a great multitude who would follow, who were to learn of her faith, her baptism, of her labours in the villages, of her death and wonderful burial. The new believers rejoiced also to look forward to the coming of the day of bodily resurrection of believers at the Lord's return.

> *Afraid? Of what?*
> *To feel the spirit's glad release?*
> *To pass from pain to perfect peace,*
> *The strife and strain of life to cease...*
> *Afraid - of that?*
>
> *Afraid? Of what?*
> *A flash, a crash - a pierced heart;*
> *Darkness - light - O heaven's art!*
> *A wound of His a counterpart!*
> *Afraid - of that?*
>
> *Afraid? Of what?*
> *To do by death what life could not?*
> *Baptise with blood a stony plot,*
> *Afraid - of that?*
>
> *Afraid? Of what?*
> *To enter heaven's rest,*
> *And still to serve the Master bless'd;*
> *From service good, to service best...*
> *Afraid - of that?*
>
> (E.H. Hamilton)

* * *

George and I made our camp one day on the hilltop near Fransisco's house while on a trip to the Camaxilo area. As we looked out across the plain below us, we saw hundreds and hundreds of Shinji approaching, the men bearing bows and arrows.

"George! Look at these men! What does this mean?" I said.

"They're armed with bows and arrows or with guns, and they're clutching hunting axes!" Just as the setting sun dipped below the horizon the last of the tremendous crowd reached the campsite, many having walked forty or fifty miles along the twisting, narrow bush path under the burning rays of the sun. Dust hovered thickly in the air, kicked up by the hundreds of feet tramping to the site. They appeared a menacing crowd, for when they smiled they showed teeth sharpened to a fine edge. The people surged toward us, trying to grasp our hands, and we thought surely at any moment the entire campsite would be swallowed up by the excited crowd shouting and gesticulating at the tops of their voices. I glanced down once more at the axes. What did they mean?

Little did we know that this was the beginning of a great work of the Holy Spirit in Shinjiland. The guns and the axes, the bows and arrows were not in any way to molest us, but to guard themselves on their trip though the wild, lion-infested country. That night as they sat down to rest and eat by fires lit on the hillside we learned that they had all come for the sole purpose of hearing the good news of Jesus and His love that we had to tell them.

"But what shall we do with so many people, George?" I asked. "Where shall we get enough food to even begin feeding them?"

"Don't worry!" Fransisco called out. "They have all brought their own food." We were concerned about preventing an accident with so many weapons laying about, and appointed a guard to supervise them all night.

What excitement! What hand clapping and expectation filled the air! It was a thrilling sight and we were deeply moved. The first meeting started at 6 pm. and continued until midnight with preaching, singing and praying, until George and I were completely exhausted. With great difficulty we persuaded the crowd to disperse and to sleep around their own campfires. The next morning many more joined the throng to hear the gospel.

Many of the crowd before us were skilled in bushcraft, men grown old in the pursuit of heathendom, witchcraft and animism with all its accompanying wickedness. There were old women, who, because they were now past the age of child-bearing, were usually the targets of diviners. Many would be in danger of being accused of someone's death, and the accusation would be followed by a swift blow of an axe on the skull. Would the gospel with its delivering power reach them first? Was there a new life opening up for these women sitting about the camp, which would provide for them not only life in heaven, but new life here, freed from the awful fears that plagued them daily?

Young children ran about, naked and covered with dust. What of their future? There was no school for them, no books. But here, praise God, was a message that would bring eternal hope to these young people, and later bush schools would be established for them all over their country, where both adults and children could learn. The government had not provided any education for these people, and it fell to the missionaries to build schools and pay teachers without any financial help from the authorities.

That Saturday evening ten Shinji chiefs faced the challenge of the gospel of Yesu. They knew it would mean a radical change in their lives, especially since all of these men were polygamous, some with as many as fifteen wives. God gave them the courage to stand up among the vast crowd that night and to invite the Saviour into their lives. Some of these chiefs not only progressed in fellowship with their Lord but also became leaders in the local churches which were formed.

In May, 1957 George wrote to "Echoes of Service" in England:

Before arriving there we heard wonderful reports of blessing, and felt that perhaps they were exaggerated, but the half was not told us. The whole district has been stirred, hundreds of people, including chiefs and diviners, and right down to the despised slaves have professed conversion. It was a wonderful privilege to spend a long weekend at this place, and to share the meetings. All day Saturday people kept coming from all directions, and well over 1,000 gathered for the night meetings.

The first meeting on the Lord's Day was announced for 7 am. but the people started coming at 5.30! We held five gospel meetings that day, with over 2,000 people present. Later we walked down to the river singing hymns of praise to the Saviour, where I baptised thirty-seven believers. I preached the gospel yet again, and how I longed for a loudspeaker!

There were no gimmicks, no films, no entertainment, no secondary attractions, but only the clear statement of Christ and Him crucified, told to a people lost in heathendom and witchcraft. Too long that tribe had waited to hear the footsteps of the missionaries bringing the wonderful story that changed their lives. Too long they had waited for the Light. At last it had come and thousands were grasping it with real joy. The first torches had been set alight and now the fire was sweeping throughout Shinji, Ruunda, Minungu and Mbangalaland. Many times George and I stood behind the vast crowds shaking our heads in amazement at this overwhelming work of the Holy Spirit.

> *Give me the love that leads the way,*
> *The faith that nothing can dismay,*
> *The hope no disappointments tire,*
> *The passion that will burn like fire;*
> *Let me not sink to be a clod -*
> *Make me thy fuel, Flame of God!*
> (Amy Carmichael)

Scores of tribespeople forsook their family idols and spirit worship and erected Prayer Houses in their villages. Group after group met daily for prayer and for the preaching of the gospel. Some believers walked as far as fifty miles to the nearest assembly to break bread on Sunday mornings, and another fifty back home. They considered it nothing to make a trek of one hundred miles to remember their Saviour!

Fransisco and other believers worked hard and erected a large hall for meetings in their village, with a seating capacity for over 800, which was quite a feat for those young converts. Not long after this, however, the terrorist war spread into the area. Christians were accused of supporting the terrorists, and traders were goaded into such hatred of the Christians that one of them persuaded evil men to burn the hall. As the Christians saw the building into which they had poured so much of their time and their meagre resources go up in flames, they were deeply shocked and saddened at the evil which instigated the fire. They nevertheless committed all this to the Lord in whom they had trusted. God had said, "Vengeance is mine; I will repay." Was

God silent and uncaring? Were the heavens turned to brass? Was God not moved in pity? Yes, he was!

> *God moves in a mysterious way*
> *His wonders to perform;*
> *He plants His footsteps in the sea,*
> *And rides upon the storm.*
>   (William Cowper)

The enemy trader who had instigated the fire, one day after this went out to the plain to hunt for game. No one knew what happened, but he was found shot dead in the bush. A pall of fear fell over the villages when people learned what had happened to him. Just as at the beginning of the work recorded in the Acts of the Apostles, God stepped in and took vengeance on those who tried to hinder the working of the Holy Spirit; God intervened in Shinjiland: "...The word of God grew and multiplied" (Acts 12.24).

The fire which destroyed the hall was minuscule compared with the spiritual fire which roared through Shinjiland in the power of God. Their land literally became "Shinji Ablaze". Crowds flocked to the meetings, carrying chairs, even their bamboo beds, as they expected to be at the meetings for several hours! These were

exciting days indeed.

Crowds of tribes-people flocked past the traders' stores, chanting "the evangelicals have taken over the country!" Then the traders resorted to making false accusations against Fransisco and George and me, and Fransisco was arrested by the local administrator. Believers brought him food and other things he needed. He was beaten several times, and was threatened with worse unless he promised to give up his preaching and praying. But the Lord stood by his young servant and gave him strength and grace to resist all these tests and threats and all the attempts to bribe him. Fransisco was a prisoner for the sake of Christ, just as Paul was long ago.

After a time Fransisco was set free. Some wondered if his God had forsaken him, and their faith wavered a little during this time of testing, but God was in full control and had noted each beating that Fransisco endured.

The local administrative official who had listened to the lies and false accusations from the traders had suddenly to face, not Fransisco, but Fransisco's God. This official's wife became so ill that no one knew if she would live. Instead of rejoicing that the illness was God's punishment of the man who had so ill-treated his servant Fransisco, Fransisco himself gathered the assembly together and they crossed the river and climbed the hill to where the official lived. They marched into his compound and asked to see him. He emerged from his house and stood on the veranda, watching the crowd of silent Christians. What thoughts must have surged through his mind as he faced the man on whose body were seen the marks of suffering he had inflicted.

Fransisco stepped forward and respectfully said, "Senhor, we would like to pray for your wife that she may have the blessing of God on her body." The administrator looked stunned. Were his ears deceiving him?

"Senhor, let us pray for your wife," Fransisco repeated. As they all bowed their heads Fransisco led them in prayer, asking God in His mercy to spare the life of this woman. During the following days she became worse, so that the official made preparations to take her to the Belgian Congo for more advanced medical help. The morning they were to leave the whole assembly turned up at their house, again asking permission for a time of prayer. Then they all accompanied the official and his wife along the way, stopping once more to commit the woman to the mercy of God. And God in His mercy spared the woman, answering the fervent prayers of the African Christians. When the couple returned home, the assembly again forded the river to gather in the compound to thank God.

God took the sweetest revenge on the witchdoctors who had rallied at the call of Satan to oppose the Word of life, by saving more than thirty of them. They turned to Christ and buried their divining baskets, were baptised and became active members of local companies of the Lord's people in Shinjiland.

We were sitting in the shade of a tree by a Gospel Hall one day when some Shinji walked past. Having never seen any buildings other than the small huts in which they lived, they stopped and stared. "I say," said one of the women, "what is the opening in the front for?" A man carrying a gun replied, "That is where you go in." Round they went for a closer inspection, and they noticed the two unglazed windows, which had been included not so much for light inside, but to let some of the smell get out! Asked another woman, "I say, what is the hole in the wall for?" Said the man, with a very knowing nod of the head, "That is where you spit out!!" And he proved to be entirely correct. All during the gospel services people appeared to be taking turns spitting out the window until we referred to it as "The Shinji Tribal Anthem".

Over the next six years I made at least eight more trips into Shinjiland. Margaret and I started out with the Wisemans on another trip later in 1957, but we had to turn back because of the illness and weakness which was increasingly affecting me, leaving the Wisemans to go on alone. In January 1958 we travelled to Cape Town where I was hospitalised and had an operation for stomach ulcers. The bad water I had often consumed on trek had taken its toll, and in March 1959 we had to return to Scotland because of my ill health. By the time I was sufficiently recovered, we were unable to obtain re-entry visas to Angola, and my days of trekking, alas, were over.

* * *

Bush Gospel Halls in Shinjiland

Ten years before this, a young man in Scotland heard a missionary report I gave regarding the deep need of the tribes of Northern Angola. His name was Willie Hastings of Ayrshire, and as he listened, the Spirit of God stirred him deeply. Why should he enjoy the comforts of home while these people lay in spiritual darkness? And so Willie and Betty Hastings were married and set off on the long journey from Scotland to Central Africa.

After several years of service in Angola, Willie was able to make his first trip to Shinjiland in 1962, and he wrote home with the following report:

"Little by little the numbers increase as the word gets around that we are here. On the Lord's Day the hall is far too small to hold the 700 odd who wait to hear the gospel. We have six and seven meetings a day, with rapt attention as they drink in every word and even sit on after the final meeting.

"That happy visit is crowned with a march to a nearby river where over fifty people followed the Lord in baptism. All of these have been saved for over a year, and some for two years, and having put their lives straight, desire to follow Him who has miraculously transformed their lives.

"We move on some thirty miles over the steep hills and down the deep valleys of the Uhamba River till we come to a large village. How encouraging to see a group of twenty four young men lined up before us who have been taught to read by the zealous leaders of that primitive assembly of God's saints. The 300 gathered are all strangers to me, but how nice to know that we are all members of the same heavenly family. Sixty of those identified themselves with Christ in the waters of baptism.

"From the opposite bank of the river they came to meet us with shouts of joy at the thought of some spiritual help. Another 400 gather together. Yes, they have come from place number one, considering the 30 miles as nothing compared with the joy of fellowship.

"After meeting upon meeting, we gather at the stream once again to witness the obedience in baptism of over 100 believers from that large area."

Willie Hastings had the gift of a Bible teacher and became fluent in the language. He had the privilege of seeing the fruit of what he had been told about years before, and what had drawn him to that missionfield. In another letter, dated October 18, 1963, he described the tremendous joy of seeing the work growing:

"We proceeded across the picturesque hills and valleys of the Upper Uhamba to the furthest of the northern assemblies. The nice hall had been completed since our last visit, with adobe and round poles, as well as a little house for us, a real testimony to their zeal and love of the things that have so remarkably changed their lives. We took them by surprise, but within ten minutes of our arrival, young men sped off to carry the news to the distant outposts. Who could forget the sight of those simple believers arriving from their villages, sometimes whole families, in order to spend some time with us around God's Word which has been so precious to them? From six, twelve, eighteen, and even thirty miles they have come (by foot), and why? Because Jesus saves! With four meetings a day and discussions between, we spent a very happy time. To hear from them of the spread of the gospel in the surrounding centres was stimulating indeed.

"The central assembly sent word of our proposed visit, the usual crowds arrived, and on our arrival, conveyed us to the house they had built beside the hall for our accommodation. With a crowd inside the large hall and another crowd half in and half out, we had the usual four meetings with a very attentive audience. In the fourth centre, how the work has grown! Several villages in an area of some 40 miles radius now have halls as large as the central one. God is blessing. With no schools for the hundreds of children, they teach one another to read.

"The climax was on Saturday night and Sunday, when we had to have two sittings in order to accommodate the people. Many had walked many miles to hear the glorious gospel which had so singularly changed their lives."

The Wisemans, Ena Bell, Tom Wilson, David Long, Willie Hastings, Roy Wood and Dr. A Stinton continued to make pioneer trips among the Shinji. By 1966 these missionaries estimated that there were between 3,500 and 4,000 baptised believers in nine assemblies, along with many others saved and awaiting baptism.

A note in "Echoes of Service", December 1966 reads,

> "Each of the nine assemblies has large "branch works" where there are many saved but where, for various reasons, the time is not yet ripe to commence assemblies - for one thing very few of the believers can read. There are thirteen devoted African full-time evangelists in the area whose position is extremely difficult and who badly need our prayers."

In 1971 when George Wiseman was allowed to re-enter Angola, he visited the Shinji, and estimated that there were over 20,000 believers in ninety assemblies, connected to thirty centres of testimony. Far from dying out during the terrible war which tore through the country, the assemblies had gone from strength to strength. Many believers carried the gospel to their own remote villages and widened the impact of God's work in that land. Truly Christ's promise is true, "Upon this rock I will build My church, and the gates of Hades shall not prevail against it" (Matthew 16.18).

Circumstances were changing, and education was reaching the Shinji so that many could read. In two trips George sold three hundred copies of the New Testament. Although the Shinji were the poorest tribe in Angola, their land was found to be rich with diamonds, and this improved their standard of living. They built better homes, opened trading stores, and cultivated larger and better fields. Yet the diamonds found beneath the ground in their land could not compare with the thousands of spiritual diamonds that we, as God's servants, found for Christ.

Time and again in later years, George and I thanked God that He had given us the great honour of penetrating the spiritual darkness of Shinjiland with the message of Life before the awful civil war in Angola wrought its evil and took countless thousands of lives. Now, although they have suffered and have often lost everything, on a Lord's Day thousands of Shinji still gather around rough bamboo tables to break bread in memory of the Son of the Infinite One about whom they once sang without knowing why. They now know, and it was our great privilege to bring the light into their darkness.

I heard His call, "Come, follow!"
That was all.
My gold grew dim,
My soul went after Him,
I rose and followed -
That was all.
Who would not follow
If they heard His call?
(Author unknown)

CHAPTER 9

Concepts of God and the Spirit World

Jungle Leaf:
  God does not crave for meat (there is no revenge in Him).

There are no atheists among Central African tribes. All believe that a Supreme Being created the heavens and the earth, and very commonly God is thought of as the Great Provider. One tribe calls him the "Nourisher". The Tswana say that *"Modimo"* (God) has helped them with the rain. The Shona call him *"Musiki"*, the Fire Creator. Another tribe says He is *"Mwene Nyaka"*, the Possessor of Whiteness. One of the most interesting is the concept of the Nyanja when they call him *"Woleza m'tima"*, the Great Caretaker of Life. Care over their daily life is always attributed to *Zambi* (God), however unknown or knowable He is, and never attributed to any idol.

One day when hunting with Little Bird, I saw a beautiful duiker-like animal (a small antelope) trotting through the forest. As I lifted my rifle to fire, Little Bird called out to me to stop. This was a *"Kongo"* he said. It is a little red animal that features much in the tribal proverbs.

"Wafwa ni Kongo, mbinga japatuka (we have died with Kongo and the horns have broken off)," he said. Little Bird then went on to explain to me his understanding of how the Kongo is a picture of the Son of God who came down to this earth. Here again, hidden among the wisdom of the jungle lore is a reference to the unknown Saviour who, they say, died, and by whose death they have been freed. Although I inquired at great length as to the origin of this element of Central African folklore, I never received a clear answer to any of my

questions. The ancient ones of the tribe only shook their heads and said that they had heard of this Mysterious One in their proverbs, but who was he? And so I was able to answer from the Bible, using the analogy Little Bird had explained, that *Kongo* (Christ) has died, and we have thereby been freed from our sins (the horns have been snapped). I later discovered that this word *Kongo* is used by other tribes to signify the Supreme Being.

The African thus does not search for God. He sees Him everywhere, but unfortunately as far off and unapproachable. I have found that the geography of a tribe's territory influences their concept of the Supreme Being. If there are hills, then they think of Him as the God of the hills. If they live among the swamps, then they form an idea of Him pertaining to water. If they have a high mountain in their territory, they imagine Him as the God of the mountain. In the low lying areas where rivers, pools and lakes abound, He is conceived of as the Water God. Sometimes He is even thought to inhabit the deep pools. Extending the idea of His providential nature, in the folklore the young men receive their brides from the water! People who die by drowning are thought to stand a good chance of finding new birth that will lead to another life.

Zambi

During the dry season, when the grass has grown to six feet or taller across sections of the great African plain, the tribespeople thatch their huts. It is a fine grass, and easy to cut with the long *panga* knives the people use.

As Little Bird and I trekked through the villages in this part of the country one dry season, we became tired and stopped to rest. Nearby a man hauled long sheaves of grass up a rickety old ladder as he thatched his hut to prepare for the downpours of the coming wet season. Seeing us resting in the shade of another hut, he climbed down from his roof and crossed over the dusty yard to speak to us.

"Yes, Father, you have done a splendid job in thatching your house, have you not?" I said.

"Yes, Ngana, but that is only the first layer of thatch which I have put on it," he replied. "I need to add a second one." As we talked together I asked what he called the work of the first layer of

thatch.

"Oh, Ŋgana, that is what we call '*Kupupika*'."

"Well, then," I said, "what do you call the second layer of thatch you will put on?"

"That is what we Chokwe people call '*Kuzamba*'," he replied.

"What, *Kuzamba*, eh?" I repeated.

"Yes, Ŋgana, we call it *Kuzamba*."

"But what does that mean," I asked, never having heard the term before, and sensing that linguistically it was irregular.

"Yes, Ŋgana, I who put the second thatch on the house am called *Zambi*. That is why it is called '*kuzamba*'."

"Zambi, eh?" I asked, really curious now, as '*Zambi*' is the Chokwe word for God.

"Zambi is my name," he said.

"But Zambi dwells in heaven; how can that be your name?" I asked.

"It is true that Zambi dwells in heaven, and He does the same as I do," said the man, "He protects us with His thatch."

What a lovely idea of the protecting work of our Sovereign God in heaven I learned that day from a heathen man on the African plains! I sat down to reflect on this fresh discovery of the Chokwe's beliefs about Zambi, whom they do not know personally. How does this Zambi protect and cover them? I thought of the rain that falls on their fields bringing their crops to maturity. This is the work of the first thatch, covering them and helping them. The hot sun that pours down on the African plains day after day - this, too is the first coat of thatch that Zambi gives them, protecting them from hunger and thirst, and from want. The second thatch that this man will put on gives him this name Zambi - the Thatcher. And God proved Himself to be that to Little Bird and to Margaret and me!

I called to the man, who was once again at work on his thatching.

"Yes!" I said, "The second thatch, do you know what that is?"

"No, Ngana, I really do not know," he said.

"The first thatch is the kindness of God taking care of you in sending the rain and the sunshine for your crops," I called up to him, "but the second one is His care for you when He sent His Son into this world to die for you. His work of salvation on the cross is His greater care of you in redemption. That is why you call Him 'Zambi' (Thatcher). He can cover you with the blood of His Son that was shed for all your sins."

The thatcher looked at me in wonder, sensing my thrill at understanding this new concept of my God who provides me with a twofold covering, one of providential care, and the other of redemptive care. After that incident, whenever I saw a thatcher busily adding the layers of thatch to his hut, this wonderful picture of the Great Thatcher came to mind. I often used it as an illustration in explaining the gospel to the Chokwe.

Just as that man was so anxious to protect his home from the wind and storms of the rainy season, so also is the Divine Thatcher willing to protect us from the coming storm of His wrath by covering us, not only with His care day by day in looking after our physical needs so well, but by protecting us by the blood of His own dear Son.

Kalunga

George Wiseman and I had to leave the interior of the country and make a long journey to the west coast one year. We took with us Paulino, an African man who had often travelled with us on pioneer trips to Shinjiland. This man had never seen the ocean, and probably never any body of water larger than Lake Kulumba in Shinjiland. Mostly he knew only the rivers. So as we reached the Atlantic Ocean and stood gazing toward its seemingly limitless expanse past the horizon, Paulino was transfixed. I urged him to come along, but he didn't move.

"Paulino, it's time to go," I said.

"Ngana, wait a little, please." A while later I told him it was late and we must move on.

"But where is the other side, Ngana?"

"You cannot see the other side, Paulino."

"But tell me, where is the far bank?" Again I tried to explain to him the vastness of the ocean, and at last he said, "Ngana, that is *Kalunga!*"

"*Kalunga*, who is he?" I asked.

"We call Zambi (God) *Kalunga* because He is like this big expanse of water. He has no bank to limit Him; He goes on and on!" And there in a nutshell is an African's grand concept of God, the One who is Bankless, Limitless, the Infinite One.

Paulino filled a bottle with water from the ocean to take back to his people in the interior to illustrate for them what he had learned of Kalunga, the One who is limitless.

Whenever I asked the ancient question among the African tribes, "What is His name, and what is His son's name, if thou canst tell?" (Proverbs 30.4) I was always richly rewarded. As one group told me,

> Here is the Inexplicable,
> Our Bull Lion Descent,
> Descend, Being of Heaven
> Unconquerable.
> (African song)

Suku

The Yao people of Malawi and Mozambique tell a folk tale that when men set fire to the grassland they forced God to retreat into heaven, and so were cut off from Him. In Zimbabwe the Shona people speak of *Musiki*, a name for God, meaning the Creator of

Fire. According to their lore, the fire was not lit by a human, but came down from heaven and it was the self-revelation of God. The Herero of South-West Africa (Namibia) speak of a sacred fire which was kept burning perpetually in the centre of the village and maintained by the Great Chief himself, who acted as a priest.

The Chokwe, Shinji and Mbangala of Angola all have explanations for the gift of fire which God made to them, but which, instead of being a help, destroyed man. The Nyanja tribe speak of their elders who climbed a mountain in order to receive fire "from above". They had to offer sacrifices of a black goat and a black chicken to the spirits. Then, taking a bunch of "*muura*" tree and "*kasanjesanje*" they waited for the fire to descend.

No doubt these stories of the origin of fire are so vivid because of the important role fire plays in rural societies which depend on it so much for all kinds of purposes, such as smoking game out of the forest, for cooking, for warmth, for light at night, and for protection from wild animals. It is not surprising, then, that such people's vague ideas of God are also linked to fire.

The Mbangala, the Songo and Ombundu tribes of Angola use the name "*Suku*" for God. Working back through the etymology of the word I tried in vain to determine its meaning. Where could it have come from? I needed to learn yet another lesson of jungle life to understand *Suku*.

The men of the bush country go hunting during the dry season when the grass is easily set on fire. Sometimes the fires get out of control, and it is terrifying to see a ten mile wide wall of fire raging across the country. During the heat of the day the animals lie down and rest, feeding in the early morning and again in the evening when it is much cooler. While the animals are resting, hunters encircle a section of the plain where they think they will trap many of the animals by starting a solid ring of fires. Sometimes the animals are smarter than the hunters, and escape before the fires trap them. These wild animals have a God-given instinct of knowing the one place where they can find shelter from the deadly fire.

Down near the edge of the river there is a small, evergreen island, surrounded by shallow water. The beasts charge through the water to reach the island haven, knowing that the fire can never overpower them there. The small duiker comes, and the enormous elephant as well as the lion. In their moment of terror in seeking a refuge from the fire, they forget their natural fear of one another. The fire roars through the bush until it reaches the water, where it abruptly fizzles out. And what do the Africans call this island of refuge? Ah, yes, they call it 'Suku'.

When I heard this, what a picture flashed to my mind as I thought of the true Suku - God, who is our refuge from the fires of judgement which are to come. Matthew 3.7 says, "Who hath warned you to flee from the wrath to come?" The question is, where shall we flee? We flee to our Suku, our Evergreen Refuge, to the One who was sinless, in whom not a spot of burnt grass is found, but in whom all is lovely and green. This is the man of Psalm 1, who is "like a tree planted by the rivers of water".

The second illustration of Suku is found in a story told by Little Bird to the Mbangala during the first year of our pioneer treks north.

Two maggots lived and worked together in the bush. One day they wandered far into the bush, looking here and there for food. Soon they found a log lying on the ground, soft from the dampness of the earth beneath. One maggot began eating the decaying log at one end, while his friend ate at the other. Little by little they chewed through the pulp until they met in the middle.

"Friend, we have eaten well, so let us go outside now and return home," said one.

"No, no, let us wait for a little time longer and eat more of this nice soft wood," said the other.

"Look, the sun is setting and we have a long way to go," coaxed the first. "Let us hurry before it gets dark and we get lost in the wood!"

"Friend, there are plenty of glow worms about, and we will be able to get home by following them in the dark, so let's wait and enjoy ourselves!" the other said. They proceeded to argue heatedly, until one gave up and announced that he was leaving and going home.

Nearby in the village the people were just warming up to one of their customary all-night beer parties. It is the women's responsibility to brew the beer, and for this they need a great deal of firewood.

An old woman came out of the village in search of wood. She wandered along, looking here and there until she noticed the decaying log where the maggots had been enjoying themselves. Overjoyed at finding such a suitable piece of firewood, she hoisted it up on her head, carried it to the village and threw it on the fire.

Now the greedy maggot who had refused to return home when his friend left had something to think about! He paid the price of delay with his life. If he had listened, he would not have perished in the flames.

At this point in his story, Little Bird, who was leaning against a grass hut, looked over at me to see if I was learning from the jungle wisdom ways to be able to clarify the gospel message for these people. Yes, I understood what Little Bird was going to say next. For the first maggot there was '*Suku*', but not for the second. "Men are the same," said Little Bird. "They help each other when their beards are burning. But it is better not to wait until your beard is burning; get out of the reach of the fire when it is still far off."

Many years later I was in the Zambesi valley to preach the same gospel of Christ which I preached in Shinjiland. But this time the response was different.

"Go away!" said an African who had been listening, "and bring us a black god! Your God is white; we need a black one!" Is God an Englishman, as Dan Crawford asked? Was His Son who came to this earth a white man? Ah, no! He was neither white nor black, but the MAN of men. So the African may stretch out his hand to Him and say, "He is mine," and the white man can do the same and claim Him as his. I sought to present neither a white nor a black God, but the God-Man Christ Jesus who left His glory temporarily to become one with us in our common humanity, regardless of tribe or language or people or nation.

The Potter and the Clay

After we had lived in a home made of sun-dried bricks for several years, I decided one dry season that I would build something stronger and more weather-resistant. The first task was to find suitable clay for making those stronger bricks, and it proved to be a lot more difficult than I thought. Several Africans helped me to search our district. For weeks we looked, but found nothing. I would have to abandon the project and content myself with sun-dried brick, I thought.

Late one night a cowherd coughed outside the house to signal his presence and that he wished to speak to me. After our preliminary greetings which can never be omitted, He whispered that he knew of a place close by where very fine clay could be found. Though surprised that we had not discovered it during our diligent search, I agreed to meet the man early the following morning before others were up and about.

The cowherd strode into the bush confidently and led me to the banks of a small stream. He stopped, rested his stick on the ground, place one foot on his stick and stood there like a stork in the wilderness.

"Ngana, look there in the water, at the side of the bank, and you will see they very best quality of clay." I stared into the murky stream but could see no clay! So I asked the cowherd to jump into the water and scoop up a sample to show me.

"Jump in there, Ngana?! No! I could never do that!" he said.

"Look, man, the water is not deep. What are you afraid of? - a crocodile, eh?" I asked.

"Ngana, I am not afraid of a crocodile, and the water indeed is not deep, but, Ngana, you certainly do not know our custom!" No, I did not.

"Ngana, we have a custom which tells that the first person to go into a clay bed to remove some will die. That is the price the first person must pay, and I do not want to die." I looked at the murky stream again, and though I didn't want to dirty my clean clothes, I knew I had to show him the fallacy of this tribal belief. As so often before in my experience, the spirits of darkness were directly challenging the Scriptures. I always tried to respect as many tribal customs as I could, but where they opposed the Scriptures, I had to stand against it and expose their error, in the strength of Colossians 2.15: "Having spoiled principalities and powers, He [Christ] made a show of them openly, triumphing over them in it [by His cross]".

"Ngana, you will die!" he cautioned, "and then what will we say to Ndona?" With a silent prayer for protection in the spiritual battle, off came my trekking boots and I slid down into the water. Yes!

The cowherd was right! There was a large bed of good clay, sufficient to make many fine bricks for a new home. I climbed out of the water and opened my small Bible to Jeremiah 18 and read to the cowherd the ancient story of the potter and the clay. There on the bank of that tropical river I unfolded to this man in a new way the ever-living story of Calvary, explaining how his Saviour went down into the waters of death to get the clay, and that He died on the cross so that He might fashion a vessel from the clay for His glory. For many days the man watched to see if death would overtake me for violating the tribal custom, but instead he saw living testimony to the power of the Great Potter who bore death so that we might be refashioned into works of beauty, to be used in His service for His glory.

As I travelled among the tribes I discovered that several have a name for God as Potter, meaning "One who works and makes with clay". Their usage is perhaps primarily metaphorical, but it gives further insight as to what these people conceive of as "God". One tribe calls Him "The Owner of the Best Clay". Some say that God used different colours of clay when He made men, and for them this explains well enough the difference of skin pigmentation among tribal groups and other races.

Evil Spirits

The spirit idols of animistic peoples are no mere fantasy of the human brain, but dark and dangerous realities of the unseen world. A young married woman lay dying in her hut, her husband at her side. I had been called during the night to attend to her, and it was soon apparent that she was suffering from no physical malady. She was convinced that she was bewitched. Her body shook, her temperature had shot up, yet no medicine would solve her problem. She died at daybreak from the fear or being bewitched.

During one trip Margaret and I made to the Minungu, we had pitched our sleeping tent at the edge of a village which stood in a small clearing ringed with dense forest. In one of the huts lay a young woman who, the villagers said, was demon-possessed. That evening the men played their drums and chanted, and the dismal noise carried on all through the night. We got no sleep, and at daybreak we visited the possessed woman. She writhed on the ground, her eyes rolling. I looked down at her and said aloud the name of the Lord Jesus. The writhing suddenly stopped and she looked up at me with a look of shock at hearing the sacred name. The tension broke, her gaze relaxed, and as her head sagged to her chest a peace and quiet came over the hut. I have never known a genuine believer to be demon-possessed, but I could often feel the influence of evil spirits as I moved among heathen people.

When new believers who have been idol worshippers burn their images, villagers watching the courageous act always stand well away from the smoke. Oh, it's not because they wish to avoid getting the smoke in their eyes, but rather they believe and fear that avenging spirits will come out and take hold of them if they are too near.

Some demon-possessed men and women exhibit superhuman powers. One day a runner came to me breathlessly, urging me to hurry over to the home of a Boer woman who lived near the mission station. She had been reared in the terrible dread of the spirits, and was now lying on the floor foaming at the mouth. I had not seen a white person under the influence of a demon before. Once again I called on the name of the Lord Jesus, and she immediately lay still. This dear woman was not only freed from demons, but she was saved by the grace of God. Some months later she confessed Christ publicly in the waters of baptism. What a joy it was to see her breaking bread every Lord's Day in remembrance of the One who had loosed her from the terrible power of Satan.

My friend and colleague George and I were conscious that the story of the Acts of the Apostles was being rewritten in Shinjiland and Minunguland. As the coming of the gospel to these territories challenged the power of Satan, he would not let his captives go easily, and we were continually aware of the forces of evil as we worked among the animistic tribespeople. It was a constant battle for which we needed the whole armour of God.

One day I invited some Portuguese friends to attend gospel meetings at the mission station. At first, being nominal Catholics, they were reluctant to come. Finally a group arrived early one Sunday morning, and they sat near the back of the hall while the believers celebrated the Lord's Supper. After having coffee in our home, we all returned for the preaching of the gospel and they listened courteously. At the close of the service one of the men said, "I've had the greatest surprise of my life today! We Catholics were taught that you evangelicals had heathen idols in your church which you worshipped. Senhor, I have looked all over your church and did not see even one idol!"

Down the river from the mission station there was a Catholic mission where the priest had a deep hatred toward anything evangelical. It was he who had told his flock that I had idols in "my" church. But Satan, using the priest, overstepped himself. A medical doctor and his wife were attending one of his services where the priest began berating the work we were doing for the Lord. This couple walked out in public protest at the slanderous statements against me. A short time later they came to the mission station wanting to talk to Margaret and me, and that day I had the thrill of leading the woman to the Saviour. With tears running down her face, she confessed, "Senhor, we knew that you had no idols in your church, and now I want to know your Saviour!" No sweeter words could ever be spoken throughout the whole world.

Idols or Christ! This educated Portuguese woman made the correct choice that day, and we were able to help her spiritually through providing suitable literature for her to read. The Evil One had lost another battle. During the short time they remained in the area, God used the couple often to meet the material needs of His servants.

> *"What have I to do with idols*
> *Since I've companied with Him?"*
> (Author unknown)

CHAPTER 10

Some African Converts

Nguvu, Chikenyoki, Gwathi, Simoni,
Samungenda, Carlos

The Hidden Duck - Nguvu

Jungle Leaf:
Don't bury a snake and leave the tail sticking out!

"How old are you?" I asked an African lad called Nguvu who leaned against a gum tree on the mission compound one day. Literally, the question is, "How many rain clouds have you seen?" To the African there are only two seasons in a year, the wet season and the dry season, so he reckons his years by the gathering clouds of the wet season. If you ask about the month of his birth the African will reply, "Oh, the corn was so high," indicating with his hand the height of the corn in the month he was born. He may also respond, "I was born in the year in which the men in our village shot the old bull elephant."

Nguvu was a young African lad who understood well the ways of bush life. He had seen great elephant marching unopposed through the forest, breaking off the branches of trees as if to show his invincible strength. Nguvu knew the proverb of his tribe, "The elephant breaks down his own firewood," and he could picture the mighty animal stomping through the forest breaking down the trees, unaware that the hunter was trailing him. A hunter will follow the elephant spoor for many miles until he has the beast clearly in sight. He wants to be sure he kills the elephant swiftly with his arrows, as a wounded elephant is a danger no man wants to encounter. But once the elephant is dead, the hunter gathers the very trees knocked down by the elephant and makes a bonfire on which to roast his flesh. Yes, Nguvu knew that proverb well: every deed brings its retribution.

Nguvu worked on the mission compound, doing various tasks in the house for Margaret, and whatever else I could find for him. In his free time he loved to take his bow and arrows and practise shooting in the bush. Often he brought home small game for his cooking pot in the evening. He also set rat traps using dirt from the anthill. Roasted rat with his evening manioc was a real treat for Nguvu. He loved when Margaret summoned him to catch a mouse or rat in the house, and became expert at this task which augmented his cooking pot.

Nguvu made his bows just as he had seen the village hunters fashion theirs. They were good bows, and Nguvu became a proficient hunter. But I laid down one firm rule for him: he must not shoot the lovely birds which made their nests in the trees near our house. What an order for a small boy to obey!

One day a little bird landed on the ground near Nguvu. He had his bow and arrows in his hand, and the temptation of it teased him. He crept nearer, bow readied to shoot once he was within range. The bird walked near one of the ducks that Margaret was keeping for another missionary, but that didn't present a problem to Nguvu.

"I'm such a good marksman," he thought, "I'll hit only the bird I want to." But alas for Nguvu, just then a gust of wind swept through the compound, deflecting his arrow directly into the duck!

"*Wolo!*" he exclaimed in fear, "My Mother! What will I do? *Lamba liami* (my bad luck)."

Now Nguvu was really in a fix. He had no money to pay for the dead duck. Although Nguvu knew his father would not spank him, he would be sent to me for punishment, and he also knew that I have a very heavy hand!

I had lived quite a time among the tribespeople before I discovered why parents never chastised their children themselves, but sent them to me for punishment.

"Go and spank him yourself," I would say, "he is your son, not mine!"

"*Tukwasenu* (please help us)," they pleaded.

And then one day I understood the relationship between this unwillingness to discipline children and their beliefs in reincarnation. After a person dies, they are believed to return to live in the body of a grandson or granddaughter.

"So you see, Ngana," they said, "this may be my own Grannie or my own Granddad, and I cannot put my own Grannie over my knee and spank her!"

And so Nguvu looked around to see if anyone was watching him. Not a fly buzzed in the hot sun. Only the grass moved slightly in the breeze. He took his little hoe and dug a hole in the earth. As he laid the duck in the hole and quickly covered it over with dirt again, he felt relieved.

"Now," he said to himself, "no one will know any better." He stamped on the freshly dug earth, scattering some leaves over the top to hide what he had done.

But wait a moment, friend Nguvu. Do you not remember the proverb, "Don't bury the snake and leave the tail sticking out?" Look, Nguvu, look behind that tree - where one of your own people is watching and has seen you kill and bury that duck. Yes, Nguvu, the snake's tail is sticking out! Be sure your sin will find you out!

The elders of Nguvu's tribe state this truth in another way: "A crime can be tracked; there is no crime that is eaten by worms." Although a hunter cannot always see an animal he is tracking, he follows the traces it leaves behind; the spoor in the sand, or the trace of blood on the leaf. In the end, the animal is found and killed. And that is why the Africans say that no crime is eaten by worms. Perhaps Nguvu had not yet learned this proverb.

The man watching Nguvu from behind the tree whispered to himself, "Hi, that child is like a goat tied to a tree. He'll never get himself loose, but he'll go round and round getting himself tied up all the more."

The following morning the sun rose and chased away the mist that lay over the river. As usual the women were up at daybreak to draw water from the river for their many tasks in the village. They sang as they marched in single file, their calabashes balanced so elegantly on their heads. Some of them had babies tied to their backs with blankets, and also a hoe under one arm. Meanwhile the men lazed about the village, talking about fishing in the lakes.

Nguvu slipped away, wanting to forget what had happened the day before. But it was so difficult to forget! He thought of the proverb which says, "The future is behind you and the past is before you." That is not what western folks think, but the proverb is correct. What happened yesterday, in the past, we see plainly, so that it is in front of us. What will happen tomorrow, in the future, we cannot see, so it is behind us. So in front of Nguvu stalked yesterday, haunting his every step. As he came past our home, Nguvu met the man who had seen his deceit.

"*Moyo, Mwane* (good morning, Sir)," Nguvu said, clapping his hand to indicate that he wished to pass.

"*Moyo, kamwana kami* (good morning, my little child)" the man replied. "See, Mwana, be at my house soon and take the calabash and go and draw water for my wife. In the afternoon you will get the axe and cut firewood for me too, all right?"

"*Sheh!*" said Nguvu in disgust, "Do you think I am your slave?"

"*Chipema, nyi* (good eh)," replied the man, "If you don't obey me, then I'll go and tell Ngana how you killed one of his ducks! So off you go and do as I say." Yes, the snake's tail is showing,

112

Nguvu, sticking out of the hole in the earth!

Nguvu bowed his head, turned on his heel and went away to draw water and cut firewood for the man who had caught him in his crime. What a tiresome task it was, being a slave to someone else. He wanted to go hunting with the other village boys. Now where would he be able to trap rats to eat as relish with his evening mush? Day after day the same thing took place. Nguvu had to work hard, for nothing.

One morning Nguvu rose early, tied his skin belt around his waist and slipped out of his hut to hunt for caterpillars, which were a juicy delicacy he particularly enjoyed. But alas for Nguvu, on the path near the mission he met his enemy once again.

"And where are you going, Mwanami?"

"Forgive me, Mwata, I'm going to hunt for caterpillars because I am very hungry," Nguvu said.

"Oh, you are hungry, are you?" the man sneered, shooting out his lip and emitting a hissing sound, which is almost the equivalent of a curse. "Get back to your work, otherwise I'll go tell Ngana of your crime!" And the man went on his way.

That night Nguvu was tired, ill-tempered and afraid. "How can I go on like this?" he inquired of his heart. "I'm not a slave, that man never bought me! My mother was never a slave. Hi! What can I do?"

The following morning, very early, he crawled out of his hut just as the duiker comes softly over the plain to graze in the coolness of the dawn. Nguvu took some leftover mush. It tasted sour, but he ate it with boiled manioc leaves and a drink of water. Away he went toward the mission. He knew that I was always to be found early in the morning in my office, reading my Bible and praying. He saw me stooped over my desk as he approached. He coughed and coughed and then clapped his hands, using African etiquette. Nguvu knew that white people have strange customs. They stand outside and knock on the door. Do they want to break it down? Are they thieves? White people can be very ill-mannered indeed, thought Nguvu. His elders had taught him to stand outside and clap his hands or cough, since grass huts have, at best, a door made of grass or bamboo, and knocking on a grass door is a very silly thing to do!

I looked up as I heard Nguvu coughing and clapping. "*Kwacha,kwacha, longeshi* (good morning to you)," Nguvu said.

"*Kwacha, kwacha mwanami*," I answered.

"Have you slept well, Ngana?"

"Yes, I have slept well if you have slept well," I said, knowing that I must follow the formalities of etiquette before Nguvu would tell me why he had come. Finally he came inside, knelt on the reed mat and again clapped his hands three times.

Haltingly Nguvu confessed how he had killed the duck, and in contrition he asked for forgiveness. But he was only too conscious of the fact that in the tribe there is no such thing as 'free' forgiveness. Every wrongdoing must be paid for. I, too, had learned this, and I had a brief inward struggle over what I should do. What would the tribe think of a free forgiveness if I gave it?

I spoke to Margaret, who promptly offered to pay for the duck. So Nguvu was forgiven, his crime paid for by another, and he eagerly went to the house to thank Margaret for her kindness and love.

The following morning Nguvu set off along the path as usual, and it wasn't long before he met his enemy. In a gruff voice the man ordered him to the river to fill his calabash. But this time he spoke to a different Nguvu.

"I'm not going!" Nguvu announced firmly.

"Not going, eh!" Anger flashed from the older man's eyes. "*Chipema* (good), I'm off now to tell Ngana of your crime killing the duck." Nguvu laughed and laughed, which angered the man further.

"You are laughing? Wait till I tell Ngana!"

"Yes, you go and tell him!" Nguvu said. "I was there before you, see! I told him and he has completely forgiven me, and my crime has been paid for!" And away went Nguvu down the forest path to hunt small rats for his relish.

Why had such a change come over Nguvu? As he confessed his crime in my office I told him the gospel story of the men who came before Jesus without just payment for their sin. Jesus paid the full price when He died on the cross. And Jesus had paid the full price for Nguvu's sin too. Romans 8.33-34 says, "Who shall lay anything to the charge of God's elect? It is God that justifieth. Who is he that condemneth? It is Christ that died, yea rather, that is risen again... who also maketh intercession for us". For Nguvu, at last the snake's tail was buried, never to be seen again.

Chikenyoki

Jungle Leaf:

The one who dies has no ears.

One harvest season there was a great commotion in our area because some chiefs' fields had been blighted and would yield no harvest. These chiefs had taken a stand against Christ and the gospel, and now they sensed that the loss of harvest was God's way of dealing with them. Africans fear what they consider to be acts of God, and their mythology bears witness that most natural disasters are blamed on God. One tribe says that God sent three pots to men, brought by a bird. Overcome with curiosity, the bird opened one of the pots, and sickness escaped. As the bird was unable to replace the lid, sickness spread among the people. One of the other pots is said to contain herbs with which to fight the sickness.

Chikenyoki was one of these chiefs who lived near the mission compound. I held gospel services in his village regularly, although I knew that his hatred of the gospel had reached the point where he detested seeing any of the Lord's servants even in his village. Time after time he spat at those of us who went there to speak to his people about the Saviour.

One morning Chikenyoki rose from his bed in his hut, sat up and rubbed his eyes. "Oh, it is not yet daylight," he mumbled to himself. "I have risen too soon from my sleep." But the sun had already risen and Chikenyoki had certainly not overslept.

"Open the door!" he bellowed to one of his wives, who responded to his command immediately. "*Kanda kucha, nyi* (it is not yet light)?" he said to her.

"*Mwanangana, vulie* (king, it is light)," she replied.

Chikenyoki was blind. He had gone to bed the previous night feeling well, and awoke without his sight. He immediately sent for a diviner to discover who had bewitched him. In this superstitious culture it is commonly believed that one person can bewitch another simply by blowing a reed pipe pointed toward the person's hut or village. When I visited Dan Crawford's grave I found some French francs lying on a corner of the stone, put there by someone who wanted to buy Crawford's supposed power to bewitch people. On further inquiry I discovered that one day, standing in "God's Acre" on the bluff above Luanza, it was alleged that Crawford had pointed his gun toward the island of Kilwa and shot dead the chief! So they believed that Dan though dead, yet spoke!

The diviner came at once to chief Chikenyoni's hut, with his basket of divining bones and assorted paraphernalia. But that day the diviner was unable to discover the culprit. At a loss, he had to admit to the chief that he did not know who had cursed him to cause the sudden blindness.

A long time passed, and one day I was preaching the gospel in the chapel on our mission compound when I saw an old blind man carrying a stick being led in by a young boy. It was Chikenyoni. Immediately after the service I approached him and greeted him. He lifted his sightless eyes to me and told me the story of his opposition to the gospel message and to the Saviour, and of his disrespect toward the servants of Christ. Now he wanted to confess his error and receive the Saviour he had long spurned. Chikenyoni believed that he had opposed God so vehemently that his blindness was God's way of speaking to him. Though physically sightless he now saw the Saviour with the eyes of his heart, by faith, and passed from death to life.

As we walked from the chapel that day, I noticed that Chikenyoni carried a bundle, and I asked what it was.

"Ngana, these are my idols... I don't want them now," he said.

"You don't want them now, Mwanangana?" I replied.

"No, because I have trusted the Saviour I no longer need them. That is why I came to the gospel service today," he said.

With a heart full of gratitude, I called some of the other Christians to gather round in a circle outside of the chapel, as we had done many times before. There we kindled a small fire, and old Chikenyoki took his bundle, untied it, and threw all his idols into the flames to be burned up. That day the old chief's experience matched that of the Scot, Samuel Rutherford, whose prose Anne Ross Cousins set in verse:

> With mercy and with judgement
> My web of time He wove,
> And aye, the dews of sorrow
> Were lustred with His love.

This old chief used to call the white folk "the kneeless people" because we wore trousers which covered our knees. Years before, the Africans had called David Livingstone "the toeless one", because he wore boots which covered his toes. How many Christians are kneeless in a spiritual sense because they do not wrestle with God in prayer for the salvation of men like Chikenyoki! He is now at home with his Great Chief in heaven, the One who sought him and saved him, and for this blind old man the Scripture has been realised, "Thine eyes shall see the king in His beauty"(Isaiah 33.17).

The Honey and the Bee - Simoni

Jungle Leaf:
> *The stinging bees are those with honey.*

Simoni was a young lad who had been reared at our mission compound and attended the mission school. His home was on the other side of the river, where his father had dedicated his life to preaching the gospel among his own people.

One day soldiers came, tied his father up, and beat him severely because of his preaching. This turned Simoni against the gospel. What was the use of trusting and following Jesus if the result was persecution like that?

One Saturday afternoon as I passed through the compound on my way to a prayer and Bible study meeting in the hall, I saw Simoni sitting by the side of the path with a calabash at his side. He was dipping his hand into it and licking rich, sweet honey from his fingers with obvious great enjoyment.

"*Moyo, Mwanami* (Hello, my child)," I said. "We are going to the prayer meeting. Would you not like to come with us, Simoni?"

"Ngana, please excuse me," he replied. "I'm eating this honey and I don't want to leave it. It's very, very sweet."

"But Simoni, leave it for just a little while, and come and hear the Word of God," I urged him.

"No, Ngana, I cannot come today," he said. And so Simoni continued to lick the rich, sweet honey from his fingers while I went on to the sun-dried brick hall to the prayer meeting. The meeting was long, as is usually the case in this land which operates according to the path of the sun rather than by the hands of the clock. As I returned along the path, I saw Simoni in the same place I'd seen him earlier. But Simoni was no longer smiling, licking his fingers and enjoying the sweet honey. He writhed on the ground, obviously in great pain.

"Simoni, what is wrong?" I asked with concern.

"Ngana, when I was eating the honey a bee stung me in the mouth," he answered. Ah, yes. Simoni had discovered that the sweet thing which had kept him from listening to the Word of God contained a sharp sting. And so I better understood the proverb, "It is the stinging bee which has the honey."

* * *

Some time after this, Simoni told me the African story of the tortoise and the monkey.

One day when the tortoise was slowly ambling along the jungle path he met a monkey whom he greeted in the usual friendly way. They chatted together as they continued along the path.

"Well, how have you managed today?" the monkey asked. "Did you get enough to eat?"

"No," said the tortoise, "it was difficult today because I was a little sick and could not go out and hunt."

"Hoho," chortled the monkey, "you had nothing to eat today!"

"Yes, friend, I am hungry, and I fear I will not be able to sleep tonight because of my hunger," the tortoise said.

"Well, come away home with me and I'll cook some food for you!" the monkey offered.

"Thank you, thank you, Mr. Monkey. This is so very kind of you," he said.

So away they went, the monkey running on ahead to start cooking the food. At last the tortoise crawled into the monkey's home and rested.

"My, you have been a long time coming to my home," said the monkey. "What was wrong?"

"Mr. Monkey, do you not know that we tortoises cannot run as fast as you monkeys?" he said.

"Oh well, I suppose that is true...but come along, as I have the food all prepared for you," said the monkey. The tortoise smacked his lips hungrily. He looked around, but he could see no food.

"Haha!" chortled the monkey again. "Look... before you eat my feast you must climb up that tree." And there, ten feet off the ground, in the crook of a tree, the monkey had placed three calabashes of delicious-smelling food.

"Please bring the calabashes down," the tortoise said, "because you know I could never climb a tree."

"No, no!" said the monkey. "Anyone who wishes to eat my food must first climb the tree!" And so the poor tortoise had to go back home not only with his hunger, but now also with great anger at the monkey for his nasty trick. He devised a plan of revenge.

"Well," said the monkey, upon receiving an invitation from the tortoise to come to dinner, "at least he bears me no malice for the way I tricked him." So when the day of the proposed feast arrived the monkey set off in great anticipation of the fine meal he would enjoy.

After the tortoise and the monkey had greeted one another, the tortoise asked him to sit down so that he could bring in the feast.

"Now," said the tortoise, "I must inspect your hands. Show them to me, please!" And the monkey lifted his two front paws for the tortoise to inspect.

"No, you cannot eat my feast with dirty hands," the tortoise said. "You must go down to the river and wash them, then come back and we'll eat together. That is the proper way to eat." The monkey washed his hands as instructed, and bounded back to the tortoise's home, very hungry now. But unhappily for the monkey, it was the dry season when the bush had been scorched with fire and the ground blackened with soot.

"Let me see your hands again!" said the tortoise. And when the monkey lifted his paws they were as dirty as ever. "Ah, no!" said the tortoise, "your hands are still dirty. You will have to go back to the river and wash them again!" Back and forth ran the monkey, each time passing over the blackened earth and returning as dirty as he had gone to the river.

While he was doing this, the tortoise ate all the food by himself. Then turned to the monkey and said, "That, Mr. Monkey, will teach you not to trick me when you invite me to a feast at your home. I did not get food because I was not able to climb a tree. You did not eat with me because you could not come with clean hands!"

As Simoni told me this story, he came to realise that it was a lesson to him. He, too, needed to "clean his hands", but only the Saviour could do that for him so that he could partake of the rich feast of God's provision. First he had learned the truth about the sting of the bee. Now his own story came home to his heart, and he found something infinitely better than rich, sweet honey when he accepted the Lord Jesus Christ as his own Saviour.

The Calabash and the Cup - Gwathi

Jungle Leaf:
   Medicine does not work where there is no wound.

Gwathi and his wife sat with me on the veranda of their small hut away up in the Zambezi valley. It was the wet season, and I had had a very difficult journey to get there, but I was anxious to reach these distant Shona people with the Message of Life. These were very poor people, badly dressed, and like all of those around, spiritually lost in the darkness of heathendom. Beside us on the veranda stood a calabash, complete with a gourd cup upside down over its neck.

"*Mufundisi* (teacher), do you know the story of the calabash and the cup?" Gwathi asked.

"I'm sorry, Gwathi, I do not know the story," I said, "but please tell me."

"As you know, Mufundisi," said Gwathi, "the calabash is used by our women to draw water from the river. Now the cup must always travel with the calabash. They are never separated. We Shona peoples call that the friendship of the cup and the calabash, because they are always together." He lifted the gourd cup from the spout of the calabash and continued.

"When the women go the wells or to the river, they need the cup to dip into the water so that they can fill the calabash from it. In many places the calabash cannot fill itself without the help of the cup. When the calabash is brought home, the cup rests on top, and when anyone wishes to drink water, the cup is again used to take the water out of the calabash. You see, Mufundisi, they have a real friendship between them, and that is what we call a "working friendship".

As I looked at the calabash and the cup, I saw a parable for Gwathi and his wife. They quickly understood its meaning, and that day from the Full Calabash they received the Water of Life through faith in the Lord Jesus. In turn they became the cup of blessing, for they then shared this Water of Life with countless tribespeople in their district. I had travelled a long way from North Shinjiland down to the hot, sticky Zambesi Valley, but there the Full Calabash, Christ in whom dwells the fullness of God, found Gwathi and made him the Cup, and a firm friendship was formed.

In time a local church was planted there, and not only did Gwathi and his wife receive abundant eternal life, but their present circumstances greatly improved as they developed a profitable industry. They were able to acquire new clothes, and became a real testimony to the transforming power of Christ there in the Zambezi valley.

Samungenda

Halfway up a valley called by the curious name of "The Valley of Heaven", George and I entered a village where the people had stooped to so low a way of life they were living like animals. At the entrance to the village were three women who were naked except for a string tied around their loins. Their heads were covered with red mud mixed with palm oil, and they were filthy. Had God's creation, what He said was "very good", sunk to the level of beasts? Two of the three women were the chief's wives.

We followed the rules of courtesy by first presenting ourselves to the chief himself. Soon he had called his whole village to sit down and listen to the gospel story, and that day became a day of decision for the chief, Samungenda. Though he had been a slave to drink, now he stood up among his own people and confessed Yesu as his Saviour. All around lay calabashes of beer, some made from honey, some from corn, some from the peelings of manioc root. Samungenda stepped over and smashed the calabashes, spilling all the beer on the ground.

The people gasped in disbelief and wonder. Why? In tribal culture, before anyone drinks from a pot of beer, he or she must pour some out on the ground as a gift, or an appeasement offering, to the family or to the tribal spirits. If this is not done, the ancestral spirits which hover over the village will be grieved, and take vengeance. The chief had therefore publicly sinned against the spirits by not offering them beer before he broke the calabashes. Had Samungenda counted the cost of turning his back against their traditional, animistic beliefs? We were impressed by his resolve and his sincerity.

Others in the village were saved, and the depth of joy and the sheer reality of their conversion made them visibly new men and women. They were no longer naked and filthy, with mud in their hair, but cleansed both outside and in. George and I enjoyed rich and happy fellowship with that company of believers in the Lord Jesus Christ.

But one day some years later, desperate and savage men, drugged by satanic power, entered the village and slaughtered the Christians. Samungenda, his wife, and many others, paid the ultimate price and gave their lives for the sake of the Saviour. They left the paltry "Valley of Heaven" on earth for the company of other martyrs in the real heaven above.

* * *

Away past Samungenda's village at the end of this Valley of Heaven, George and I set up camp where people had been ostracised because of leprosy. Some had their fingers eaten off by that dread disease. Others had their feet eaten away so that they hobbled about on their heels. Day by day they hunted the bush for berries, leaves, roots and field mice, as they could not handle a hoe in order to cultivate manioc or corn.

We held our usual type of meeting with them all, and at the end of the gospel message that night, an old man who was completely bald stood up on his heels. He told of their miserable existence and their rejection by the other tribespeople. But here was One who lovingly welcomed them – His name was Yesu. This man accepted the invitation of the Great Healer into his life. He then led George and me over to his idol house and started to throw out the idols. We had never seen so many in one house. The leprous old man gathered all thirty-seven together and lit a bonfire. What a bonfire it was! The grace of God bringing free salvation began to encompass more of the needy bushdwellers right there in the Valley of Heaven.

Months later these believers obeyed the Lord in baptism, and subsequently each Lord's Day the Christian lepers limped several miles down the valley to partake of the Lord's Supper, no longer cast out, but graciously received by their fellow Christians.

The attitude of Angolan tribes toward leprosy is reflected in their words for it. Among the Shinji it is called the "King's Disease" because in their tribal tradition the first man to contract the disease was a king named Mbumba. The Shona of Zimbabwe use the word *Maperembudzi*. *Mapere* are hyenas, and *mbudzi* are goats. When I inquired why they use the double barrelled name they said, "Mufundisi, you know the ferocious nature of the hyena and how it attacks our goats, tearing the flesh and eating it bit by bit! That, Mufundisi, is why we call this disease 'hyenas and goats'."

Carlos

One afternoon I was preaching in a village when I noticed a man slinking into the shade of a mud hut and listening attentively to the gospel story.

"Ngana," he implored me at the end of the talk, "no one cares for me – I'm a leper. Look at my hands and feet. Ngana, please help me." Forsaken by his wife, cast out by his relatives, this man who was probably in his late fifties cried out from a wounded heart. Gently I pointed him to the great Healer of broken hearts and to the One who gathers in the outcasts. Leprosy was eating his body away, but shame and desperation were eating his very soul away.

"Look, He loves you; He died for you," I told him. "He too has marks on his body, marks of the nails by which He was crucified for you."

"Ah, Ngana, this is *maji* (oil) for my heart," he said. "Did you really mean that Yesu said, 'Him that cometh to Me I will in no wise cast out'? "

"Yes, the Saviour is the great *Mukwa-Kukungulula*, the great Gatherer of the Outcasts," I said.

"I've heard God thundering in the sky, but did He really have a Son? Tell me again." So once more I told the desperate man how the Saviour died to save him. Old Carlos knelt on the ground reverently, confessed his sins and committed his life to the One who loved him just as he was. He rose from his knees a new man, with a new hope for the future.

I built a house for Carlos to live in. He applied himself to learning to read, and showed a burning zeal to learn more about the Saviour. As person after person drifted into the village, Carlos became an ardent evangelist, going from hut to hut and leading men and women to Christ. Early in the morning he called them to prayers, telling them of the heavenly *maji* that had healed his heart and life. He lived to see others baptised and gathered into a local fellowship, breaking bread in remembrance of their Lord. Carlos was among the finest of the firstfruits gathered in by the Great Harvester.

A special day came in the life of Carlos when His Excellency, the Governor General, heard of our work among the lepers and came to see them. I took him out to the leper village and presented him to dear old Carlos. A retinue of attendants followed the governor, but they remained at a distance. His Excellency was visibly moved but kept his distance from the lepers too, and when he saw the ravages of the disease on their bodies, he courteously withdrew. Carlos was waiting for a new body, because "nothing that defileth" will ever enter into heaven, and that includes leprosy. He was buried in a shallow grave in the forest, but it was a triumphant funeral, and the forest seemed to echo back the prayer and praise of his fellow Christians as his poor body was laid to rest.

* * *

Another time I saw a man crawling on hands and knees as I entered the leper village. He made painfully slow progress.

"Friend, why are you so tired and emaciated?" I asked.

"Ngana, I have crawled for days and days because I heard that there was good medicine in the mission for me, a leper." I was deeply moved as I looked at the man squatting on the ground with no hope in his eyes, pleading for mercy. He described his long, torturous crawl over a jungle trail. What agony he must have suffered, physically and mentally, never knowing when a lion would pounce on him as easy prey.

> Can we whose souls are lighted
> With wisdom from on high,
> Can we to men benighted
> The lamp of life deny?
> Salvation, oh, salvation!
> The joyful sound proclaim
> Till each remotest nation
> Has learned Messiah's name.
> (Reginald Heber)

Miss Jean Park, a nurse from Lanarkshire, Scotland, was commended to join us in the work of the Lord and for some years she worked among these poor, neglected lepers. Though highly trained in her medical speciality, she also helped to mix the mud to build their houses. Her hard work and her kindness left an indelible impression on these outcast people. The African proverb says, "Misery cannot be chased away with a hunting club." No, it takes Calvary love to touch and heal the misery of such as lepers.

Mr & Mrs Allison and Miss Jean Park

Jean Park's House at Camundambala, built by Crawford Allison

CHAPTER 11

Bullets, Beer, and the Bible

Africa has been described as the place of the three "Bs" : the Bullet, the Bible, and the Beer.

Beer

First came the beer, which has always been part of the African way of life. It is made from grain or honey, and even remote jungle villages boast rustic skills in beer making. Beer is a continent-wide curse in Africa, and it is much to the discredit of white settlers that beer drinking has been further encouraged. Many European immigrants have profited from selling hard liquor to Africans, and in many districts drunkenness has escalated at an alarming rate. Before native people drink of the beer, they must first spill a little on the ground to venerate the ancestral spirits, and it is also poured out as a drink-offering to appease the spirits when certain forms of sickness afflict villagers.

The Pig Pen

Jungle Leaf:

*The little pig turns its snout up
because it saw this from its mother.*

Chitanutanu was a man of the fierce Chokwe tribe which inhabits Angola, Zambia and Zaire. He was powerful in physique, and knew no fear of man or beast. Accustomed as he was to living a rough life in the wild bush country, he was enslaved to many types of vice. Beer-drinking became the chief of these, and he had no regard for what time of day he leaned against his hut and lifted a full calabash to his lips. This habit of Chitanutanu's conflicted with tribal custom which dictates the time of day beer-drinking should be done. Chitanutanu didn't care.

On a particular day Chitanutanu had gone with his wife to cultivate their bush patch. Usually the men chop down the trees where the women want to plant crops, but they hardly ever uproot the stumps and get rid of them. He carried his hoe and a bow and arrows. Possibly he reflected on the African proverb which says, "The hoe never tells a lie." If a man uses his hoe regularly it will be free of rust, but if the person is lazy, the hoe will tell the story. Chitanutanu worked for a while, but as it was a particularly hot day, he returned home just as the sun at noon beat down with its fiercest heat. Since he had carried home a load of firewood along the jungle path he was also tired and very thirsty when he reached his hut. Throwing his load down, he called out to his wife to bring a cup of beer.

"My husband, how foolish you are to think of drinking beer while the sun is still overhead," she replied. "Why don't you wait until the sun has gone down just a little?"

"*Sheh!*" He said in disgust. "Woman! Look at your head and look at your eyes. Bring me beer NOW!"

"Enough! Enough!" she said. "You are foolish, but I will bring the beer." And Chitanutanu rested in the shade of the hut. His wife brought a calabash of strong beer and placed it at his side on the ground. As he began to drink he also began to scold his wife.

"You, woman, you are not the whole hoe. You are just the handle!" She bantered with him in like manner until she realised that his speech was becoming slurred and he was not thinking clearly. Beer affects a person much more forcefully in the heat of the day. Chitanutanu soon toppled over and lay on the ground, while his wife, used to such behaviour, went about preparing the evening meal. Not even the thudding of the stick in the large wooden mortar disturbed Chitanutanu from his drunken stupor. A passerby quoted a local proverb, "To be drunk is to be like a king," and laughed as he went on his way. But Chitanutanu was soon to discover that he was anything but a king.

The cool of the evening brought respite to everyone in the village, and a soft breeze lifted the red dust in the village circle. The cattle that lay under the trees all day, sides heaving because of the stifling heat, rose to their feet, rubbed their heads against the trees and started to bellow. They, too felt refreshed in the cool of the evening. But Chitanutanu slept on.

"You, man, you are foolish!" mumbled Chitanutanu's wife as she looked over at him, the evening meal eaten and cleared away. The sun set, a golden ball of fire in the west, and the sudden tropical darkness blanketed the village till dawn. Twilight is but a moment, and is referred to as "the time when you mistake your own relatives".

Now it became quite cool for Chitanutanu and he awoke, sat up and tried to see where he was. His vision was still blurred by the drink, and there was not a flicker of light to help him figure out where he was. He stared into the darkness.

"*Whe, whe*! Where is my house?... *Ewa* (yes), I see it ... over there, eh?" He staggered to his feet and fell again. Up and down a few more times ... oh ... it was easier to lie still. Chitanutanu slept on. Some time later he again awoke, rose to his knees and crawled forward. Soon he bumped into a stick door, pushed it aside, and after he was a bit inside, he lay down and went back to sleep.

In tropical Africa it becomes cold at night during the dry season in June and July. This coldness caused Chitanutanu to stir in his sleep. He felt something warm at his right side and thought, "*Chipema* (good), even my wife has not forsaken me in my trouble. She lies at my side." Again he stirred and felt something warm at his left side and thought, "Hi! My daughter is at my other side." And he again fell asleep in the comfort of having his wife and daughter with him.

Just at dawn, when the elephant goes washing in the river, he awoke, sat up and rubbed his eyes. "Hi! Where am I?" he cried. He was not in his hut, and his wife and daughter were not next to him. Chitanutanu sat in the middle of the pig sty, with two fat and filthy pigs as his companions. He remembered hearing grunting during the night and thought it was his wife's snoring! Ah yes, this is the condition to which sin brings people – the muck of a pig pen.

"*Wolo!* (oh dear)", said Chitanutanu as he sat up. "My whole body is covered with the dirt of pigs, and I smell like a pig!" Just then his wife came out of her sleeping hut and saw him sitting in the pigsty. She laughed.

"Ha, Ha! That is what you deserve!" she said. But she told him to hurry and get out of the pigpen before others saw him who would laugh also, and who might give him a new name like SaNgulu, "the father of the pigs"! Chitanutanu leaped out of the sty and ran to the river to wash the terrible stench from his body.

Back in the village and much sobered by his experience, Chitanutanu began to think of the words he had heard from the missionary, words of a Saviour who had come to save him from this very pig pen of sin by coming to die for him. Right then he decided that this was the cure for his disease of drinking. He would become a new man by becoming converted.

Chitanutanu's tribe have two words meaning "to turn", or which mean "conversion". One means "to turn aside", while the other means "to turn about and head in the opposite direction". Ah, yes! Chitanutanu knew which word would describe what he wanted! He wanted to turn his life completely about and to leave his drinking and all his other heathen ways.

Some time later a visitor from England came to Chitanutanu's village and met him, now baptised and participating in the local church services. The visitor remarked how deeply impressed he was when Chitanutanu, without shoes but with great dignity, rose at the Lord's Supper and gave thanks for the bread, then passed it to the believers. It was not eloquence of words but the quiet reverence which impressed the visitor so much that day in the heart of Africa. Chitanutanu's story has been written in tract form in several African languages, and many people in different central African countries have received the Good News of salvation in Christ through this witness.

Proverbs 20.1 says, "Wine is a mocker, strong drink is raging: and whosoever is deceived thereby is not wise." And in 1 Corinthians 6.9-11 we read, "Be not deceived ... drunkards ... shall [not] inherit the kingdom of God. And such were some of you, but ye are washed ... in the name of the Lord Jesus."

When older folk in the villages see a person like Chitanutanu given to drink and brawling they say, "A polecat cannot smell its own stink."

* * *

Drink is not the only vice in the bush country of Africa. Often the men who accompanied me on my treks were not believers, and they would bring out their pipes and smoke at night after I'd gone to sleep and was supposedly unaware of what they were doing. They sat around the blazing fire pulling in great drafts of hemp smoke, often from a communal pipe. Hemp is so intoxicating that quite often someone would topple into the fire in a drunken stupor. In fact, they use the same word for drinking and smoking, so that they say they "drink" beer and they "drink" tobacco.

It was a great joy for us to see the transforming power of the gospel when many others like Chitanutanu were converted and redirected their lives to serve the living God, abandoning those evil habits which damaged their lives and had enslaved their souls. The gospel is the message of life and liberty for all who believe.

Bullet and Bible

The bullet is a constant menace in Africa, as it has been since the old pioneers introduced it to shoot game, and since slave traders and many colonialists abused it on the African people. It is a sad fact that many Africans are still being killed by bullets, some in political causes and others as martyrs for their faith in some regions of this unsettled continent.

Thank God there is also the Bible. It is being translated into many more languages and dialects, and it is bringing spiritual life to those who will accept its living message. Unfortunately, however, the Bible is used by some along with animism to create cultic beliefs. For the most part Angola was mercifully protected from the many false cults that blossomed in other parts of Africa, but on one occasion some followers of a cult that practised baptism crossed the border and came into our area. Somehow they managed to get hold of several New Testaments in the local language. When the Portuguese rounded up these folks they found the New Testaments, and naturally linked me with the cult because they knew I did Scripture translation into the African languages.

I was called before a Portuguese official to be interrogated. He expressed nothing but hatred for me and my work. Then came the most outlandish accusations, that I was busy smuggling, and inciting the people against the Portuguese. The grilling went on for several hours. I learned that the official had been trained in Germany and knew the tactics of the Nazis. Although some of the Portuguese traders spoke up boldly in my defence, and the chief of police affirmed my testimony, it was to no avail. But finally I was released. God's mills of justice grind slowly but relentlessly, and in due time this unjust high official found himself behind prison bars!

* * *

After independence in 1975, Angola began to suffer from various cults which misused the Scriptures in the way Satan did when testing our Lord. At one time a godly elder was taken by heavily armed, Bible-hating men to the gable end of the Gospel Hall, where they pointed their rifles at him. What would the elder do now, as he stood there with his Bible in his hand.

"Why," muttered the captain, "the man must be mad!" And lifting up his voice the elder sang,

> *Face to face with Christ my Saviour,*
> *Face to face, what will it be?*
> *When with rapture I behold Him,*
> *Jesus Christ, who died for me.*

Here were the Bible and the bullet meeting together, with no doubt about the Bible triumphing over the bullet.

Ngunga and Bells

There was a young man called Ngunga (the bell), who was taught in the mission school and proved himself to be an effective messenger for Christ. He travelled far and wide with the good news of salvation and was loved by many. But he was hated by those who resented the loss of their trade as new converts forsook their old heathen habits. He often tramped through the villages with me, helping with the preaching.

In his twenties and married, he was called by his Master to pay the supreme price of Christian service, and do in death what he could not accomplish in life. One night the enemies of the cross used their own version of the bullet. Feigning kindness to him, they cooked mush made from manioc and laced it with deadly poison. Oh, the agony of that poison, with no one to comfort him! But Ngunga was not alone, because for him whose name meant the bell, as the last peal on earth was tolled, the bells of heaven rang out when Ngunga met his Saviour face to face.

I wept when I heard of the cowardly act, for Ngunga was one of my spiritual children. Ngunga himself was a heavenly bell, ringing out his testimony and bringing the good news of salvation to prevent souls from going to hell. His enemies thought that by killing him they had silenced the message, but he left behind him many other Ngungas who still sound out the story of the Saviour's love. Again the Bible triumphed over the bullet.

> Far, far away, like bells at evening pealing,
> The voice of Jesus sounds o'er land and sea;
> And laden souls, by thousands meekly stealing –
> Kind Shepherd, turn their weary hearts to Thee.
> (F.W. Faber)

To call the people to various meetings, sometimes the village church used a native drum, sounding at dawn each morning to announce that the hour of prayer had come. I also used as a gong a heavy piece of railway track which I brought from the railhead - it was heavy! Once we brought back from furlough a real ship's bell. The ship had been scrapped and dismantled near Edinburgh, and its bell was salvaged and given to us by a kind brother. After much use, however, it became cracked, and the sound was never the same!

In December 1943, the Chinese melted the first bronze for what eventually would be "the largest bell in the Orient". Weighing 44,000 pounds it was to be housed in a tower on a mountain in Anwek. It was called "the bell of hell", and was to be sounded at regular intervals by Buddhist priests to "awaken souls sinking into the inferno of the lower regions".

More Bullets

Many of those who believed the gospel and accepted Christ in Central Africa became martyrs for their faith as they fell under a hail of bullets. Others where clubbed to death, marked out for attention because they carried a Bible and followed its principles. Some Christians were forced at the point of a gun to cook meals for the fighters, and were later killed by the opposing forces for doing so. Some of the men were roasted in the fire after being

135

shot, and their wives were not only forced to watch, but to eat a piece of the body.

One day Margaret and I were surrounded by men holding rifles.

"Who are you for?" they screamed at us. I stared into the barrel of the rifle. One false move and I knew I would meet instant death. A man took the pin out of his hand grenade and my heart beat more quickly.

Bullet or Bible? Ngunga and the other martyrs had faced this trial. Their enemies, looking at their slain bodies, laughed and thought that they had gained the day. Now Margaret and I stood where they had been.

"We are neither for the whites nor for you," I answered quietly, amazed by the fulfilment of the promise that the necessary words would be given by the Master Himself in the moment of trial when I was humanly speechless.

"We are for no political party; we are for Christ," I said.

"We've warned you!" the man shouted again.

"Come into our hall and we'll tell you what we preach – not politics, but Christ," I said.

"Enough, enough!" They lowered their rifles. Then I heard myself saying, "Put the pin back in the grenade – it might go off!" and the men left.

* * *

Devilish devices were invented by wicked men to break the Christians' resolve to stand firm in their faith. One of the most shocking, and reminiscent of what was faced centuries before by the Covenanters in my native Scotland, was the trial by fire. Young Christians were lashed to stout poles as if they were pigs, then held over a large fire and roasted. This was the final effort to try to force them to deny their Lord. And yet the men who perpetrated such evil called themselves "Freedom Fighters". I knew a young man who bore this trial. After his torturers had tied him to the pole he begged them to tie his New Testament to his breast.

"Why?" they asked roughly.

"Because I love God's Word and I believe in the Saviour!" he cried.

The bullet or the Bible? "Fear not them which kill the body, but are not able to kill the soul: but rather fear him which is able to destroy both soul and body in hell" (Matthew 10.28).

The Angolan martyrs died triumphantly. Cremation is never practised by the tribes of Central and Southern Africa, as it violates the people's concept of the spirit world. Only evil witches are burned to death. But these people looked on Christians as worse than witches, and thought they deserved to be slowly roasted to death.

> *Few men venture out beyond the blazed trail;*
> *'Tis he who has the courage to go past this sign*
> *That cannot in his mission fail.*
> *He will have left at last some mark behind*
> *To guide some other brave exploring mind.*

Robert Louis Stevenson wrote, "No man is of any use until he has dared everything." These brave Angolan martyrs blazed a trail and dared to give their all.

CHAPTER 12

Trees, Water and Crocodiles

Trees

Jungle Leaf:
   A tree does not heal where there is no disease.

Before I left Scotland I took some dental training. I knew this would be most useful in furthering the work of the gospel in Africa. One Friday afternoon a knock at the door told me a European waited outside, as no African ever engaged in the weird custom of knocking on a door! There, indeed, stood the local Roman Catholic priest, hand on his jaw, suffering from a severe toothache. He sat silently watching while I boiled my extraction instruments and prepared an injection. Just as I asked him to open his mouth he drew back and said, "Oh, Senhor, I've forgotten that this is Friday, and if you extract these teeth I won't be able to say mass on Sunday!"

He left quickly, and I stood holding a wasted injection, thinking I'd never see him again. I was wrong. The following week he reappeared at the door, but this time he was not wearing his clerical robe.

"Senhor Padre," I said, "what about your clerical robe? Where have you put it?"

"Senhor, I know you are Protestants, Evangelicals," he said, "and I did not want to come into your home wearing my Catholic robes, so I took them off and hung them outside." And there, sure enough, outside I saw his robes hanging on a tree!

138

As the priest sat with forceps in his mouth, unable to answer back, I thought what a good opportunity I had to speak to the man about the Saviour! But I completed the extraction successfully, and then when it was over he listened to what I had to say. Then he admitted, "Senhor, I have never read the Bible. I don't even own one. Could you get one for me?" What a pleasure it was to write home to a close friend of mine in Scotland, who sent out a Bible immediately. And what of the tree where the priest had hung his robe? I asked that it never be cut down, but that it remain as a testimony to the priest's conversion, a symbol of his hanging all the empty ritual that robe represented on the Tree where the Saviour died for him.

Many years later a friend of mine went to the continent of Europe to visit some war graves. As he wandered about in one of the cemeteries he noticed a priest also searching gravestones for names he knew. They exchanged greetings, and when my friend discovered that he had come from Angola, he mentioned that he had a good friend named Crawford Allison who worked there.

"Crawford Allison?" asked the priest. "I know him well! He extracted my two teeth and helped me to find the Saviour!" Reaching into his pocket he pulled out his Bible and said, "This is the Bible he gave me. I read it all the time!"

* * *

Slogging along in the heat by the edge of Lake Mweru in Congo was no easy hike even for a seasoned veteran of the bush, but I persevered that particular day because I was searching for something. Earlier in the day I had talked with an old African who had accompanied the pioneer missionary Dan Crawford on his great treks. It was thrilling to listen to stories of the adventures of this servant of God in the very parts of Africa where I was now travelling. The story that peaked my interest most was of a tree which Crawford called *The Witness Tree,* and all the more so because I had also read of it in Crawford's famous book, *Thinking Black.*

When, after much searching, Dan Crawford found a suitable

site on which to build a mission compound, he and the local chief stood before a designated tree for the African equivalent of the signing of the deeds. They carved a square in the bark, then each fired a bullet from his gun, and the "wounded" tree thus became a living witness to the fact that Crawford had been given the land on which to build a mission station.

It was with much interest, then, that I searched for this tree as I stood near the cliff at the edge of Lake Mweru and looked toward Chipungu where Crawford had begun his work in the area. I was not surprised to find it, as one of the characteristics of a witness tree is that it must never be felled. And as I stood there I thought of another Tree on which a Wounded Man died, and which became a living witness to a deed ratified in heaven of a finished work of salvation. I called the tree "the wounded tree of Africa", as it grew far above the waters of Lake Mweru, living testimony to a settled deed, and bearing in its body the wounds.

* * *

Down in the Zambesi valley I visited another tree, this time one associated with David Livingstone who explored the Zambesi and much of Central Africa to open a way for the progress of the gospel of Christ. In one of his journals, David Livingstone wrote that the only time he desecrated the flora of Africa was when he carved his name on this giant baobab tree. Since then many people have carved their names on this tree as a mark of gratitude to Livingstone for his pioneering work.

Near the village of Chief Chitambo in the Lake Bangweulu area, in the eastern part of what is today known as Zambia, Livingstone's heart was buried beneath yet another witness tree. Dan and Grace Crawford visited that site to show their appreciation for the work of their Scottish predecessor who gave his all for the healing of the sore of Africa. Unfortunately this tree was later destroyed because some had desecrated it.

* * *

These last three trees in Central Africa each bear an individual testimony. The first is a wounded tree, testifying to the fact that a deed had been signed and sealed and delivered. It reminds us of our Saviour's cross. The second at the edge of the Zambesi, is a reminder of the work of Livingstone, a great servant of Christ, and bears the names of many people who appreciated what he did. But the third tree in a lonely spot, tells of the man's life worn out at the age of sixty, given and poured out to death for the sake of others. David Livingstone's heart was buried there in May 1873, then his body was preserved and eventually brought to be buried in Westminster Abbey in London. On his tombstone there you can still read the verse which sent him to that dark continent: "Other sheep I have, which are not of this fold: them also I must bring" (John 10.16).

* * *

A bald-headed man sat in our home at the mission one day. He was somewhere around fifty years old, and had walked from a heathen village near the Shinji country. He was the first Shinji I had ever seen.

"Ngana, I want to be baptized," he said. This was a surprise from a man who had come such a distance.

"That is good, but when did you trust the Saviour?" I asked.

"I, Ngana, yes, I trusted in the green tree."

"The green tree? What do you mean by that?"

"Ngana, I heard you talking in the gospel service about a green tree and you said this was a picture of the Saviour," he said. "You know, Ngana, I have lived in a land where we have a lot of dried up trees and we lack green trees. When you talked of the green tree I remembered our village with no green trees in it."

"What do you think of the green tree?" I asked. He laughed, but in a subdued voice.

"The Saviour who died for me, that is my green tree," he said. Then I remembered the verse in Luke 23.31 from which I had preached, "For if they do these things in a green tree, what shall be done in the dry?" Here was this man from the far Shinji country saying that he was a dry tree but Christ was a green tree! What a perception he had, having lived and hunted in a dry land where green trees were so hard to find, and understanding that spiritually the Saviour is as an everlasting Green Tree in a dry and parched land!

* * *

Trees are integral to the life and ancestral worship of the Bantu tribes. At the Sacred Tree, often ringed by a fence, sacrifices are made as the people try to approach their ancestral spirits. The area around the tree is considered holy ground. I saw many such trees outside Shona villages, where the people carry their offerings of meat, mush, blood and beer. The ritual takes place in the very early morning at a time when they say 'the elephant washes'. The offerings remain under the tree until afternoon, when the people return. If sugar ants are in the beer, or crawling on the meat or mush, it is a sign that the ancestral spirits have accepted the offerings and are happy. The mush is then given to young children to eat, but never to older people. The beer is given to an old man or woman. Should there be no sign of the sugar ants in any of the offerings, it means that the ancestral spirits are grieved and refuse to accept the gifts. Such refusal instills much fear among the villagers. How good it was to tell these people of another tree mentioned in 1 Peter 2.24: "His own self bare our sins in His own body on the tree, that we being dead to sins, should live unto righteousness: by whose stripes ye were healed."

Water

Similarly water is of great significance in tribal life throughout Central Africa, both physically and spiritually. During one trek I became lost as I trekked through Minunguland with my carriers. We were into our third day's journey along the jungle path without finding drinking water, and we were becoming desperate. There are no rivers in this region either, only wells scattered here and there, but we could not find one. We had been harassed by lions, and were tired and also in need of protection from these marauding animals as the forest light faded with the approach of night. Just then I saw a small pool of stagnant water right in front of me. We dropped to our knees and the men drank quickly. I tried to filter the dirty water through my handkerchief first, but although the water saved my life, I was plagued with chronic dysentery for many years after this. In such situations it is better to shoot a buck and to squeeze the rumen for its liquid, but of course that day there was not a buck track in sight!

Yet another time George and I were trekking away up north in Ruuandaland, the territory of a break-off tribe from Rwanda. We stopped, amazed, in front of a grove of palm trees. Palm trees, hundreds of miles into the interior away from the salt breezes which are essential to the growth and maturity of the coconut palm! They even bore clusters of coconuts. A local missionary lady laughed, and called to her gardener.

"Bring a hoe and dig around this tree," she told him. And so he dug a circle about three feet away from the tree. There lay the secret. Bags of salt had been buried around the trees' roots. "Now climb up and bring Ngana a coconut," she told the man, and he shimmied up the stately trunk and returned with a fruit. The milk was somewhat tasteless, but refreshing. And here was another parable for George and me to use. Apart from the salt of the Word of God there can be no fruit-bearing in Christians' lives. Salt, a precious commodity in Shinjiland, in Minunguland and in Ruuandaland, was now available to these people in a spiritual sense as well, through the message of Life which we had come a far distance to deliver.

It is not surprising that so many African proverbs concern water, especially drinking water. "Dig your well before you feel thirsty", and "The one who guards a well will never die of thirst", are commonly repeated. I added my own to the list: "He is wise who boils his water before drinking", since some tribes buried their royal dead in the rivers. They would select a stream and dam it up, then dig a shallow grave in the exposed bed downstream before releasing the dam again.

On a long trek into Mbangalaland one of my missionary colleagues rested beneath a tree near a village, and asked for water. The villagers gladly obliged, and returned quickly. But when my friend saw the container in which they brought the water he immediately vomited. The water was offered to him in the skull of a soldier who had recently been killed!

One other concern I had when accepting a drink of water from anyone was that I should not accidentally spill any of it. When a chief drinks, he takes the gourd cup from the person kneeling before him and tilts it slightly to allow a little to spill on the ground before he drinks. This is an ancient ritual in deference to the ancestral spirits, and of course I wanted to be sure that no one ever had opportunity to mistake my clumsiness for appeasing an ancestral spirit!

"The water that I shall give him shall be in him a well of water springing up into everlasting life" (John 4.14).

The Shining River

We were forcing our way through tangled bush country, scratching our legs on the thorn bushes that grow so prodigiously everywhere. All the while we were on the lookout for lions. At once a herd of antelope pounded past us nearby, and although we could not see lions, we knew they had caused the stampede.

Late in the afternoon we arrived at another village, and again set up camp and prepared to share the gospel message around the campfire that night. As darkness fell suddenly, the way it always does in Central Africa, I heard the people talking among themselves of a shining river. Curious, I asked them in which direction this mysterious river lay.

"Oh," they said, "it's not far away from here, but no one goes there now." And as far as they were concerned, that was the end of the matter.

After another gospel meeting early in the morning, I was keen to push on for I hoped to cover a good distance toward the next village before the heat of the day became too intense. As usual, the carriers dallied, not wanting to leave until the dew dried alongside the path. How they hated the dew clinging to the long grass and soaking them as they brushed past it! I thought again of the shining river the villagers spoke of the evening before.

"Yes, Ngana, we can take you there," the carriers agreed, and we left the path, forcing our way through dense jungle growth. Soon we came to the banks of a large river, and sat down to rest.

"So this is the shining river, is it?" I asked, unable to understand why the muddy brown waters in front of me deserved such a lofty name.

"Yes, Ngana, this is it," they said. "When you walk into the river you will understand." Gingerly and slowly I waded into the water, hoping no crocodiles lurked in the muddy shallows. As I came to deeper water in the middle, I suddenly saw something. It shone! It really did! I dived down and grabbed at the shining objects on the sand. *Mama yami!* I held two lovely diamond bearing stones! I looked again, and there were more! Undoubtedly they had washed from the slopes of the bank further up the river, and there they lay.

I waded back to the bank, knowing that I could not keep the diamonds, but it was a thrill just to hold these precious stones.

The men crowded around me to look at the gems. They too, thrilled at the sight of such beauty, and also understood that this wealth could never be theirs because it already belonged to another. As we stood there I thought of how these diamonds represented what we as believers in Christ have received.

Placing one of the stones on the ground, I held up the other and said, "Yes, men, we know the great Chief as our Saviour.

He is our Diamond which we possess forever. I cannot take this one away because it is not mine; it belongs to someone else. The Great Chief, our Saviour, who is our Diamond, belongs to us for all years. He actually belongs to us. You see, men, we can say, 'The great Chief as Saviour is mine'!"

Placing the first diamond stone on the ground I picked up the other and told the men it reminded me of the Holy Spirit who indwells us.

"Listen my men," I said, "you remember your own proverb? 'Riches are like the dew that vanishes when the sun rises.' The Great Chief who is Saviour, and the Holy Spirit who indwells the believer are beyond any riches of this earth, even these beautiful and precious diamonds."

After a long while I rose, picked up both diamond stones and tossed them back into the Shining River. I then took my Bible and showed the men that this is my Shining River where long ago I discovered my two splendid Diamonds, Christ as my Saviour, and the Holy Spirit to dwell in me.

We left the river, and the men found the path once more. They sang as they walked along, "Oh Great Spirit, give us goats, give us sheep. Give us many children that we may be rich." I listened to their chant and thought how strange this land was. Would the message of Life about the Great Chief, the Saviour, never penetrate their heathen minds and change their values? Ah, but their values were not really different from those of the Scottish people I knew so far away. Here in the jungle song was the familiar expression of the shining river the whole world seeks for - wealth in this life, and ignoring the world to come.

* * *

Margaret and I received an unexpected visitor one Sunday morning, a Portuguese man who arrived at the mission station with neither suitcase nor explanation as to why he'd come. Margaret cooked him breakfast, and when the hour for our first meeting came, I gave him a Portuguese Bible and hymnbook. He attended two services that morning, had lunch, then asked me to take him part of the way to the administrative offices. A little more than half way there I left him, but my son David watched him and saw that instead of continuing on down the path, the man turned off into the bush.

I was very busy with other meetings at the station that day, and the incident slipped my mind. The next morning a soldier arrived to say I was to report to the Portuguese Administrator right away. We soon covered the eight miles to his office, and the Administrator asked if we'd had any visitors at the mission the day before. All visitors to the district were meant to report to the Administrator in person. I still didn't remember the Portuguese man, and thought he must be alluding to a possible visit from some of our missionary friends from the south.

"Senhor, please think well," he said. "Did you not have any visitor yesterday?" Suddenly the image of the Portuguese man who had gone off so mysteriously flashed into my mind.

"Ah," said the Administrator, "that man is a diamond smuggler. We know you, Senhor, you have lived many years in Angola. Please go back to your house and search around your doorway, as that man may have planted diamonds there to implicate you!" I hastened home and searched thoroughly, but found no diamonds anywhere. Margaret and I often wondered what the man did with the Bible we gave him, and whether he thought seriously of the words he heard that Sunday as the gospel was presented to him.

The intrigues and attacks of Satan were always with us, following our labours for our Master who had sent us here. But from the dark depths of heathendom there came many spiritual diamonds for the crown of the Saviour, and this offset our many trials and disappointments.

Crocodiles

Jungle Leaf:
The stream crosses the path; the path crosses the stream;
which is the elder?

In African mythology the crocodile frequently represents cunning,

147

but seldom human beings, or any thing for the good of man. Certainly the crocodile's behaviour demands that people be very careful when crossing any river, deep or shallow. As the proverb says, "If you have not looked down, do not cross the river." Any wary traveller knows this well. The crocodile lies still in the murky shallows, looking like a log, waiting for some woman to stoop with her pitcher to draw water from the river or the pool where it lies. I've seen crocodiles shot and opened up, and inside are bangles of women whom the crocodile has killed and eaten.

Another proverb illustrates the crocodile's behaviour. "The crocodile does not live on raids; its food comes along the water way." Raids are left to great hunters like the lion and the leopard. Instead, the crocodile waits for its victim to come to him. Almost submerged, only its eyes and a part of its head show while it waits, often hiding among reeds near the river bank. Even a large crocodile cannot eat a whole adult at once, but what it cannot eat it hides in a hole in the river bank where the body cannot be washed away. And so the crocodile has another meal prepared. Hunters who are after crocodile skins, especially the soft skin of the belly, cut a channel running from the reeds where the crocodiles typically lurk, to lead it into a well concealed trap.

River barricaded against crocodiles during baptism

A young woman attended a gospel service which I conducted in a village on the banks of a large river one day. She listened carefully to the message of salvation, but at the end she lifted her basket on her head and left. I watched her as she descended the slope to

148

the river, and felt saddened as I wondered if she would ever hear the gospel again. So many of the villagers I met and preached to heard the message only once. She called out to the ferryman to cross from the other side of the river to get her. After much haggling as to the ferryman's pay, he poled his dugout canoe out into the river toward her. I watched as she climbed in with her basket and they began their return journey.
"*Tala! Tala!* (Look! Look!)" called some of the villagers. In mid stream a hippo had emerged, put his head under the canoe and thrown the man and woman into river. While hippos can't eat their victims, the ever-wily crocodiles lurk nearby to benefit from the hippo's meanness. The only call I heard that day was, "*Hatoka, hatoka* (She is lost, she is lost)." I called some men and we searched the river in another canoe, but we never found her body.

Another day a woman came down to the river to draw water, and as she stooped to dip the calabash into the water a crocodile's jaws snapped around her, its huge sharp teeth gouging her flesh as it attempted to drag her into the deep water. A crocodile never kills its victim outright, but grips the person firmly and drowns them. The woman cried loudly for help, and her friends nearby grabbed sticks and smacked the crocodile on the nose. It let her go, but she still remained in danger of dying from blood poisoning contracted from that crocodile's bite.

Ah yes! The proverbs are true. "In a pool where there are crocodiles you swim only once," they say, and "the lips of the people do not miss the mark" – their warning is dependable.

* * *

Our boys, Kenneth and David, attended boarding school at Sakeji in distant Zambia (then Northern Rhodesia).We so much looked forward to their times at home with us on holiday. On one of these occasions we took them camping to a place near a large river where there were "singing sands". How the boys loved rising each morning from their camp beds and going down to the sands. There they played, listening to the sand "singing" as they walked along slowly. They fished and took long walks with us along the river banks. And always, they begged to jump into the river to cool off. The answer was always a definite "No!"

One day they were going back to camp by the edge of the bank when the same plea came to me yet again to allow them to go into the shallows and swim. It looked so inviting to the boys. But "No!" I said yet again. I was hot from carrying my rifle, so I leaned it against a tree and took rest for a few moments, while Margaret and the boys went on ahead. As I looked down at the river I noticed a ripple, and then, very slowly, a nose protruding. Yes, it was a crocodile! It lifted its head out of the water as it swam along noiselessly following Margaret and the boys with its narrow, cunning, shiny eyes. I took careful aim and fired, but since the crocodile's head seems almost as hard as steel, two shots accomplished nothing more than frightening it out in to the murky river depths. The boys got a tremendous fright and learned a necessary lesson. There were no further pleas to go into the river!

* * *

In Job 41.1-10, the Bible mentions a creature which resembles the crocodile and concludes with this advice, "Remember the battle, do no more."

The Monkey and the Crocodile

Jungle Leaf:
> *The thread always follows the needle.*

Away up north in Shinjiland there is a lovely lake surrounded by rolling hills. George Wiseman and I often camped with our men at the edge of this beautiful lake. But we were always wary of the night-time dangers lurking nearby - in the form of hippos, which mostly made a lot of noise, and which were attracted by our camp fire. To us it appeared as if these wild creatures of the water were curious about the two white men daring the dangers of the lake which held so many mysteries.

Near the edge of this vast lake there grew a tree whose branches spread out across the surface of the water. It was the chosen home of a certain monkey, allowing him to swing out over the water without fear of toppling in. As we watched this monkey and his neighbours swinging from branch to branch, our African friends told us some of their tribal proverbs concerning baboons and monkeys. These creatures are favourites in jungle lore.

To compare a human to a baboon is an insufferable insult, yet they repeat proverbs such as, "Big baboon, fold your tail up so that the little ones may fear you", and "The baboon is ugly to look at but it does not eat dead things". People set traps for baboons, but they are known for their extreme cunning. In one jungle story the baboon is outwitted by the hare, but this story is seldom repeated. Both baboons and monkeys are generally credited for their cleverness over all other animals. At the same time, the monkey is often detested by the African because of its destructive nature, raiding gardens and destroying crops until the people's anger cannot be contained.

Sitting around village camp fires at night I have heard many stories of the escapades of baboons and monkeys. Exaggerations, of course, abound. But baboons have been known to outwit even lions of the forest with their cunning. I heard stories of baboons catching humans, tying them up and slapping them until they died. Such a story told from time to time wakens in the human breast a genuine respect for these forest dwellers. The following story is told of the very monkey who lived in the tree overhanging the lake near which we camped.

* * *

The monkey often threw fruit to the crocodile, and a friendship between them grew and was cemented firmly. One day the crocodile swam up to the tree and called out to the monkey.

"You have been very kind to me for a long time in sharing with me the fruit of your tree, but you have never seen all the wonders of my home here in this lake. I would like to give you a ride on my back and show you what my home in the deep is like," the crocodile said. The monkey was not flattered or interested, but remained in his fruit tree. Another day the crocodile arrived under the tree again and called out to the monkey to come and talk to him.

"Do you not feel how hot it is up in that tree?" the crocodile reasoned. "Come down and climb on my back and I will give you a lovely, cool ride in the water."

The crocodile often gave the monkey invitations like this, and one day the monkey agreed, and swung nimbly down onto the crocodile's back. Off they went, out into the lake, with the monkey enjoying the cool ride. What a difference from the hot branches of his home in the tree! Suddenly they were joined by some baby crocodiles who swam alongside on the right and on the left. The monkey listened to them as they swam along singing.

"Hi, friend!" he called to the crocodile. "We've gone far enough now; I can hardly see my home in the tree from this distance."

"Friend Monkey, are you not enjoying yourself?" chortled the crocodile.

"Oh yes, I'm enjoying myself on this cool ride, but I want to get back to my home in the tree now," said the monkey. He listened to the baby crocs swimming at his side as they continued with their singing.

"What are they saying in their song?" the monkey asked the crocodile.

"The chief of our tribe is sick, the chief of our tribe is sick; he needs a new heart," replied the crocodile.

"Oh, my!" said the monkey in fright. "I wonder when I'll be able to return to my home in the tree."

"The chief of our tribe is sick and needs a monkey's heart; the chief of our tribe is sick and needs a monkey's heart," sang the baby crocodiles. The monkey began to shake with fear.

"How can I escape? They want my heart! They have deceived me!" he thought to himself in panic.

"Hold on! Hold on! Stop!" the monkey cried.

"What do you want?" asked the crocodile, as the babies turned to see what was happening.

"I've left my heart at home in the tree!" the monkey shouted. "I want to go back and get it. It is in the tree!"

"You came without your heart? What a stupid monkey to leave your heart behind you in the tree of fruit!" said the crocodile.

"I have no heart to give your chief, since it is left behind in the tree," said the monkey again, looking very sorrowful. The crocodile thought hard. Could he go to his chief with a monkey who had no heart? No, that would be a crime, and he would be made to pay for it.

"All right," said the crocodile, "I'll take you to your tree so that you can fetch your heart." And he swam around in a big circle and glided off back toward the monkey's tree. As soon as they reached the shallow water, the monkey gave one huge leap and landed safely on the shore. He clambered up his tree as fast as he could, high up into the foliage of the branches. The crocodile and all of the baby crocodiles lay in the shallow water with just their long snouts and their eyes showing, waiting for the monkey to find his heart and come back. A long time passed, but no monkey appeared from the tree.

"Friend Monkey! Where are you? Have you found your heart yet?" the crocodile called.

"It is right here, in the tree, in the centre of my body," came the monkey's high-pitched voice. "This is my home where my heart lies and I am not coming to you and leaving the place of my heart."

And so the monkey managed to outwit the crocodile. The Bible says, "lay up for yourselves treasures in heaven ... for where your treasure is, there will your heart be also" (Matthew 6.20-21); and "set your affections on things above, not on things on the earth" (Colossians 3.2). The monkey was safe when his heart was in the right place.

CHAPTER 13

Lions and Dogs

Lion

Jungle Leaf:
The severe frost made the tortoise climb a tree.

One very dark night people from the Songo tribe gathered around a flickering campfire to listen to the gospel message. Their village nestled on a hillside overlooking the Jambo River, in a remote district where few visitors ever ventured. They listened intently to this strange white man who spoke their language, and who carried neither sleeping tent nor gun. And there I sat on a small stool, all alone and without a gun, and suddenly found myself facing the King of the Jungle!

Before the beast chose to move, I sprinted toward a grass hut, only to find it already crammed with sixteen men. They squashed back and let me stand against the flimsy grass door, which of course provided no protection whatsoever from a lion. I heard the lion breathing right outside. It sat down and then stretched out. All night it lay there while we ached with weariness from standing so squashed and unable to move. About four o'clock the lion gave a great grunt, stood up and walked away. I also gave a grunt of relief and opened the grass door, only to see the lion standing a short distance from the hut. Much to my surprise it began to imitate the call of a goat. I had never heard of a lion doing such a thing. It bleated until a goat appeared and became the lion's breakfast in place of me.

The Songo carriers who accompanied me on that trip could not be coaxed out onto the jungle trail the next day until about ten o'clock for fear of the lion. The path dipped down from the hillside into a valley of dense jungle. As we walked along, the lion returned with his lioness, and the pair kept pace with us all day, one on either side of us. Terrified, the men huddled together in a tight single file, and trotted along the entire day within touching distance of one another.

That night we reached the safety of another Songo village where the chief offered me the use of a hut. Upon inspecting it, however, I discovered that my choice of companions lay between lice inside and the lion outside! The choice was easy. I kindled a small fire and lay down outside. As I was drifting off, I heard movement, and was most relieved to find that it was only the youngest carrier creeping out of his hut to join me by the fire.

The lion did not trouble us further, but some years later I was vividly reminded of this event in the Songo village on the banks of the Jambo River when Little Bird told the following story of the Lion and the Goat.

The Lion and the Goat

One day, according to Little Bird, the goat wanted to change so he could become a lion. He called all of the jungle animals together and told them of his wish. The leopard told him that if he truly desired such a change, he would have to roar like a lion, eat like a lion and walk like a lion. In other words, the leopard told him, he would have to learn all the lion's ways.

So Goat hurried off to try to learn all of these new habits, but he could not. The task was too hard for him. He said, "I'll roar like a lion!" But his voice was too weak. "All you animals, hear me! I am a lion! I am a lion!" But the animals laughed at him and made a fool of him. No one believed him.

One day the goat met the ape in the forest. "I say, Mr. Hundu," said Goat, "what should I do to change myself into a lion?"

"Listen to me, Mr. Goat," he replied, "take a piece of paper and write on it, 'I AM A LION', and then tie that to your horns so that all the animals will see it."

The goat did as he was told, but still the other animals made fun of him. He arrived at a house and asked if a lion lived there. Immediately he heard the fearsome roar of lion and he thought, "*Mala!* (goodness) That is my echo!" Boldly he entered the house, and Mr. Lion jumped on him and killed him. Yes, the goat could not change himself into a lion. Only by being born as a lion could he follow the lion's ways.

Little Bird used this story to great effect in illustrating the gospel message, choosing as his text John 3.7, "Marvel not that I said unto thee, Ye must be born again."

The Lion and the Rabbit

Jungle Leaf:
   It is in the silent pool where the crocodiles live.

Man-eating lions are scarce, thankfully, and are not easily tracked in the African bush, as they are usually old and cannot hunt game like the younger ones do. Nevertheless they are still to be feared greatly, because once a lion has tasted human flesh it poses a permanent danger, always craving more.

Gathered around the flickering campfire whose comforting light penetrates only a few feet into the blackness of the African night, the people recount their tales of the King of the Beasts.

One such tale involves a male lion out hunting for food for the lioness and their cubs. He stole along silently and swiftly as is the lion's custom when he is scenting game. He hunted for a long time, and although he saw no game he saw a man walking along the path to his field where he cultivated manioc.

The lion waited just at the bend of the path, scenting the air as the man approached, unaware of the danger to his life. With one leap the lion pounced on the man and ripped his skull open with his massive claws. Satisfied with himself, he stood gazing down at the large dinner his family would enjoy that day. Just then a rabbit emerged from the bush and stood next to the lion.

"*Moyo, mwane* (good morning, Sir)," said the rabbit in a timorous and shaking voice.

"*Moyo yene mukepe* (good morning you small thing)," replied the lion. "What do you want here?"

"My, you are strong! Did you kill that man?" said the rabbit.

"What do you want?" roared the lion again. "Wait! You stand here and watch this man while I go and call my wife and hungry cubs to come and eat some meat."

"Yes, mighty Lion, I'll stand here and watch this man till you get back with your wife the lioness."

Off bounded the mighty lion and was soon lost from the rabbit's sight. He had good news to tell his wife and cubs!

Mbalu the rabbit also stood and looked at the man. He knew that he must guard the meat carefully because it belonged to the King of the Jungle, and after all, who was he, Mbalu?

He lifted his eyes and scanned the sky. He saw vultures circling high overhead, waiting for their chance to swoop down and snatch off a piece of meat. Mbalu knew the ways of the vultures well, and he puffed himself out to look as important as possible while he stood guard. But Mbalu, too, was desperately hungry. What should he do? If he ate a piece of the flesh, the King would know immediately when he returned. Huh! Mbalu was tired of eating leaves. He wanted meat!

Mbalu studied the man's body intently and noticed his ears sticking out from his head.

"Well," he thought, "I could just nibble at one of the ears and that would be enough for me......just a little." So he hopped nearer and licked the right ear. Mmmmmm! It was good. He took just a small nibble. That was even better. "*Chipema* (that is good)," he said to himself.

Mbalu nibbled and nibbled until the right ear was completely nibbled away. "*Kuyema!* (that was sweet)," he said. "Now if I could just nibble at the left ear until it, too, is completely eaten away, the king will never know what is missing."

Does Mbalu not think of the wise saying of the elders, "A

cockroach sent to fetch the milk never returns?" So Mbalu ate both of the man's ears before the king returned. Then he sat back on his haunches to wait for the lion. Very soon the lion came bounding along the path with his lioness and cubs. Mbalu started to tremble as the lion stood with his legs apart surveying the body of the man he had killed.

"*Yena!*" he screamed at Mbalu, "Where are the man's ears? You have eaten the ears! Now I'll kill you and eat you too, Mbalu!"

"Just a minute," squeaked Mbalu in a terrified voice, "let me tell you..."

"Tell me what? You have eaten the ears, have you not!" the lion said.

"No, no! People don't have ears like we have," said Mbalu. "They have no ears like King Lion!"

"*Mahuza!* (lies)" replied the lion.

"No, no! I tell you! Please run off to the village and see for yourself that people have no ears."

"Mbalu," said the lion, "you are very cunning. You will run away when I go to the village!"

"No, friend Lion, I'll stay here with your wife the lioness. She will guard me until you come back." So at last the lion agreed with Mbalu, and away he went like the wind toward the village.

The lion knew the path to the village well because he had crossed over it many times while hunting duiker. He also knew that in this village the people were not living at peace with their chief, and were angry with him. The chief had told them that very morning to dig a deep ditch around his manioc field to keep out the wild pigs. They had only completed part of the job and had left to go hunting for wild honey.

"I tell you, my people, you simply have no ears!" the chief cried out to them when he discovered they had disobeyed his command. King Lion came closer and listened.

"No ears, I tell you, no ears!" the chief roared.

"What?" the lion thought, "no ears?" Did he hear properly?

"I told you to dig that ditch and you have no ears!" the chief said again. The lion hardly breathed as he listened. It must be true. People did not have ears like animals have! Away ran King Lion once more to find Mbalu. He apologised to the rabbit and asked his forgiveness because he had learned that people like the man lying on the ground before them have no ears. And so Mbalu hopped off having saved his life through his cunning, and he had also had a good dinner.

So it is that many people metaphorically have no ears; they do not listen to the voice of the Saviour. As I listened to the tale that night around the camp fire, I thought of another African proverb, "Ears are for hearing and not for digging in the manioc field."

* * *

Some years later I came upon a number of men who really had no ears. They had been summoned to a different village by an arrogant white official, but they refused to go. They had work to do in their own village, their necessary work of cultivating crops to provide them with their food. A person who does not work in the field will soon be left to die.

Such blatant disobedience angered the white man and he sent soldiers to bring the men to his office. The official handed the soldiers paraffin tins and ordered them to cut off the men's ears with knives. The men later told me that the tins were full with their ears. They were given a wad of cotton wool soaked in disinfectant to cover their gaping wounds and then were sent home. Flies came in swarms and tormented them while their festering wounds were trying to heal. What a cruel sight to see these men with no ears! Such wicked deeds were commonly perpetrated against the innocent Africans in those wild parts of the continent during colonial days.

How many of us would lose our ears if God behaved that way toward us for not listening to him? Hebrews 3.15 says, "Today if ye will hear his voice, harden not your hearts."

As the man telling the story of the lion and the rabbit finished his tale that night, the embers of the campfire burned low. He stopped and looked around at us all and grunted, "Eh, someone else's ears do not hear for you."

"What?" I asked, "say that again."

"Someone else's ears do not hear for another person," he repeated.

Now it was my turn to tell these people the story of God's love in the gift of the Saviour, for I remembered something else I had learned. One of the tribes calls the ear 'the pierced one', because they say it has a hole where the voice can penetrate. After I had finished I asked, "Does His voice manage to penetrate your ears?" Indeed, are our ears the pierced ones God wants them to be? Psalm 40.6 says, "Mine ears hast Thou opened."

The Calabash and the Lion

Jungle Leaf:
Two roosters cannot crow standing on the same pole.

The bottle gourd plant of Africa, when hollowed out and dried, is known as a calabash, and serves a variety of purposes in rural societies. All over Africa women use calabashes for drawing water. It is a lovely sight to see the women returning from the river at sundown, walking erect with the full calabashes balanced expertly on their heads. To prevent the water from spilling as they walk, they place thick grass or fine twigs in the neck of the calabash. These gourds also serve as containers for beer and honey and anything else, even for the Diviner's divining bones and other paraphernalia used in his trade.

Because of its important place in society, the calabash features prominently in African folklore and proverbs. For example, "It is the calabash which is full that is heavy", means that a poor man who is intelligent is greater than a rich man with a less fertile mind.

An African who had accompanied Little Bird, George Wiseman and me on many of our long treks among the Shinji tribe of northern Angola, told this story one evening in a village where the people had gathered around the campfire to listen to the gospel message.

"Listen," he said, "and I will tell you the story of the calabash and the lion. There once was a lazy man named Saulengami who was married to a very industrious woman. Instead of hoeing his field or fishing in the river or hunting with the other men in the forest, he just lay around his mud hut. The elephant grass had grown right up to his house because he was too lazy to clear it away with his hoe.

"There was also a tree stump right in front of his house, and though his wife repeatedly asked him to dig it out and take it away, he was too lazy to get up and do it to please her. Do you know, folks, why we call a lazy man a 'white man' in our tribe? Because he lies on the ground, never washes, and the dust of the dry season clings to his body until he becomes white with the fine dust. That is why we call a lazy person a 'white person'.

"In the end, Saulengami's wife refused to cook for him and he became thinner and thinner. Now he was sick, but his wife would not help him because he was so lazy. One day he told his wife that he would go off to his sister's village some distance away from his house, up the hill.

"He was walking along the path when two fully grown lions sprang out of the bush and stood on the path in front of him. He stopped, shaking with fear. He saw no hope of escape. While the lions stared at him he began to plead for his life.

" 'Look,' he said, 'if you kill me now you will not find much meat because I am very thin; it would be better for you to let me go until I am fatter. I am going away to my sister's village where she will fatten me with mush and meat. When I get back, you can kill me.'

"The lions conferred and agreed to let him go, on condition that when he was fat and returning home, they would kill him and eat him then.

"With a deep sigh of relief, Saulengami hurried away from the lions. Sure enough, when his sister saw him so thin, she hastened to cook his favourite food for him. He stayed with her for three months and became fat again. His face shone with health.

" 'Now,' he said to himself, 'what about my return home? I promised the lions that when I became fatter they could kill and eat me.' So he wrestled within himself because he knew that the lions would be waiting for him on the path home. The only thing he could do was to consult his sister. After all, at times women have good plans to help men in difficulty!

" 'Ah, I know what you should do, my brother!' she said. 'I have a large calabash in my field, so large no one has seen one like it before. I'll take you and put you in the calabash and seal it so the lions won't be able to see you. Since your house lies away down the hill, I'll roll the calabash past the lions and they will never know you are inside!'

"Saulengami was grateful to his sister for such a good plan of escape from the waiting wild beasts of the jungle. She went to her field and brought the huge calabash to her house, where she scooped out the seeds and cleaned it. She was expert at this work which she had done many times with all the gourds growing in her field.

"The morning of Saulengami's departure arrived, and he crawled into the calabash. Then his sister took resin from a tree and sealed the calabash so that no one could see Saulengami. At the top of the hill she whispered to him not to speak a word until he was safely home. Then she gave the calabash a powerful shove and sent it rolling away down the hill.

"When the two lions heard the sound of the rolling calabash they jumped out of the jungle to see what it was. They had never heard such a strange sound before. As it rumbled past they leapt out of the way, and then they followed it.

" 'Hi, I smell a man but I cannot see a man,' said one.

" 'Yes, I too smell a man but I cannot see a man!' said the other. So they followed the calabash all the way down the steep hill.

"Do you remember the tree stump which Saulengami refused to remove because of his laziness? Well, the calabash rolled at great speed right to that stump and slammed into it. The calabash broke in pieces and Saulengami spilled out. The lions saw him and lost no time in tearing him to pieces and eating him.

"That stump," the man explained, "is like the sins you refuse to forsake. You try to forget them, to escape from them, but in the end they will be your undoing, just as the stump was the undoing of Saulengami. Your sins have grown like that stump, but by His death for you, Jesus can take them away so that the Lion, Satan himself, will not get hold of you and destroy you. We have a saying, 'Don't drive yourself into the mouth of a lion,' which is just what Saulengami did by refusing to take that stump away."

Silence enveloped the jungle village that evening as the preacher sat down, and I had learned yet another lesson in presenting the message of the Son of God to these jungle dwellers. Their own folklore and parables illustrated the truth far more effectively than I could ever manage to do.

* * *

One day while out in a village with Margaret, I was offered a welcome calabash of water, but as I raised it to my mouth to drink, the foul smell stopped me. We discovered that the fault lay not with the water, but with the calabash, which was new. It

163

had not been cleaned properly, and the rotting gourd flesh infected the water. That same evening I referred to this incident to illustrate to the African believers how one must live a clean life. The Christian is like the calabash containing the pure Water of Life, given by the Lord Jesus, but if the calabash is not clean, how badly the water appears as it comes out to the village people - they will not want to drink it! We must be clean vessels, fit for the Master's use (2 Timothy 2.21).

The Africans tell a story of a miracle calabash which was owned by a poor widow. When she was in need, the calabash always contained sufficient meal for her porridge, or water to mix her porridge. The supply never failed until her enemy discovered the secret, and smashed the calabash. The story is, of course, reminiscent of the barrel of meal and the cruse of oil belonging to another widow, in 1 Kings 17.

The Spotted Dog

Jungle Leaf:
  Wounds on the tongue cannot be healed.

One evening Little Bird, the carriers and I approached a village after a long and very tiring trek through dense bush. We erected my small tent and kindled a fire on which the men could roast the bush rats they caught to eat along with their manioc. We ate, and in polite tribal custom each man belched as loudly as he could to indicate that he had eaten and was satisfied. In this society it is simply impolite to accept a meal without belching to express gratitude to the host or hostess. With my proper Scots upbringing I found this one of the more difficult customs to embrace!

Since this was lion country, every precaution had to be taken against the marauders' nightly raids, so we built fires to form a circle so that each man could sleep between the fires. The tired men soon slept soundly with the warmth and comforting crackle of the fires at their backs.

Suddenly I was startled awake in my tent by the cry, "*Ndumba* (lion)!" I dived through the canvas opening in time to see the hindquarters of a large lion disappearing into the surrounding darkness. He clenched one of our carriers in his jaws, dragging him off into the night. Although a number of us ran after them, the night was too dark and the bush too dense for us to catch up with the lion. At first light of morning we found only the mauled body of the man. Some parts of his body had been completely eaten. Silence brooded over the village that day, and I stayed for the burial of the victim.

Since Little Bird was with me, when the villagers gathered around their fires on the second evening, he told them this story. "Folks, listen to what I am going to say to you... wounds on the tongue cannot be healed. The man who was killed by the lion had wounds which he could not heal."

"What wounds had he? Wounds on his tongue?" called out some of the folks.

"Yes, that man had wounds on his soul which he could not heal, and no one could give him the proper medicine." The people waited. They had never heard this strange message before. Then Little Bird told them a story from their own folk lore.

"One day a hunter decided to go into the bush to hunt for animals as he was tired of eating leaves with his manioc. He wanted meat. On the way he met a hare who said to him, 'Where are you going, Mr. Hunter?'

"The hunter looked carefully at the hare and replied, 'I am tired of eating leaves with my mush, so I am on my way to hunt game.'

"The hare said, 'Look, Mr. Hunter, have you no dog. You know a dog is a useful animal to help track a wounded buck.'

" 'No, I do not have a dog or anything else except my trusted bow and arrows.'

" 'Well,' said the hare, 'I have a good hunting dog near my home, so if you wish, I'll sell it to you for an easy price, eh?'

" 'Good,' said the hunter, 'let us go and see it before I pay anything.' Off they went, the hunter and the hare, to examine the dog.

"Before he met the hunter, the hare had seen a leopard crouched high in a tree, waiting to kill small antelope as they crossed the narrow jungle path under the tree. The leopard often sat there. When the hunter and the hare arrived at the tree, the hare said, 'Do you not see the dog here?'

" 'Yes!' replied the hunter, 'I see the dog sitting up in the tree. It is a spotted dog. My mother, I am in luck today! What a fine dog it is! I'll be able to track many animals with it.' Then the hunter and the hare started to heckle over the price to be paid. Eventually they reached an agreement.

" 'What is the name of the dog?' asked the hunter.

" 'It's name is, *You will die with what you know,*' the hare replied. And the hare ran off immediately, leaving the hunter staring up into the tree at the spotted 'dog'.

" '*You will die with what you know,* come down and go along with me!' called the hunter. But the leopard sat silently in the tree. He didn't move an eyelid or a paw.

"Just then a traveller rounded the corner in the jungle path, and was amazed to see the hunter calling to the leopard in the tree. 'Hi! What are you doing there?' the traveller called.

" 'I bought this dog from Mr. Hare,' the hunter replied, 'but it refuses to come down from the tree!' The traveller glanced once more into the tree and yelled, 'Run for your life! That is not a dog, it's a leopard!' But the hunter refused to move. He believed he owned a great spotted dog and he wanted it to obey him.

" 'What's its name?' the traveller asked.

" '*You will die with what you know*' said the hunter. At that the man fled for his life, leaving the hunter pleading with the beast to come down from the tree. He flung stones at the 'dog', which greatly angered it. Suddenly the leopard sprang out of the tree onto the hunter's back and killed him instantly."

Little Bird leaned forward and spoke more softly to the attentive villagers, the whites of whose eyes shone in the flickering firelight.

"You, too will die with what you know," he said. "You know that the wages of sin is death; you know that there is a God up in heaven. Yes, you know all that. But there is something you don't know. Listen and I'll tell you all.

"God had a Son whom He sent down to this world to die for you. He Himself was sinless, and He offered Himself as a sacrifice because of what you know - your many sins. Yes, your sins you know. These will eventually destroy you, but this something you do not know can save you. Trust Christ who died for you."

When Little Bird had finished his story the people appeared as if they were holding their breath, wondering what he would tell them next. I visited that village again on several occasions, and found there a group of people who that very night confessed what they knew, their sins, to God, and who trusted in the One whom they did not previously know.

Yes, those folks could not treat the terrible wound in their souls caused by sin, but this One, the Lord Jesus Christ, brought healing and eternal life to them.

* * *

The old saying runs, "Can the Ethiopian change his skin, or the leopard his spots?" (Jeremiah 13.23). Yet I have seen many Africans trying to change the colour of their skins by rubbing on a white ointment - a hopeless task! One day an African bride arrived for her wedding with her face as white as flour! Indeed it was flour, which she had rubbed on to change her colour. Likewise the Africans say that if you wish to catch a baby leopard, always carry a gun, because even a baby leopard attacks in the same deadly manner as a grown animal.

* * *

One day a burly Dutchman well over six feet tall arrived in our part of the country announcing his intention to hunt lions. I told him that we never hunted lions because they hunted us, but the Dutchman was not to be put off. Away he went with an African helper.

Not far into the bush he saw a pride of thirteen lions together. Instead of singling out one lion, he foolishly lifted his rifle and shot into the pride. Unfortunately for him, he hit a lioness, and his shot merely wounded and enraged her. Before he could reload, she sprang for him. Thoughts of a mission nurse's advice to him to go on a diet must have flashed through his mind. To run fast was out of the question, and even to try to climb a tree out of the reach of this locomotive of fury was unthinkable. Why had he not lost weight as instructed! In a flash the lioness was on his back, knocking the rifle out of his hand. The African lad grabbed it, took aim and shot the lioness dead.

When I saw the wounded Dutchman he said, "Put your fist in the wound in my back." His fat had saved him, for the lioness had bitten deeply into a large chunk of flesh on his back, but had not reached his vital organs! What was the first thing this man asked for while recovering? Yes, he asked for a Bible. I had great joy in giving him a copy of the Word of God, and telling him the message of the gospel that had brought me to this jungle of Africa.

* * *

There is a proverb which says, "When a lion is fierce it eats couch grass." That is another way of saying that a jungle-wise person will be on the lookout for the lion which is silent because of hunger.

The Hunting Dog

Jungle Leaf:
> *Green maize abounds at the home of those*
> *who have no teeth.*

African hunting dogs are scrawny creatures which are kept permanently on the scrounge as the villagers believe the dogs will never become good hunters unless they are hungry.

Local mythology is rich with tales of such dogs, which were

always associated with the jackal. Legend has it that the two were hunting partners until the dog met man, to whom he swore allegiance, and thus became man's loyal friend. No hunter ventures into the wild bushland to hunt without a dog at his heel. Sometimes the dog can be impaled on the horns of a wild buffalo, or attacked by the antelope which also knows how to use its horns to advantage to keep the dog away. I have also seen such a dog meet a sad end when its owner ties a rope around its neck and pulls it through the water to attract a crocodile. Crocs love the tasty bite of dog, but sometimes instead of the hunter getting the croc, the croc is faster and gets the dog. Lions raided one village near us for a considerable time and pounced on almost every dog prowling around. One cannot read *Jock of the Bushveld* by Percy Fitzpatrick without a twinge of admiration for Jock's adventures.

Despite his popularity, the dog is never personified in African mythology. In the modern city townships the African likens the dog to the transistor radio in that if you tramp on its tail, it is the mouth that barks. In their analogy, the transmitting station is the tail, and the radio itself the mouth that barks! In other words, the dog, like the radio, never takes initiative, but is obedient to a higher power, receiving commands.

During the time the pioneer missionary Robert Moffat worked among the Tswana tribe, there lived a dog so skilled at hunting that the villagers rarely had to feed him. It was swift, tracking wounded animals and bringing them to bay so that the hunter could catch up to deliver the mortal shot. Such dogs circle the animal, keeping out of reach of horns and vicious hoofs, always barking to help the hunter find the prey. Some dogs hunt by sight and others by smell, rather like people, some of whom live by faith, never seeing their object until the end of the trail is reached, yet others walk by sight.

No one was more committed to the task of bringing the Scriptures to people in their own language than Robert Moffat. One of Africa's greatest pioneer missionaries, he endured extreme adversity in bringing the gospel and the Scriptures to the Tswana, whose language is spoken over a vast area in Southern Africa. Moffat became well known as a diplomat and chiefs could trust him as a man of his word. When Moffat began work among the Tswana he had great difficulty discovering their word for God. Unlike most other tribes in Central and Southern Africa who have one or more words for God, even if He is the Remote One whom they do not know, the Tswana had become so culturally distant from any concept of a creator-God that they had almost forgotten His name. Under Moffat's ministry many of these people came to Christ and were transformed both inwardly and in lifestyle.

People who knew him were accustomed to seeing him with his ever-present pencil and paper, checking and rechecking words and phrases. Sometimes his head must have ached in performing this arduous task. Although he never tired of asking questions to obtain the linguistic information he needed, often he would just sit listening to the menfolk in the palaver place. He also frequently strolled in the quiet of the African bush, refreshing his mind. He often wondered why God had chosen him for the task of translation when there were so many others better qualified academically than he. Yet he always concluded that it was God who had reached him, chosen him and sent him forth to these wild parts as His messenger, that the excellency of the power might be of God and not of Robert Moffat.

On this particular day the dog was prowling in the village looking for a scrap to eat, when it sniffed at a book open on a low stool. This was a new smell to the jungle village. To try it to satisfy his hunger, the dog grabbed the book and tore out several pages with his teeth. It ran off with the pages and promptly swallowed them.

"Oh, my mother! What shall I do now?" the dog's owner cried, returning just as the animal and the pages disappeared behind a hut. Off marched the man to see Moffat, who had recently completed the first translation of the Bible into the Tswana language.

"*Dumela Rra* (good morning, sir)," the man said, careful to observe strict African etiquette with Moffat, who understood his people's ways so intimately. "Excuse me, *Moruti* (teacher), you have committed a crime," he said.

"A crime? What kind of crime have I committed?" Moffat asked.

"Moruti, you see this dog? It was an excellent hunting dog with me in the bush. I cannot count the number of animals which it has brought down with its skill. When it smells blood it hangs on until it corners the animal, allowing me to get a shot at it. Now look what you have done, Moruti!"

"Now what have I done? Your dog looks fine as I see it," Moffat said.

"No, Moruti, you were never near my dog, but it found a Bible lying open on a stool. It took some of the pages and has swallowed them!" Puzzled, Robert Moffat looked the dog over more closely and could see nothing amiss.

"Moruti, did you not translate this book into our own language? Yes, Moruti. Truly you have a great crime. Do you remember the drunkard who was saved and changed and he no longer drinks beer? And the woman who was always stealing from other people? She has not stolen anything for a long time?" The Tswana stood accusingly, his legs apart, holding his dog on a leash.

"But," reasoned Moffat, "If your dog ate another man's Bible, I'm not responsible for that, am I?" Moffat, though he understood so much of the ways of these people, was baffled.

"You, Moruti, wrote this book and it has changed these people so that they no longer do the things they did before. No, you must pay me for my dog. He has swallowed these papers which have changed him! Now he will no longer hunt, but will just stay in the village."

What a testimony to the transforming power of the Word of God in the lives of tribal people! Ah, yes, one day in the future the animals will be changed by the word of their Creator, and the lion will lie down with the lamb; but for the present it is in changing the hearts of people that God is interested. The jungle proverb, "Green maize abounds at the homes of those who have no teeth," reminds me of all the green maize we have in the Word of God in our favoured western world, but so many have no teeth, no desire for it to change their lives.

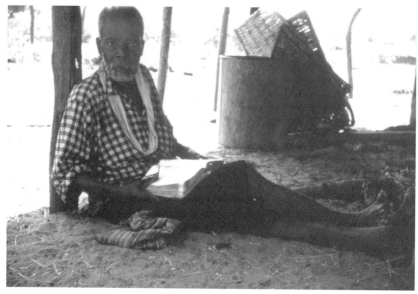

A changed person - old Chingumba studying the Bible

CHAPTER 14

Chiefs and Antelopes

The Chief and the Poles

Jungle Leaf:
   A tortoise is never burdened by its own shell.

"*Moyo, Ngana*," said the man who hurried towards me where I was waiting for him on my veranda. "Ngana, the king is coming!" he exclaimed, "and I am his forerunner to prepare you for his coming!" And the following morning, the king indeed arrived, along with his retinue who sang and danced all the way up to the house.

The village people had prepared gifts of fowls and goats and corn, together with other items fit for the king. These he was very pleased to accept from his subjects. He wore a leopard skin and a seashell necklace, and held a fly switch in one hand. A servant attended him, ready to do his bidding.

I knew this king, named Sauwa, and had been able to begin a spiritual work in his village, where there was now an assembly of men and women who had trusted the Saviour. Nearby stood another chief whose name belied his character: *Same Neka* (The Greeting One) - he went about with a stern scowl on his face! He strongly resisted the advance of the gospel, and treated his people cruelly. The contrast between the two struck me forcibly that morning. Same Neka laboured under the burden of his chieftainship, whilst Sauwa went about calmly day by day, apparently secure in the knowledge that his people loved him.

Since one of the tribe's words for kindness really means "softie", and kindness is often scorned as mere softness, the kindly chief, Sauwa, must have had a nagging fear that his people's willingness to obey him might only be feigned. He decided to test some of them.

Some Central African chiefs have attained notoriety for the kinds of tests to which they submit their subjects, and particularly the younger men. For example, should a young man wish to marry the chief's daughter, he must achieve a difficult goal, such as kill a crocodile which is known to have killed people in the vicinity. Sometimes he will be required to take the "test of poles". A large pole is sunk into the earth, and the man is told to climb it. As he starts to shimmy upward, dancing girls leap about the base of the pole, attempting to divert his attention. It is difficult for a young man to resist looking at the scantily clad girls whooping and cavorting about, but one who is diverted from his task of climbing the pole immediately fails.

Sauwa's test was different. He called certain of the young men of his village and instructed them to meet him at a village far from his royal capital. Each was given a long pole which he was told to carry with him to the distant village. This meant struggling for many days with a very awkward burden through thick bush country and over swollen rivers, since it was the wet season.

"Hi!" they shouted, "that is easy, just to carry a pole along the way!" And they set off at a good pace, full of youthful enthusiasm. The first day's journey went well, but when they started out the following morning they found the poles weighed a little heavier. They might have recalled the local proverb, "A chicken does not weigh heavily inside the village, but on the path." Soon they began to grumble, and by the end of the second day they were divided as to what they ought to do.

"Let's cut off part of the pole because it is too heavy for us," suggested one. "After all, the chief will never see that we have done this, will he?" Wiser young men objected to that idea, and they slept that night around the camp fire with the poles untouched.

The third day, however, as they pushed through a particularly thick section of the jungle, some sat down and cut a bit off their poles, comforting themselves with the thought that the chief would never know what they had done. The next day they chopped off a little more, and some who had resisted the temptation the previous day began to hack at their poles too. Only two of the party felt that to cut their poles would be a disgrace, and they struggled on with them full-length. But what a struggle it was!

Finally they arrived within shouting distance of the royal village, but there remained one large river, swollen and dangerous, to cross. Cautiously they edged out into the turbulent water and found it deeper than they had thought. Ah, yes! Now these tiresome poles would be useful! But those who had chopped their poles found them of no help. They could not touch the river bed, and these young men were swept away by the swift current.

Those who had valiantly persevered the entire journey with the long poles found that the poles were long enough to dig into the river bed to steady them, and they were able to cross safely. There on the other side the people of the royal village were waiting to greet them, and to congratulate them on obeying their chief despite the great difficulty of the way. They had passed the test.

Around the evening camp fire I have heard Little Bird apply this story of the chief and the poles to teach scriptural truth.

"Yes," he said, "the poles are the Word of God which Ngana has brought to us and by which we are tested. We all want to arrive safely in the presence of our Chief in Heaven, and receive a welcome from Him. How can we do this? Well, we must carry our pole responsibly and not tamper with it or damage it. We must never cut out some of the Bible and say that we do not believe in that part. We dare not discard our pole; we must keep it intact until we have come to the end of our march through this land."

The preacher also reminded us of the warning in Revelation 22.19, "If any man shall take away from the words of the book of this prophecy, God shall take away his part out of the book of life, and out of the holy city, and from the things which are written in this book."

* * *

The carriers sang as they carried their loads down the jungle trail one day, when a small bird landed on the trail right in front of the leading man. To an African, a bird means meat for the pot, and they are always on the lookout for it. The carrier hurriedly dropped his load and his pole and darted forward to catch the bird, which appeared lame. But the bird quickly soared away! Birds often play tricks like this with people on trek, and the Africans call it, "*tula muhamba* (put your load down)".

"Don't you put down your load or your pole, because you need them on the way," Little Bird would tell the people. "When you get to the last test, the river of death, how will you get over without your pole?" And in the jungle proverb, "Death can be told to an ox but it never takes heed. A person can flee."

The Chief and the Bridge

Little Bird told the story of the chief whose land was divided by a deep river, a river so turbulent with rapids that the people were not able to cross it at all. One part of the tribe was thus cut off completely from the other across the river. The chief spent many sleepless nights worrying about this.

The chief's son became so concerned for his father's sadness and worry about this division, that he started looking for a tall tree that could be felled to serve as a bridge across the river. After a long search he found a tree tall and strong enough, right near the river's edge. He felled it skilfully in such a manner that it landed right over the river, and he merely had to chop off the protruding branches to make it suitable as a walkway over the water. This was all done during the dry season when the river was not in flood. All of the people on the far side were then encouraged to move to the chief's side of the river so that the tribe could be together. They would have to hurry as the wet season of heavy tropical rain was approaching, and the river would soon be flooded, making crossing this bridge impossible.

Some of the people were glad of the opportunity to be close to the chief, and hastily crossed to be reunited with him and with the others of their tribe. Great feasting and celebration continued for many days after they arrived. Others, however, had built new huts on the far side of the river, and they were reluctant to obey the call of the chief's son to leave their huts and move across the river.

One day news came that those who delayed were to come under the jurisdiction of another chief who was well known for his cruelty. Upon hearing this alarming news, some of them rushed to try to cross the river, only to find that its waters had risen in flood and the tree-bridge had been washed away. They were thus taken into the kingdom of the cruel chief, and had no further opportunity of being reunited with their old chief and with their friends.

Little Bird used this story effectively, just as he did with so many other fragments of jungle lore, to communicate the gospel. Little Bird travelled all over the jungle paths to shout the warning for people to cross over and to be reconciled to the King whose Son had prepared the bridge by His death on the cross for them (2 Corinthians 5.20).

The Antelope

A storyteller in the wilds of Africa is a crowd-drawer. The Africans say, "A fig tree does not go after the birds but the birds come to the fig tree." The following story is typical of those which my companions, particularly Little Bird, would tell to the people gathered around the fire in a village at night. They so wonderfully illustrated the gospel message I was trying to convey.

"You know the antelope which we have here in these great plains which God has given to us?" the storyteller would ask.

"Yes, we know them well. That is where we get meat when we are lucky enough to kill an animal, or when the ancestral spirits are kind to us!" the people responded.

"My people, listen well to me, as I am going to tell you all the story of a baby antelope." No one stirred as the story unfolded to the crackling of the bright fire in the middle of the darkness. The forest was silent, and the children slept on the ground where they had slumped over, tired from their day's activities such as catching flying ants to eat, and playing among the grass huts.

"There was once a herd of lovely antelope which roamed over the vast plains which the Creator has given us. You know, my people, that these animals always have a watcher which stands guard while the others are grazing, their heads bowed to the grass. When they travel from plain to plain they have a rear guard too, as lions are always on the prowl for a tasty meal of antelope. These graceful creatures can never take a chance, and they must particularly watch their young.

"Young antelopes frolic and run all over the place, and at times they have to be butted by the horns of their mothers back into their place in the middle of the herd, where they are safe."

The people listen attentively to this familiar scenario. The older men occasionally give a grunt of satisfaction as the preacher tells the story in their own language. The skilled story teller knows where to lay the stress, and how to build up the atmosphere of the story towards the climax of the message, according to the storytelling customs of the tribespeople.

"One of the young antelopes named Mwana-tengu ran with the others, but he was not satisfied with his life. He looked at the other older antelope and thought, 'What a bunch of squares!' He saw the horns of the older antelope all growing backwards in the usual manner, and he decided that he wanted his horns to grow forwards so that he could see them!

" 'Wahepuka, mwana (you are a fool)' his mother Nakatengu replied when he told her of his wish. She scolded him because of his pride, wanting to admire his own horns, which none of

178

the other antelope could do. The young fellow pestered Nakatengu every day until she became tired of his pride and at last gave way to his strange idea.

" 'Enough, child!' she said. 'If you want your horns to grow that way, let it be done.' Sure enough, his horns started to sprout and grew towards the front instead of to the back like any other young antelope.

" 'Look at me, hey! Look at my horns!' he shouted to the others, tormenting them with his pride. 'I'm with it; you are just a bunch of old squares!' Some of the younger ones talked about following this new fashion of life, but listened when their elders reasoned with them against it.

"Mwana-tengu ran about on the plain showing off his horns to everyone and making himself a perfect nuisance. When he fought with the other young antelope he had an unfair advantage, as with his horns pointing forward, no one could lock horns with him. They grumbled bitterly about this.

"Then one year the rains refused to come. You know, friends, here in our land sometimes the rain refuses to come for months and months. All the pools in the forest had dried up. The rivers, too, had no water left in them, so all the animals wandered about seeking pools where they could drink. They searched in vain. Although antelope can smell water a long way off, this year there was neither sight nor smell of any at all.

"Even the great lion and the swift leopard could not find water to quench their thirst. What about the elephant who needs so much water for himself? You know our saying that 'he who guards the well will never die of thirst', but there was no well to guard.

"One day the swift leopard climbed a hill, and in a hole in a rock he discovered a deep pool of water. 'Ha!' he said, 'what good fortune is mine today.' He stooped and drank and drank until he was satisfied. Then he thought of his companions who were all dying of thirst down on the plain. Bounding down, he announced the good news that he had found water, life-giving water for all to drink freely. The lion gave one mighty grunt of relief and padded off quickly in the direction shown him by his friend the leopard.

"The hyena listened and thought, 'Well, this might be a trick, but I don't know.' He was cunning and not willing to believe the good news, but he went off to explore. When the small duiker nearby heard about the water, he started without hesitation to climb the hill. Even the huge elephant turned and lumbered along as fast as he could upon receiving the good news that would save his life.

"Ah, friends, what about our Mwana-tengu? He too heard the same news and heaved a sigh of relief as water was what he wished for above everything else now. So he made off at a good speed and was soon among the other animals climbing the hill. In their deep need for water the animals lost their fear of one another. The lion went with the duiker, the leopard loped alongside of the buffalo stomping up the hill, as they pressed toward their common goal of finding water.

"One by one they stooped to drink from the small pool in the rock, and all were soon satisfied. Mwana-tengu, with his horns proudly sticking out front, approached the pool. He lowered his head, but - oh! as he bent down his horns struck the rock. He couldn't get near the water.

" 'Try the other side,' the other animals called out to him. So Mwana-tengu circled the pool and approached the water from the other side. Alas! he could not get near the water.

" '*Mangweseke nawa!* (let me try again!),' he pleaded in desperation. He tried placing his head in every position and at every angle, but to no avail. He stood back, looking longingly at the pool, his tongue hanging out of his mouth. None of the other animals could draw the water for him and give him a drink.

"You know our proverb, 'Water that is drawn by another person never quenches your thirst.' You must draw the water for yourself." The preacher waited for a moment to let the truth grip the minds of his listeners, and then he repeated, "You must take for yourselves; no one can take for you."

"The antelope backed away again, his head down now in sheer

despair. What could he do? This pool was his last chance to save his life, and he couldn't get near the water because of his horns. There was no other pool of water but this to save his life.

" '*Chisako chami!* (my bad luck!)' he fumed. Yes, he wanted to be so clever and fashionable, and now he was paying for it. He backed away, turned around, and with a heavy heart started slowly down the hill knowing that he was leaving behind him all hope of life. Out there in our sun-scorched plains he wandered till every bit of strength went from him. He lay down to die, his sides heaving in the heat on the plain.

"Look, above him are vultures, circling, waiting. They smell death and are coming to feed on the carcass. And soon there was nothing left of him. The vultures picked him clean.

"Folks, what kept Mwana-tengu from the life-giving water? It was his horns which were growing facing forward. These kept him from the water of life.

"Fellow tribespeople, what keeps you from the Saviour who is the Water of Life? It is your sins, which are like Mwana-tengu's horns. What does the Bible say to us? 'Your iniquities have separated between you and your God, and your sins have hid His face from you' (Isaiah 59.2).

"What can you do? Your 'horns', unlike those of the young antelope Mwana-tengu, can be taken away so that you may reach the Water of Life."

"Say to Him (the Lord), 'Take away all iniquity, and receive us graciously.' (Hosea 14.2). Behold the Lamb of God which taketh away the sin of the world" (John 1.29).

The Lion and the Honey Guide

There was once again an extended dry season in the land when there was very little drinking water, so, according to the folklore, the animals and birds had a conference to decide what they would do. Their solution was to dig a deep hole, down to the water table. But the honey guide refused to dig. "I have my honey which is very sweet, and I don't need water," he said.

Day after day the animals and birds worked hard at digging their hole until the water started to seep up and they knew their lives were saved. They were all satisfied and revived by the fresh water. All except for the honey guide. Though he longed for it desperately there was no water for him. Every time he came near the drinking hole he was chased away. The animals chose the brave lion to guard the hole.

The lion lay down near the water and kept one eye open to watch for the honey guide who regularly came and perched on a tree nearby. By this time the honey guide was dying of thirst, and decided he must make a plan to get the lion away from the hole long enough for him to have a drink. So the honey guide flew to his honey supply and came back with a small amount in his beak, which he dropped in the lion's mouth.

"Hi! Where did you get that nice sweet thing? What do you call it?" the lion asked.

"We call this honey, and I have more of it in the forest where I live," the honey guide answered. And so the honey guide started to tempt the lion.

"Little honey bird, can you give me more of this sweet thing you call honey?" asked the lion.

"I could, but I have only a little," said the bird.

"Away you go and bring me a lot more!" demanded the lion.

"If you want more you will have to do as I tell you," the bird said.

"What do you want?" the hungry lion enquired.

"You must let me tie you to this tree and after that you will be able to eat a lot of honey," the bird replied. Down he came from his perch, and he tied the lion to the tree with a strong cord. Then the bird hopped over to the water hole and drank his fill. The lion roared with rage when he realised that he had been cheated, but to no avail!

The Africans interpret this story as an analogy of the Water of Life and Satan trying to keep people from it. If someone wants the Water of Life, they must first see that the enemy who keeps them from it is already conquered by the power of the Lord Jesus Christ.

Jungle note

There is a story about the cricket and the birds, all of whom were called by the king of the jungle to come and get their wings. The cricket delayed, because he stopped to eat a tasty meal he had found along the way. By the time he arrived at the appointed place all the birds had received their wings and had flown off. The king refused to give the cricket any wings because he was so late.

When the bush fires raged during the dry season, the birds spread their wings and escaped from the fierce fire. What about the poor cricket? He could only jump a short distance and was overcome by the fire in no time. He lost his life because he refused to come immediately at the king's command. So it is with free forgiveness for us in Christ being offered today. Those who delay in receiving salvation from eternal death may never have another chance.

CHAPTER 15

Sacrifices, Idols, Sticks and Staffs

"For we wrestle not against flesh and blood, but against principalities, against powers, against the rulers of the darkness of this world, against spiritual wickedness in high places" *(Ephesians 6.12).*

Poison

Jungle Leaf:
   The fly does not land where there is no open sore.

Trouble had broken out in a village upstream on the river Chikapa, some thirty miles from our home at the mission station. Heathen people who disliked the effects of the gospel among their fellow villagers were persecuting the Christians. Idol worship, veneration of the ancestral spirits, and other heathen practices were now in danger of being set aside since many had turned to Christ. An intense battle between the forces of evil and the new power of Christ's gospel raged in that village.

I started off from the mission compound at daybreak and took only one short rest in a river village so as to arrive at my destination before dark. Thirty miles on foot is a strenuous day's journey. The sun set and found me still on the trail, but not long after dark I reached the village and immediately I saw something which made me feel sick. Right in the centre of the village a large pile of wood burned, and on top were two human bodies.

I knew the man, a lame man, and with him burned a woman I didn't know.

As the gruesome story unfolded I learned that the two had been accused of witchcraft and of having caused the death of the village chief. The diviner had divined with his paraphernalia and these two had been found guilty and were condemned. They had been given the traditional poison cup, and death, a horribly painful death, followed. The smell of the burning flesh was so acrid and nauseating that I asked my carriers to build our camp outside the village and upwind of the fire.

That evening as I rested in the jungle clearing, a woman approached carrying two plates. One of them held manioc mush, which, to the uninitiated in jungle life, has a strong, repulsive smell. Only by forcing myself continually was I able to learn to eat such food, since it is the staple diet for much of Central Africa. Strangely, although so common, it is not indigenous, but was introduced by the Portuguese from Brazil. Manioc is a root shaped much like a sweet potato, from which the people make both cassava and tapioca. Margaret also learned to make starch from it.

The smell of the mush, however, was insignificant compared to the contents of the second plate the woman offered me. There, complete with heads and tails, lay three lovely long rats! They lay boiled and white in their gravy, ready as a delicacy of the first order, sent to me by the chief. I knew that whatever the chief sent I had to accept with gratitude. To refuse would be a transgression of African etiquette. I waited until the woman had returned to the village and handed the rats to my travelling companions who devoured them eagerly.

By morning the funeral pyre fire had died down, and only the bones of the victims remained among the ashes. And there in the centre of the village clearing were two idols about five feet high. They had been anointed with fine flour and dripped with the blood of animal sacrifices. I was overcome with joy mingled with deep sadness as I stood between those idols and told the people of the precious blood of Christ, the One who had come to save them. Today in that village there is a church of men and women who trusted in the saving blood of the sacrifice of Christ for them.

Sacrifices and Idols

The bush dwellers of Central Africa are accustomed to seeing and offering blood sacrifices. Sometimes they pour the blood of the sacrifice on an idol which represents the ancestor spirits, and offer a drink offering of beer or rum. This is followed by the "communion meal" at which the meat of the sacrificial animal is eaten. This is a reminder of the peace offerings of the Old Testament, and provides a wonderful bridge to proclaim the story of the Evangel of Christ the Son of God.

Then there was the "reconciliation offering", when men who had been at enmity with one another would kill an animal or fowl, catching the blood in a basin. When they had cooked the meat each man in turn ate some of the various parts of the sacrifice, symbolically restoring the relationship between them. The "sacrifice of friendship" is also common among these tribes, another blood sacrifice to seal the pact of friendship. I learned that the word for "friend" is literally "blood friend".

The custom of sacrificing white animals prevails when a crime has been committed against someone, stemming from the idea that when the crime is confessed and forgiven, the white sacrifice represents a white heart on the part of both the sinner and the sinned. Black animals or fowls, on the other hand, are sacrificed to appease the dead rather than the living. According to tribal belief, ancestral spirits often become upset with living relatives and must be mollified by a blood sacrifice.

* * *

During one trek in Shinjiland, George and I set off to hunt on a plain where we knew there were antelope and small duiker. The local village headman decided to bring his old gun and join us in the hunt. We soon spotted a duiker grazing quietly quite nearby. George lifted his powerful rifle, took careful aim and fired. He was always a better shot than I was! As the duiker toppled over, the headman took off running, yelling, "*Hamba liami, hamba liami*! (my idol, my idol!)*"* Before we left his village that morning he had anointed his idols with the blood of sacrifice. And here were George and I, who had prayed to the Most High God to assist us in the hunt to satisfy our hunger, listening to a heathen man claiming the honour for his *hamba* (idol) which he had anointed with the blood sacrifice!

George would have none of that nonsense, and set to do battle for the honour of the name of Christ right there in the middle of the African plain. The idol toppled over like Dagon of old. The mere blood of an animal sacrifice could never answer the prayer of the needy, but the blood of the man Christ Jesus has fully satisfied every need once for all, and that day the physical needs of the messengers of the cross were met.

Over the years more than thirty witchdoctors were converted and brought into fellowship in the assemblies in Shinjiland. They burned their idols and divining baskets and turned to the living God. However, as the civil war spread, sad to say several of them were killed by terrorists and are now with their Saviour in heaven.

Diviner at work

* * *

While some tribes in Central Africa emphasise the cunning of the baboon, the Shona of Zimbabwe believe that the possession of a baboon spirit can confer healing powers practised by witchdoctors in the villages. I have found a surprising number of links between the Old Testament and the customs, proverbs and folklore of these heathen African tribespeople.

One Central African tribe protects sacred groves where no tree may be chopped down. A fugitive can flee into these groves and find protection from anyone pursuing him to take his life. Of course this reminds one of the Cities of Refuge established in the time of Joshua. However, in the African groves, sacrifices are offered to the gods, sacrifices of unblemished rams. Part of the meat is left for the god at the foot of a tree, and the rest is eaten by the worshippers. This too, is reminiscent of an Old Testament custom, the Peace Offering in Leviticus 3.

Where did these tribes, spiritually lost in heathendom, ever learn such things as we read of in the Old Testament? How did they know of a sacred day, perhaps a Thursday or a Friday? Such mysteries remain among the customs of these people, but they provide yet another wonderful means for explaining the true message of forgiveness through the sacrifice of Christ who is our only refuge from the wrath of a holy Creator-God. Through research in later years I learned that with the migration of tribes south through Ethiopia and over the lakes, the people had brought with them snatches of the great story of Calvary, perhaps from their encounters with Jewish culture and history. The rest had been lost in the dust of tradition.

Ouma

Our story switches now from the northern wilds of Angola to the highveld of the Transvaal in South Africa, near the close of the nineteenth century. A group of white South Africans, Boer farmers, determined to be free of British control and had fled across the Orange River into the Transvaal to get beyond the influence of the British flag. Now events had rapidly changed and the British had reached that promised land. The Boers were an independent people, building their own nation through hard work. What they had fled from had now overtaken them and the hated Union Jack fluttered in the strong winds of the Transvaal highveld. What would be their future? Would they ever merge into the British nation? Their answer was a defiant "No!" They would never yield their young nationhood to the British.

The men deliberated at length in their farm homesteads, and decided to trek once more rather than subject themselves to the English gold and diamond traders. Patrols scouted west, checking the route they thought they would take, but the reports were not encouraging. However, the men were hardy, used to saddle and gun, and the women were used to a hard life. So the wagons were made ready and the oxen yoked together. The men mounted their horses with their rifles at their sides. The great Dorsland trek had begun.

Trekking by ox wagon was slow and laborious, and the burning sands made the going difficult. Inside the canvas-covered wagons the women endured intense heat and discomfort. At times the weary travellers stopped to scoop a grave in the sand and leave a loved one buried in the desert. God-fearing, independent people were these Boers, most of them farmers, explorers, and stoic adventurers. The desert seemed to challenge and envelop them. Eventually they reached southern Angola, which some regarded as their Promised Land and settled there. Others travelled on northward to central Angola and built homesteads. Yet another group trekked even further north and built mud huts for themselves, content to plough fields with their oxen and live a simple life on the boundaries of Shinjiland. It was there I found them.

The women hoed fields and the men hunted game to supplement their diet. Carrying a blanket, a rifle and a frying pan, these men set off into the bush on their frequent hunts. They built grass shelters to protect them from the heat of the sun, and from rain in the wet season, but the hard life resulted in all of them contracting tuberculosis. These people had almost unconsciously adopted many African customs, many of which were graceful and displayed the delightful manners of the people. Like the Africans they never knocked at the door to announce their presence, but clapped or coughed outside until someone appeared. Likewise they extended both hands to receive anything offered to them, and the womenfolk curtsied as their African sisters did. Unfortunately, they also absorbed some of the evil customs of heathendom, which only the power and love of the Redeemer could break. Some of the women had fallen into the satanic trap of witchcraft, and the whole company of big-game hunters with their wives had stooped very low, both physically and morally. But they were of stoic character!

One day one of their young married women walked over to the mission station to have her teeth attended to, and I saw she needed them all extracted. I was preparing an injection to numb her jaws, but she refused, saying, "Ngana, take them all out, I can stand it!" Resting her head on a tall chair, I extracted all of her badly decayed teeth. She never winced one bit. She left and walked back to her mud house as if she had merely paid a social visit! The men were just as fearless in the hunt, facing lions and great buffalo without wavering. But their spiritual need was great, so I commenced gospel meetings in their homes. It was an uphill battle, month after month. The Seed was sown, but with no evident result.

At last a lame married girl put her trust in the Saviour, and I had the joy of baptising her in the river and seeing her join the local church fellowship. A short time later she died in childbirth, and how glad I was that she had found the Saviour in time.

One day I was summoned by Ouma Klopper, a very old woman who lived alone in a small mud hut. Her daughter had become involved in witchcraft, and had then been possessed by a demon. As I entered Ouma Klopper's hut that day I noticed that, although there was no furniture, the floor had been freshly re-done with manure and smeared with the blood of an ox in preparation for my visit. Ouma was dressed in black with a Dutch hood.

"*Goeie more, Ouma, hoe gaan dit?* (Good morning, Granny, how are you?)" I asked in Afrikaans, her native tongue. The light of the gospel message had penetrated her soul and she was ready to kneel on the blood-smeared floor and pour her heart out to a Saviour who had sought her for so many years. She was 82 years old at the time, and had set out on the Dorsland Trek at the age of six months! What great rejoicing there was some six months later when Ouma obeyed the Lord in baptism in a local river. The late Mr. W. Stunt of Echoes of Service was with me when Ouma Klopper was baptised. She was so heavy and unsteady on her feet that it took two men to lower her into the water. She then met with Christians on the Lord's Day to break bread in remembrance of her Lord Jesus. Fifteen more of this group trusted Christ and followed Him in baptism. But one after another they succumbed to disease and passed into eternity.

Ouma's daughter made a profession of faith in the Saviour, but as time went on I saw that it was empty. She continued in her witchcraft and demon possession, and although she was never given the poison cup test to prove her authenticity, she was feared by the local people. In some tribes witchcraft is hereditary but in others a person can become a neophyte and learn the craft. Among qualifications for such a person to be initiated they must symbolically die, be buried and raised from the dead. A shallow grave is prepared, the neophyte lies in it and is covered except for their head and toes. Tribespeople dance around the grave, and then the person is symbolically raised up from the dead. In African custom, such a one becomes a new person and receives a new name! The similarities between Biblical truth and many of the perverted heathen customs continually amazed me as I travelled through central Africa.

I wrote to some Afrikaans Christians in Paarl, South Africa, telling of the circumstances of these poor people, and in Christian love they sent clothing, medicine, and food supplies. Afrikaans books, too, were sent for the children to help them with their reading, for at home they read in their own language. The children also came to the mission compound where they attended classes taught in Portuguese.

Sticks and Staffs

One day while I was trekking through the forest I came across a stick lying in the path. I examined it, knowing that it had been placed there on purpose. When the carriers caught up, they said, "Ngana, we must turn back; this stick is a sign of danger ahead!" Leaving a stick on the path is an African custom used to warn people from approaching their village along the present route. To transgress against the customary warning was unthinkable to the carriers, so they immediately turned back to seek another approach to their destination. They could not brush the stick aside because it was connected to their veneration of ancestral or tribal spirits. As we tried to push through the forest undergrowth they explained their fears to me.

"Yes," they said," if we took that stick away we would die by witchcraft." The terrible fear of the power of witchcraft haunted them every day until they knew the liberating power of the gospel. The European says, "Don't walk under a ladder," while the Central African says, "Don't jump over the stick." Superstitions are universal, but in animistic cultures the power of the Evil One is commonly evidenced in many physical ways.

Often we saw small sticks lying at the doorways of mud huts in the villages. They were placed by a "hunter", someone "sniffing out" a person guilty of some alleged crime, especially a death in the village. The so-called hunter would lay a stick at the door of the accused to indicate to them that were considered guilty for the death. No one would stoop and remove the stick in case they, too, would be suspected of being involved.

A woman from the far-off Minungu tribe, five days march to the west, arrived at the mission station one day. She was a slave fleeing from her master and her hard toil. We gave her a home and a job drawing water, cultivating fields of manioc, and being useful around the house. Gradually she seemed to forget her awful years of slavery. Week by week she listened to the gospel and eventually she received the Saviour, was baptised and received into the local fellowship of the church.

One night, some strange men crept into the station, laid a stick at her doorway, then broke down the door and captured her. Early in the morning when the people on the station were passing her hut on their way to morning prayers, they saw the stick and knew immediately what had happened to her. The stick told them that a slave had been recaptured and returned to her terrible life of slavery.

* * *

Some of the Portuguese officials who were located in remote places became a law unto themselves and would send soldiers to capture Africans and force them to do free labour. Also in the north-eastern part of Angola where there were diamond mines owned by the powerful De Beers Company of South Africa, white entrepreneurs forced the African people into unpaid service while they themselves became very wealthy. Each chief had to supply a certain number of able-bodied men each month, who were then sent to work in the diamond mines. If a chief failed to fulfil his quota, he was beaten with a stick shaped like a cup with perforations through it. This exploitation and cruelty, of course, caused deep-seated resentment among the Africans. If they refused to go, they were cruelly beaten with a stick. Margaret and I saw some of these men, Africans who were our friends, who had been beaten on their hands and feet till they were neither able to stand nor crawl.

One of the elders from the local church on the mission station, who had lived a godly life serving the Lord among his own people, was abducted from the station one dark night by a wicked "chefe do posto" (local administrator) and beaten. When I finally found him, he was trussed up from his shoulders to his ankles. I was so furious at coming upon him in this distressing condition that I whipped out my bush knife and cut him loose.

Now I was in trouble for having interfered with the chefe. The captors pointed their guns at me and shouted threateningly. I cried out to the God of heaven for help. Slowly the guns were lowered and the shouting ceased. Then the soldiers marched off with the elder, taking him to the Fort some seven miles away. I received a summons to see the chefe, and walked the seven miles to the Post.

The man's crime was that his brother had been kept at the Fort for free labour and had managed to escape. The administrator was punishing this man for his brother's "crime"! When they arrived at the Fort he was thrown spread-eagled to the floor. The men hit him with sticks on the soles of his feet over sixty times, until the feet were split and bleeding. After that they did the same to his hands. When he could no longer stand or crawl, they released him. The following morning he managed to start out for his home at the mission station with his wife's help. Along the way they stopped several times and she heated water over a fire of sticks to bathe his hands and feet.

Such severe and unjust treatment was common in remote regions of Africa. Thousands of young men fled the district and settled in what was then the northern Belgian Congo (Zaire) and Northern Rhodesia (Zambia) to avoid forced labour and the tyrants who demanded it. The Africans never forgot the brutality of those sticks, and it was incidents such as this which sparked off the war of liberation which shook the whole of Angola. Recrimination was such that the white people had to flee from the land in fear of their lives. The cries of the poor and oppressed and their unjust suffering in time brought terrible retribution.

A group of men from the province of Bie were taken away to the mining area of north-eastern Angola, and among them were some believers. They commenced meetings on their own, and the work of God through them grew steadily until many thousands of men and women were baptised and gathered into local churches in that area. Missionaries had to obtain a special permit to travel there, and among the first who visited were W. Maitland, L. Gammon, and R.S. McLaren, who greatly helped and encouraged these assemblies. Later Mr. Donald McLeod visited frequently, and that sphere became his special work. He was fluent in Chokwe, the most widely-spoken language in the mine region. I also had the joy of ministering the Word of God to the Christians there several times.

* * *

During one trek into the remote Shinji bush country George Wiseman and I learned the following story of two men who had gone to the diamond mines under forced labour conditions for eighteen months. When their time was completed and they were allowed to return home, they tied all the possessions they had accrued during their eighteen months into loads they could carry, and set off through the bush towards their village.

The men hurried along the familiar path, unaware that a hunter had dug a game pit across it. Suddenly they both tumbled into the pit. Fortunately for them, although the pit had been shaped so that they were unable to climb out of it, there were no spears in the bottom. They shouted and shouted for help, but there was no response. Only the birds in the trees nearby heard, and became excited. After some time, a hunter passing by heard the birds chattering agitatedly, and was alerted that all was not normal along the path. Then he heard the noise in the game pit, and approached cautiously.

"Wait a moment!" he shouted down to the two men. "I cannot manage alone - I'll run to the village for help."

So the men waited in the terrible silence of the bush, suspecting that the hunter would never return. They knew their own people well, and according to custom, the villagers would suspect the hunter of having caused the men to fall into the pit. Rather than take the chance of being blamed, the hunter would probably never mention having seen them, and they would never see him again, they thought.

Much to their surprise, however, the man who promised to go

for help did so, and within an hour he returned with several others. The men made a strong rope of tree bark, and lowered it into the pit, calling out, "Catch hold of this rope with your two hands! Hold tight!"

The first man looked at the precious bundle he had carried for several hundred miles. What would he do? To grip the rope with both hands meant he couldn't hold onto his possessions. He had a choice. Either he accepted his life without his goods, or he could remain in the pit with them and die. Letting go his bundle, he gripped the rope and was pulled up onto the path. The second man reasoned differently. He steadfastly refused to abandon all of the things he had acquired at the diamond fields.

"*Hichika muhamba we* (leave your load and get saved from death)!" pleaded the men. Again and again they called to him, but to no avail. He would not leave his bundle behind. The law of the jungle prevailed, and the man was left to die slowly in the pit.

In Psalm 40.2-3 David wrote, "He brought me up also out of an horrible pit, out of the miry clay, and set my feet upon a rock, and established my goings. And He hath put a new song in my mouth, even praise to our God: many shall see it and fear, and shall trust in the Lord".

* * *

I had always thought that a rifle or shotgun would be the best means of safety while trekking through the African bush, but I soon learned that I was wrong. The humble African staff proved to be the most useful weapon for my help and protection along the way. In the morning when preparing for a long trek, I saw that each of the carriers was provided with a staff. Just as Little Bird had done with his load of tobacco on his trip to sell it, each carrier placed his load on his shoulders, then slipped his staff over his right shoulder and under his load, giving himself leverage, and reducing the strain on his shoulders as he jogged along at a good pace all day. At night around the campfire I would often tell the carriers about my spiritual staff given to me by my Master, which helps me carry my burdens every day of my life. "Thy rod and Thy staff, they comfort me" (Psalm 23.4), is strength and comfort indeed for the weary traveller on the road to heaven, and the lesson was, "Never leave your staff behind, but take it to ease your load along the way."

When we reached a river where there was no bridge or ferry, each man took his staff in his hand in order to test the depth of the water. He would not go in without it. The staff steadied him as he moved carefully over the rough river bed and kept him from being swept away with the current. He learned to lean on it heavily. Sometimes a carrier would stop and thrash the water with his staff, alerting others that a crocodile was lurking beneath the surface with only his nose showing, waiting to clamp his jaws over a juicy traveller! The thrashing also frightened the crocodiles away. Many times I looked back at such a river safely crossed and thought of another weary traveller, Jacob, long ago who said, "With my staff I crossed over this Jordan" (Genesis 32.10).

Pushing on along a bush path after rain I knew that danger always lurked in our way. At such time snakes usually come out of the undergrowth and lie waiting in the path for their prey. With my faithful staff I have whacked many a snake a swift blow on the head, making an end of it. Another Scripture often came to mind at times like these: "The God of peace shall bruise Satan under your feet shortly" (Romans 16.20). Yes, full victory awaits me and all my carriers and my thousands of friends in Africa who have trusted the Saviour.

With steady pace the pilgrim moves
Toward the blissful shore,
And sings with cheerful heart and voice,
'Tis better on before.'

His passage through a desert lies
Where furious lions roar;
He takes his staff and, smiling says,
'Tis better on before.'
(Author unknown)

197

CHAPTER 16

Cowboy Katie

Jungle Leaf:
The path with thorns is the one that leads
to chieftainship.

"*Bom dia, minha senhora* (good morning, lady)", I said with a welcoming smile, answering a knock at our door one sweltering hot day.

"I don't speak Portuguese!" she snapped. Ah, she was English!

"Good morning!" (this time in the correct language, but with a Scottish accent!) "Where have you come from?" I asked.

"Oh, I came from London on my bicycle," she replied as off-handedly as if English women cycled from England to the Angolan jungle frequently for an afternoon's pleasure. "Yes," she continued, "after leaving England I cycled down through France and then Italy. From there I crossed to Egypt and travelled all the way down the east coast of Africa until I reached Johannesburg."

"What, alone?" I asked, incredulously.

No reply.

I took hold of her heavily laden cycle to assist her, but she shook my hand away and pushed it herself through the sand, talking as if she had just returned from a short afternoon's spin in the English countryside. And then I listened and learned her unusual story.

Away back in a London club, this five-foot three-inch woman of racehorse build and about fifty years of age, took on a bet for a thousand pounds that she would cycle all the way to the south of Africa and back again! The heat of the moment passed and then she realised what she had let herself in for. But with stubborn English courage she set out with a thirty-five pound bundle tied to her bicycle, fully anticipating success in her venture.

After reaching Johannesburg she had turned northward, cycling through Rhodesia (now Zimbabwe) and Zambia, then west until she reached our mission compound here in Angola. She stood before me now, her hair matted with thick dust from travelling those jungle trails in the dry season. Her face was burned and peeling from exposure to the tropical sun.

Margaret greeted the woman warmly, thinking she was another of the Portuguese women who came to have teeth extracted. What a pleasant surprise to hear an English accent! She hurried to prepare a bath, and our visitor spent so long soaking in it that Margaret became worried that she had drowned! Finally Margaret had a look, and there sat Cowboy Katie, carefully reading a Portuguese grammar!

Over a cup of coffee we learned more of her story. She had become fascinated with the explorations of David Livingstone, and had determined to follow the so-called Livingstone Trail west from the interior as far as she could. Livingstone had crossed Africa from the mouth of the River Zambesi on the Indian Ocean, into Angola, and on to the town of Luanda, on the west coast at the Atlantic Ocean. That epic journey took two years, most of it on foot, and was fraught with difficulties of every kind. Tribal peoples were hostile, the climate was inhospitable, and disease frequently ravaged his body. Our mission compound had been built very near the site where that brave Scot had to barter for his life with the wild tribespeople who had never seen a white person before. And so she had come to us.

"Now where do you sleep?" I asked.

"Up the trees," she said casually.

I looked at her five-foot three-inch stature and asked, "How?"

"Come on outside and I'll show you both," she said. Within a few minutes she had hauled a heavy piece of rope from her bag, lassooed a tree branch and, pulling the rope tight, clambered up the tree trunk with great dexterity. She then made a cradle bed with the rope, lay in it, and peered down at us, smiling broadly. What a woman! I didn't tell her that a lion or leopard can easily leap that distance, as can a flying snake. She told us that the night before, she had arrived at a village where lions had been seen prowling. The chief, feeling a responsibility to protect a white person visiting his village, gave her a body guard, but she misunderstood, and, terrified, she sat up the whole night between two fires! She produced her passport for us and removed any lingering doubt that she had indeed made the whole amazing trip by bicycle.

We had Bible reading and prayer with Cowboy Katie daily, but she was restless, anxious to get away on her long trek over another wild part of the country. She showed no interest in spiritual matters. Over the years we had several visitors from abroad who also weren't primarily interested in the Lord's work, including a professor from the University of London, who came with his wife to study African languages in our area. At the time we lived in a home built of bamboo and furnished with bamboo beds and chairs. Even the canoes that carried people on the rivers were made of bamboo, which made them easy to paddle. The professor's wife was particularly taken with the fascinating process of baking bread, as she was unskilled in bushcraft. Since the professor and his wife shared our home and our food, we considered it a golden opportunity to share with them also the Word of God. Night by night we read with them as we committed ourselves to the care of the Lord.

Margaret baked for Cowboy Katie so that she would have fresh food for at least a little farther on her journey. According to local custom I offered to escort her over the river and to travel a few miles with her, but Cowboy Katie would have none of it. She would go it alone. How differently the African Christians responded to the truth that when their Lord raptures the church He will do so according to their own custom by coming part way to meet them in the air! "Hi! is this not our custom?" they asked, "never to let anyone arrive at your home alone, but to meet them on the way?"

So Cowboy Katie left early one morning on a seven hundred mile journey through the bush and jungle to the coast. I thought of the dangers that lay ahead of her, and of one particular experience I'd had in Minunguland when lions had chased me. I had been blockaded by them in a village for two days until they changed their minds and gone elsewhere for their food.

Cowboy Katie had hardly been gone two hours when an African soldier ran up to my office, panting.

"Ngana, you are wanted quickly! The Portuguese administrator at the Fort is calling you!"

I accompanied him on the seven mile walk to the Portuguese fort down the river, where I found the administrator sitting in his office with none other than Cowboy Katie, who was reading a novel. On the desk lay a revolver and several bullets. Apparently she had cycled down to the river to cross in a canoe. An African approached and placed his hands on her handlebars to help her into the canoe. Imagining that she was being attacked, she made another blunder. She whipped out the revolver she kept hidden in her blouse and pulled the trigger. Fortunately the bullet jammed in the gun barrel, and a couple of Portuguese traders who were also waiting to cross rushed over and disarmed her. They had brought her to the fort where she was held in custody until I should arrive to translate from Portuguese to English.

"Now," said the administrator, "I want you to translate for me what I think of this English woman!" Cowboy Katie never batted an eyelid as I relayed the official's scathing remarks to her as accurately as I could.

"Ngana, I am going to risk giving this woman back the revolver and the bullets," he concluded. This was indeed a great risk, as no one knew what Cowboy Katie might do further along the trail.

I stood outside with my friend the administrator and watched Cowboy Katie tie a very dirty and ragged hat on her head and mount her cycle. With a saucy shake of her head and a wave of her hand she pushed off downhill towards the river once more.

That night she climbed a tree and carved the following "letter" to Margaret and me: "Ngana and Ndona, your Christ to whom you pray is nothing but a big joke to me."

Christ... a joke? Had this supposedly civilised woman from London not seen what Christ had done among the wild tribespeople of this continent? Ah, the irony of it! Here lay this woman asleep on the Livingstone Trail, a product of a great university, but without one glimmer of spiritual light to penetrate her mind and bring peace to her soul. When she arrived at Luanda the British Consul wisely shipped her back home to England, and in the end she lost her thousand-pound bet. Cowboy Katie took up chicken farming in the south of England, and we never heard any more of her.

Many other people besides adventurers have crossed the heart of Africa. Traders try to sell to the Africans things that bush dwellers do not need. Imagine selling toothpaste to the village African who has sparkling white teeth without the help of twentieth century chemistry! The villager cuts down a little reed which grows in his forestland, beats it with a wooden mallet, and presto! he has a fine toothbrush!

Game hunters too have been attracted to this great continent to seek fine trophies for themselves. In so doing they have menaced the bushlands, killing off vast herds of wild game, all for the love of adventure and the love of money. It often saddened me to see the Boer game hunters carrying nothing but a rifle, a blanket and a cooking pan, willing to live in the bush for months on end, when so few were willing to do the same thing to bring the good news of the gospel of Christ to the people living in darkness.

"The path with thorns is the one which leads to chieftainship," says the proverb. Cowboy Katie's trail was certainly a thorny one, and so was the Boer game hunter's. But such paths did not lead to chieftainship. There is Another, however, who chose the long path of thorns which has led to a wonderful Chieftainship. Christ is the Chief whom we follow on the path He blazed for us, His messengers. We take our example from

Him: "Looking unto Jesus the author and finisher of faith, who for the joy that was set before Him endured the cross, despising the shame, and is set down at the right hand of the throne of God" (Hebrews 12.2). There are the many thorns on the trail of Redemption, and there is also the Chieftainship!

Long the blessed Guide has led me
By the desert road;
Now I see the golden towers,
City of my God.
There amidst the love and glory,
He is waiting yet;
On His hand a name is graven,
He can ne'er forget.

Who is this who comes to meet me
On the desert way?
As the Morning Star foretelling,
God's unclouded day?
He it is who came to win me
On the cross of shame;
In His glory well I know Him
Evermore the same.

O the blessed joy of meeting,
All the desert past!
O the wondrous words of greeting
He shall speak at last!
He and I together entering
Those bright courts above;
He and I together sharing
All the Father's love.

He, who in the hour of sorrow
Bore the curse alone;
I, who through the lonely desert

Trod where He had gone;
He and I in that bright glory
One deep joy shall share:
Mine to be forever with Him,
His, that I am there.

(trans. from Paul Gerhardt)

CHAPTER 17

Slavery

Too Late

Jungle Leaf:
The hare who keeps its ears down is caught by the dogs,
while the one putting them up, hears.

An emaciated African woman sat listlessly on the ground, her dulled eyes sunk deep in her face. I recognised what this pitiful sight meant as I'd seen it many times before on my treks among the jungle villages. These were the eyes of a slave.

Another time I met a group of men and women walking along in single file, all tied together at the waist by a strong rope. Such a dreadful sight was much more common when the Arab traders wielded sufficient power to capture and enslave these people. They forced them to work without pay, and usually with little or no food, or sold them to the great slave markets of the "civilised" world. Time and again I wrestled within concerning the concept of civilisation. Is this what civilisation looks like?

There is an old trail leading through central Africa to Tanzania called 'the trail of bitter memories'. The name was coined by gangs of slaves whom the Arabs drove on foot, like animals, to the east coast where they were sold. At each camping place where they spent the night, the slaves planted seeds of the date palm. The stately trees grew, and reminded all who later travelled along that trail of the bitter years of slavery and of the terrible cruelty to which so many thousands of African men and women were subjected, often to the point of death.

Sakatoka

Sakatoka was a household slave, held by a master who belonged to the same tribe. Sometimes men became slaves because of a bad debt, and sometimes the inhuman desire of holding complete power over another person prevailed. While the proverb says, "The animal can be enslaved, but a human being can choose for himself," there is much evidence across Africa to contradict this. And it was to end this very evil, this "open sore of the world" as he called it, that Dr. David Livingstone gave himself and gave his life to the heart of Africa.

The chief who owned Sakatoka was a very powerful man in the northern part of Angola. He also owned many other slaves, but Sakatoka was his favorite. He always received the easiest tasks to perform each day inside the village. He was never sent far away to the banks of the Quango River to cut out salt slabs, the main source of revenue in those days, and carry them back to the chief. Such a hard task was left to the men who had been born into slavery. These men became jealous when they saw that Sakatoka always had the easy tasks to do. They were also jealous that he received meat to eat with his mush, while they had only boiled manioc leaves. To vary their diet they had to catch a mouse or a rat.

One day there was a great commotion in the village. Strangers bearing heavy loads on their heads filed into the clearing and made their way to the palaver place. They unpacked their loads and sat on the ground, legs stretched out African fashion. They had come a long way, they said, five days' journey along jungle paths, through crocodile-infested rivers and across the vast plains. Had they come to barter? the villagers asked, observing the large loads on the strangers' heads.

"No, we have not come for purposes of bartering," they responded. And for another half-hour the ceremonial greetings continued as the people fulfilled the local customs of politeness. They conduct themselves with great decorum as they receive strangers, as confident of what is culturally appropriate as any western diplomat would be receiving guests in his culture.

After some time the guests were served '*kasumbi wa yimbunji*' (the chicken of the stumps). The meal receives this strange name from the journey the visitors have just ended. All along the jungle paths the travellers have encountered tree roots growing over the trail, and they regularly stub their bare toes against the roots. When a tree falls over, the people seldom bother to chop it up and remove it. They simply walk round it, creating a new twist to the path, and inevitably they encounter a new root system. Villagers also believe that the more twisted a path becomes, the more difficult it will be for the evil spirits to reach the village. I always knew that I was nearing a village when the path was becoming more and more twisted in the forest. When the journey is over, and the last toe has been stubbed, travellers are offered "the chicken of the stumps" so that they can forget the stubbing of their toes in their enjoyment of the freshly roasted fowl.

The villagers slept that night without hearing the reason for the travellers' visit. In the morning the chief summoned them to his courtyard where all the people sat on the ground. Only the chief sat on a stool, as is the custom, but there at his right side sat a slave. I had recently been teaching these folks the glorious truth of the finished work of the Son of God on the cross, and that He is now seated at the right hand of God in heaven. Now here sat a mere slave at the right hand of the chief! I must have had a puzzled look on my face, because the chief called out to me, "No, no, Ngana! You must sit on my left hand as that is the place of honour. The right side is the place of a slave." Here the slave served as an armchair for the chief! There were no theological connections to my teaching, and I was certainly not looking for a place of honour! After everyone had settled, the strangers asked permission to speak, which was granted by the chief.

"Great 'Kangwili' (Big Leopard)," they said, "we have come to redeem our relative who is living with you as a slave. We have brought loads of 'upite' (riches) with which to purchase his liberty."

The chief sat silently, his eyes greedily surveying the unopened bundles of riches. "Upite," his heart whispered to him, "that is what I want."

"Let me see what you have and I will give you my decision," he replied. Now the African is highly skilled in the matter of bargaining. He can spend hours at such a task without feeling tired. Since there are no clocks in forest villages, and life merely follows the path of the sun across the sky, there is no pressure of time to make you hurry. The travellers untied one bundle at a time and removed the articles one by one, not allowing the chief to see everything at once. At last the laborious procedure ended.

"Call Sakatoka," the chief demanded, "and let him be asked what he wishes." A young man ran off bearing his urgent message as the chief and everyone in the village waited. The messenger relayed the summons to one younger than he, who set off and found someone yet younger! This familiar game is part of the cultural fabric whereby the importance of eldership is established. Every privilege is given to the older person, so even younger people constantly seek ways to show that they are older than someone else.

At last the message reached Sakatoga. He came at once, and knelt on the ground, clapping his hands but looking downward as a slave was expected to do. Then he scooped dust off the ground and rubbed it on his chest in obeisance to the chief.

"Here I am, Great Leopard," he said. "I have come to you."

"See, here are your relatives who have brought the price of your freedom. The full price is here before me. Get ready to go," the chief said.

"Great Leopard, forgive me. Honour be to you. I cannot go," said Sakatoga. "I cannot leave you as I am your favourite slave.

Let me stay with you."

Sakatoka's relatives cupped their hands over their mouths at hearing this plea, and exclaimed how foolish he was. They mocked him for his decision. Here they had worked long months, even years to accumulate sufficient wealth to approach the chief for Sakatoga's freedom, and now he refused it!

"*Upinji* (slavery) eh!" Sakatoga continued. "I have a good life. I am well fed and looked after in the compound of Great Leopard. I am never beaten as the others are. You say '*upinji*'? What if I come to you? I will have to go hunting and do all your hard work. I will have to hunt for beeswax and boil it to sell at the trader's store. No, I am not coming with you, my relatives. Just leave me alone with Great Leopard."

Sakatoga crawled backwards out of the presence of the chief. When he was out of sight he rose to his feet and left through the grove of banana plants in the village.

Sadly Sakatoka's relatives left also, recounting all that had happened at the chief's palaver place. Their loads seemed much heavier now than when they had first come along the twisting path. The leader was so engrossed in his sad reflections that he stubbed his toe on a root in the path. Everyone stopped while one stripped some barkrope from a nearby tree and bound up his toe. Still it bled profusely, so they searched for a certain leaf which all jungle dwellers know will stop bleeding when applied. Then they went home sad at heart, while Sakatoka the slave continued to enjoy his life of ease in the compound of the chief Great Leopard, *Kangwili Munene.*

The wet season ended. Although the rains ceased a cold wind whipped across the land. At such a time the Africans of the bush country are susceptible to much sickness. The winds pierce through the walls of their grass huts and there is no place where they can escape its chill. They become ill with what they call "stabbings" - pleurisy or pneumonia. And so Great Leopard became sick with an attack of stabbings.

The African medicine man, the Nganga, was called immediately. First he had to determine if an ancestral spirit was grieved with the chief, causing his sickness. Or perhaps some person had bewitched him. So a chicken was paid to the medicine man, who killed it and offered its blood to appease an ancestral spirit which might have been offended. Then the Nganga had the women brew some beer and pour it out on the ground as a drink offering to the ancestral spirits, which hover over the village incessantly. The African must take great care not to offend the spirits, as they hold such power over his life. Since the African has no direct contact with the person he calls God, believing Him too remote from his thinking and life, he believes he goes to God through his ancestral spirits.

After completing the religious ritual the medicine man made incisions on both sides of the chief's chest, and rubbed in a black power made of ash and chili plant. He boiled certain medicinal roots and fed the liquid to the chief morning and evening. But the chief did not get well.

As his temperature rose he perspired so profusely the women bathed his body with calabashes of cold water. The Nganga watched, shaking his head. If the chief Great Leopard had been a younger man he would have prescribed more drastic treatments, but the chief neared seventy years of age. He had seen seventy rain clouds during his life, and now death was calling him.

The chief thought of a proverb he had quoted to his people many times, "On the other side of death there are no prayers." Did the eagle of death take only the chick? Did it not swoop on the mother too? "Ah, Great Leopard," the chief thought to himself, "the eagle of death is swooping over you! You will be snatched away as easily as a mere chick. Death has no chief!"

In the early hours of the morning before the horns of the sun were seen shooting over the horizon the chief knew he was dying. He did not hear the cock crow. Yes, he was glad he was leaving many grandchildren behind him. Did not his forefathers teach him that the one who leaves grandchildren behind is assured of a proper place in the next world? And so the chief Great Leopard passed into the next world of which he knew so little.

Great Leopard's relatives came to prepare him for his burial. They brought his bow and arrows, which must accompany him to his grave. And then they thought about their tribal custom that a chief cannot go to his grave unaccompanied. Someone must go with him. Why not a slave?

Sakatoka sat in his hut enjoying his leisure and a plate of stiff porridge when two men clapped their hands outside to announce their arrival.

"Sakatoka! Come out!" they shouted.

"Hi," he thought, "how dare they shout at me, the favourite slave of the chief Great Leopard!"

"Come out at once!" they yelled again. Sakatoka rose and stood in his doorway.

"We have come to get you, slave!" They held thick ropes in their hands.

"Come to get me?" he laughed.

"Were you not the favourite slave of chief Great Leopard?" They leered at him, then swiftly grabbed him and bound his hands behind his back. As they led him away they told him the chief had died shortly after the cock announced the new day.

"Send for my relatives who have the price of my redemption," he pleaded. "Send quickly and they will come!" But Sakatoka was too late. The proverb says, "Delay has a leopard," meaning that the one who delays along the jungle trail is always in greatest danger because of the lions and leopards waiting to pounce and kill with one strong death leap. Yes, Sakatoka had delayed too long. He would accompany the chief to his grave. Once more he fell on his knees begging for his life, but in vain.

"*Chipema* (good)," the men said, as one lifted an axe and split Sakatoka's head open with one swift blow. Then they threw his body into the chief's grave.

There was no need for Sakatoka to die, because the price of his redemption was there for him. His people could '*jichika muya*' - establish their blood relationship with him. But he died because he failed to avail himself of their offer. He chose not to be redeemed and set free. How well this event illustrates the great story of redemption. Hebrews 2.14-15 reads, "Forasmuch then as the children are partakers of flesh and blood, He (Christ) also Himself likewise took part of the same; that through death He might destroy him that had the power of death, that is, the devil; and deliver (redeem) them who through fear of death were all their lifetime subject to bondage."

In order to redeem us, Christ established blood relationship with us while we were poor slaves of Satan. Ah, and much better than the bundles of goods which Sakatoka's relatives brought to the chief, Christ paid the full price with His own precious blood. "Ye were redeemed... not with corruptible things, as silver and gold... but with the precious blood of Christ" (1 Peter 1.18-19).

Jungle Leaf:
> *No one can put his finger in his mouth*
> *without it becoming wet.*

* * *

Another time a young African boy came running into the mission compound. He was running to us for refuge. Although he was only twelve years old he was a slave. He had run away from his master, and came to us for help. Margaret and I were overcome as we looked at the emaciated little boy with an abject look of terror in his eyes. Here he stood, without love, without protection, and with no chance of schooling. He was merely a chattel for those who owned him. He would work for the rest of his life without reward.

Very soon men in pursuit of him arrived and demanded his return. I offered to pay the price of the lad's redemption. They laughed.

"What?... *Jichika muya wenu!* (tie your genealogical belt). Tell us of your blood relationship with the boy!" Here we stood, a Scottish man and woman and a little African lad. There was no way I could claim relationship to him. I could pay the money, but I could not claim relationship therefore I could not redeem the boy.

I told the people that day of Someone who came to redeem us from our sins, of One who became our relative. He from the great heaven, became a baby boy, grew to manhood, and paid the full price of our redemption upon the cross. Yes, I found great joy in telling that message, but I felt utterly helpless in the face of the gulf between the African lad I wanted to redeem, and myself. I could perhaps begin to think black, in Dan Crawford's terminology, but I could never become black and effect redemption.

Only One Thing

Jungle Leaf:
  The one who applies a proverb gets what he wants.

Kapinji sat on the ground weaving a reed mat, clad only in a small, tattered cloth. A thick layer of dust covered his body, indicating that he was poor. In his tribe poor people are called "white ones", often because they lie about on the dusty ground in the dry season, having no fields to hoe.

In fact, Kapinji was a slave. His life had been spent in the service of the chief who owned him, *Sakanjamba* (the Father of the Elephant). Kapinji went out to the forest patches to cultivate corn, manioc, peanuts and various types of squash. He worked hard in the hot tropical sun. For seven months or more in the scorching dry season, the prevailing hot wind blew fine dust into his eyes, ears and mouth. Kapinji also had to watch for monkeys who delight in raiding well-cultivated fields for their food. Other times, destructive baboons invade the fields. They break off whole ears of corn, rip them open to see if they are ripe, and throw much of the crop to the ground, wasting it. Kapinji watched for them particularly in the mornings which was their usual time to raid. The tribal saying goes, "To chase the monkeys away from danger is easy, but the one who tries to chase people away from danger has more trouble."

Kapinji was present for the Lord's Supper one Sunday when the table had been set appropriately with a loaf of bread and a cup of local African wine. Suddenly, a monkey sped across the compound, leapt through one of the unglazed "windows", snatched the bread off the table, and disappeared into the bush! The elders eventually caught the monkey and sentenced him to death, providing meat for a Christian widow's dinner!

Often Kapinji had to draw water in a calabash from the crocodile-infested river. This, he knew, was the work of the women in his tribe, women who balanced the calabash on their head and walked so gracefully back to the village. Kapinji also had to cut firewood to keep the fires going in Sakanjamba's compound. He had never seen a hospital or a school, yet he could tell me the name of any tree growing in the lovely woods surrounding the village. He knew the names of many of the medicinal roots almost as well as the witchdoctor. Occasionally his life was brightened by a journey with the men out to the vast plains as they went off hunting.

On this particular day as Kapinji sat weaving, a shout came, "Kapinji! Kapinji! Come here quickly. The King wants you!" He jumped up hurriedly, tucking his loin cloth around him and ran to his master.

"Hi!" he thought, "why should I hurry? Perhaps it may be another beating from the chief. My mother, what will I do?" Yes, it was likely that he would get a whipping with a hippo-hide switch, or perhaps with a green sapling, cut fresh from the forest, which could dig cruelly into his flesh.

"Out of my way!" he shouted to the dog lying on the path. When he reached the chief's courtyard he found most of the village people gathered there. The women sat on the ground weeping and wailing, pulling at their hair, while the men sat nearby in silence, with grave faces. Even the young people were quiet.

"*Kuma* (dear me)," thought Kapinji, "the heavens have

thundered indeed." He was taken to a large hut and told to enter. No slave had entered this place before. Trembling at the sight of Sakanjamba, who lay motionless on a bamboo bed, Kapinji fell on his knees and clapped three times, as is the custom of his people. He lifted some dust from the ground at the side of the chief's bamboo bed and rubbed it on his chest as a sign of obedience. Again he clapped his hands, always looking downward in respect. Yes, King Sakanjamba was dying. The elephant which had roamed the forests was laid low. Kapinji remembered that the king had often quoted the proverb, "Death knows no partiality."

The chief lifted his hand calling for silence. Kapinji's fears mounted. "Why," he thought, "I may be accused of witchcraft! My mother, what will I do!" Kapinji knew the fate of those accused of witchcraft. If he escaped the poison cup test, bringing a slow and painful death, then he may be given the boiling water test, in which the accused has to dip his head into a cast iron pot of boiling water. If he survives, then he is declared innocent!

King Sakanjamba spoke slowly in a weak voice. "Children, listen to me," he said. "I have called you because I want to tell you of my last wish." Breathing heavily as the malaria sapped his life, he spoke again. "My wife, my son, my slave, listen to me. I am a rich man. I have many fields and many houses and many sheep, goats, and cattle." He paused. "I am leaving all that I have, my slaves and my houses and my fields and my goats, pigs, sheep, everything I have, to you, my slave Kapinji." He fell back on his bed, exhausted.

"What, father?! Leaving all to a mere slave?" cried his son, Chisale. "I'm your son!"

"And I'm your wife!" cried the mother. "What have we done to you that you should leave all to a useless slave?"

But Sakanjamba was adamant, and refused to change his mind. All that he owned now belonged to Kapinji. The wife rolled on the ground, foaming at the mouth.

"May the spirits of our ancestors curse you and forsake you and never intercede for you!" she said. Fear fell on those present, as such a curse is the most dangerous utterance ever to be made in an animistic culture governed by ancestor worship. After resting a while Sakanjamba spoke again.

"My son, Chisale, when I have died and gone to our fathers, the elders of the village will call you on an appointed day and give you the chance to choose one thing for yourself out of all the riches I am leaving to Kapinji. Remember, only one thing!"

"Only one thing!" cried Chisale. "Only one thing, and the useless slave is getting it all!"

By and by the king died and was buried down near the river in the tradition of his ancestors. Since one of the names for God is a water-god, it was fitting that all royalty should be buried near him, but slaves are buried in the upland far away. And so the eventful day arrived when Chisale was to make his choice. He rose early at the time his people call "the washing of the elephant", as the elephants all go down to the river to wash at daybreak. Chisale splashed water on his face and hurriedly dried his hands on a leaf from a nearby tree. As he walked through the forest he was too preoccupied with his momentous decision to notice the splendid brace of beautiful African pheasant among the trees. And though he was skilled in bushcraft he did not notice the warning call the birds screeched. Not even danger from a wild animal distracted him from musing on his coming choice.

"What should I choose?" he mumbled to himself over and over. Just then an old African woman approached him on the narrow forest path, carrying a bundle of firewood on her head. He didn't see her.

"*Moyo, mwanami nyi* (good morning)," she said. "What is wrong with you... have you lost something?

"No, Mother, I have not lost anything," Chisale replied. But his face told the story of his grief. She urged him to tell her of his problem.

"Yes, mother, I'll tell you. Today I have to make a choice." And so Chisale, the king's son, told the old woman his sad tale. To his surprise, she laughed and laughed. "Well," he thought, "she is making a fool of me."

"Come closer, my child," she said. "I'll tell you what you should choose." And she whispered a word in his ear.

"Hi! Mother!" he cried, jumping up. "That is what I will choose! Thank you, thank you!" He transferred the bundle of firewood from her head to his own and carried it back to the village for her. He thought of the proverb told to him by the leaders of his tribe, "The elephant who does not take advice gets his tusks growing out of his mouth." Ah no, he, Chisale, would be wise and take this old woman's advice!

Chisale hurried over to the palaver place in the centre of the village where the men usually gather to eat and to talk long and solemnly after a day's hunting or fishing. A crowd waited for him, eager to know what he would choose from all his father's wealth. Some said, "He'll choose an ox so that he can pay the bride price and get a wife." Others said, "No, he'll choose a house which is well fortified against the wild animals which prey on our village."

At last Chisale rose, clapping his hands three times in ceremonial manner, the fingers of one hand crossing the top of the fingers of his other hand. This was an act of respect to the older villagers present.

"Yes, I have chosen one thing," said Chisale, "only one thing of all that my father, Sakanjamba, left before he died and went to our ancestors." The people leaned forward, eager to hear what was coming. Slowly and deliberately Chisale walked over to the slave, Kapinji, and placed his hand on Kapinji's shoulder.

"Well, out of all that my father left, I choose this slave to be mine!" The people gasped in astonishment. Women trilled with their fingers in their mouths, and the men clapped their sides in sheer delight. Young men ran to fetch their drums hanging on a tree, and beat them in joy. Ah yes! What a wise choice the old woman had instructed Chisale to make that day. In choosing the slave, Chisale got all that his father had left. All of his riches, the cattle, the sheep, the goats, the pigs, the houses - all were now his because he had chosen one thing - the slave Kapinji.

Romans 8.32 says, "He that spared not His own Son, but delivered Him up for us all, how shall He not also freely give us all things?" If we choose Christ as our Saviour, then all God's gifts become ours by faith. There are some people who want the forgiveness of sins, they want eternal life, but they do not want Christ. But without choosing Him, none of these blessings can be ours. When we receive Him, they are all ours. He is that one choice we must make. As the African proverb says, "If I choose two hares at the same time one will escape, or perhaps both." So it is with folks who want what this world has to offer for the present, and also the blessings of eternal life for the future. But Christ calls us to make Him our one choice for both the present and the future - our only choice!

The Martyred Slave

A woman who had been a slave since childhood fled to the mission compound and lived there for a number of years. Daily she heard the Good News, and one day she yielded her life to the Saviour who had died for her. She was baptised and received into the local fellowship of Christians, and became an exemplary member of the African Christian community.

As she cultivated her fields day by day, fear yet stalked her, for she lived in constant dread of her former masters who still owned her. One night these men crept into the mission compound, found the woman, tied her up with ropes, and forced her to walk down the narrow, slippery trail to the wide river Chikapa. The ferryman did not want to be associated with this evil deed, but the men bribed him to leave his canoe in a place convenient for them, while he hid in his house.

The slavemasters poled out into the river with the bound woman lying in the bottom of the canoe. Knowing what was ahead of her, she preferred death, whether in the jaws of a crocodile or by drowning. As they approached the middle of the river she rolled over, capsizing the canoe, and toppled them all into the water. The men caught their breath, then dived deep to pull her out, so intense was their hatred and determination to control her. They managed to hold her head above water and swim to the far bank, after which they marched five day's trek into the heart of Minunguland.

There she was judged, and forced to take a test to determine her guilt. One common test was to have the accused put their hands into a pot of boiling water. If the person received no burn, they were innocent; if they did, they were guilty. Another test was a gourd of poison. If the accused who swallowed the poison didn't die, then they were declared innocent, but if they died, their guilt was established. This dear sister in Christ was poisoned, and she died a martyr for her faith rather than follow the heathen customs forced on her by her slavemasters. What a welcome she must have received from her Saviour, as she joined the great throng in heaven who will sing, "Worthy is the Lamb that was slain."

CHAPTER 18

Death, Fire and Resurrection

Death

Jungle Leaf:
Death has no pathway through the forest.

Among the Bantu tribes in Central Africa, there is no uniformity of ideas about the hereafter. Some tribes conceive of death according to station in life. Such ideas typically divide people into three groups for burial. First, the common people are buried in the usual Bantu manner and, as the Bantu say, their spirits hover over the villages which have known them. I never discovered how long the spirits are alleged to remain in the vicinity, but clearly there is no thought of anything eternal in their activities.

The second group comprises those convicted of being witches, and who are therefore a great danger to the tribe. They are buried in some hole dug by a night animal. The third group is comprised of lepers, who are thrown into the river. According to legend they become hippos. Generally the hut of the deceased is destroyed by fire or pulled down. If the spirit of the dead one is known to be troublesome, however, and not at rest, then further rites will have to be performed.

Other tribes bury their dead along with food and weapons in order to provide for their journey to wherever they are going beyond the tomb. Some believe in a literal happy hunting ground where there is no lack of game meat.

Water and rivers hold a great deal of significance in African mythology, and are also linked closely to beliefs about death. Some tribes speak of "the river of death" over which a departing spirit must pass. Words for God include "Ferryman" and "Steerer". When the great river Zambesi floods annually the people say of God that He is the "Flooder". When a person is sick and crosses a river he must offer water to God in an effort to obtain healing. *Kalunga* (God) pervades water, the rivers, and finally, the sea.

Malawians speak of the crocodile-men who live in the rivers and bring death to many. People living near the rivers are constantly in fear of these evil beings, which feature prominently in local mythology and parallel stories of leopard-men in other mythologies.

In the very north of Shinjiland there flows a river called "River of Heaven". What an irony that this river has brought death to so many who try to cross it! One time when George and I trekked along this valley my legs broke out in festering sores which refused to heal until we left the so-called "Valley of Heaven"!

The "other world" to some is "somewhere north" while to others it is "somewhere in the west". A few tribes avoid lakes and rivers because they believe the spirits of the dead are there. In many places when a death occurs the whole village flees to a new site. The fear of death and the hovering spirits are partly responsible for the semi-nomadic lifestyle of many tribes in Central Africa.

Fire

Jungle Leaf:
  When the arrow craves for meat it speeds from the bow.

African mythology explains the origin of fire in the story of the hare who climbed up to heaven along a thread which the spider had spun for it, and stole a ray of the sun which he brought back to earth. It was the same spider who spun a web reaching up to the sky when the animals complained that they had no wives, because, said the spider, "all the good wives come from heaven"! So up the spider's web climbed all the animals, and found themselves wives!

George Wiseman and I loved to sit round a campfire when such stories are told, especially in the far north country where the cape buffalo roam freely, as the sun like a ball of fire sinks quickly in the western sky behind the bushlands. We always had a special affinity for this out-of-the-way region where men and women had been waiting for centuries for someone to tell them the message of the cross. In a sense, it was our "ain countrae".

We had already visited this particular village, preaching the gospel. George had spoken to a young man about his need for salvation, and of the Saviour's love for him. George, standing six feet tall, towered over the boy and said solemnly, "Now, perhaps you may die tonight, and where will you be after death?" The young man was visibly startled at such words. Six months later, when we returned, the people came running out of the village to meet us calling, "No! Pass on! Pass by! We do not want you in our country!" After some discussion we learned that the young man to whom George had spoken had indeed died that night, and it was believed that we had bewitched him.

Over time God did a wonderful work of grace in this village, and now we sat around the campfire telling what the Bible says of the Last Judgment when all those who have rejected Christ will be cast into the Lake of Fire. The people started to clap their hands in delight instead of crying out in horror.

"Ha, ha!" they cried, "Judgement! No! Not judgement, but rest and health forever!" More and more puzzled at how they could have misunderstood what we said, we wondered if we had blundered in our use of the language.

"Lake of Fire! Why we already have one here in our country!" they said. We asked them where it was.

"Oh, far away in that direction... we take sick people there and they are healed," they said. Slowly we realised that what they were talking about there must be a spring of warm healing water. And so it was. I had to think of another term with which to refer to the scriptural pit of fire and judgement, so as not to confuse the Shinji.

* * *

Later that evening, Little Bird recounted the story of the hippo and the fire.

The hippo and the fire had been close friends for many years, for they had made a pact between themselves. Often the hippo came to his friend the fire to chat with him, but the fire never returned the visit.

One day the hippo asked his friend the fire, "Why do you never come to me and visit me and have a chat with me?"

"Friend," replied the fire, "it is good for you to come to visit me, but for me to come to you would be very difficult indeed. If I came you would be terrified."

The hippo returned to his home in the river, but after a few days the fire decided that he would indeed visit Hippo as he had requested. When Fire started out on his journey the whole area around him started to blaze. All the vegetation and trees were burned up due to his fierce power as he swept past. Nothing was able to stand in his way. Great clouds of smoke rose to the heavens and all the animals of the bush fled in terror.

Hippo was sitting down resting in his home in the river where it was so nice and cool for him. Suddenly his nostrils twitched as he smelled the approach of his friend Fire. Hippo lumbered out of the river to meet him. Then he heard the crackle of twigs burning and he saw bright flames licking the trees and the tall grass.

"Hi!" he called out, flames all around him. "This is a dreadful thing that is happening to me today!" And he turned and tried to run in hippo fashion toward the safety of his home, the river, with all the speed hippos are capable of! But the fire had come around behind him and his way was blocked. He ran in every direction without finding a way of escape from the flames. Hippo was too late, and he perished. Fire went back home in a different direction destroying everything in his path.

Little Bird interpreted the gospel through the tale this way: "Yes," he would tell the villagers, "if you had never left God who is your real home you would not be in danger of perishing in the flames of the fire of judgement with which you have made friends." Little Bird stooped at this point to pull a burning brand from the village fire. He suggested to each person in the front row that they should hold the wood in their hands, at which, of course, they recoiled in horror. And so Little Bird proceeded further to relate the following event to drive his message home.

Kanjaviti and the Dwarf

One dry season when the tall elephant grass was as dry as tinder, Kanjaviti and six of his friends decided to go hunting on the plains. All the vegetation had withered because no rain had fallen for more than six months.

The men arrived early one morning at a village where an African evangelist named Dwarf was preaching the gospel in a small grass

church building. They filed in with the village people, listened to the message from God's servant, then hurriedly picked up their bows and arrows and spears to reach the hunting plain before high noon. That is when the sun is directly overhead and the heat fiercest, and the animals lie down in any shade they can find to provide respite.

After spotting some game, the men quietly encircled a large area around the resting animals, then torched the long dry grass. The circle of flame frightens the animals to escape through one corridor the men leave fire-free, and as the terrified animals thunder past, the men shoot arrows at close range.

All of a sudden the men looked up, as terrified as the animals. A deafening noise like a whole railway-yard of trains was approaching. It was no train, but a wind storm which had suddenly arisen and was roaring over the plain, sweeping up the fire in its power and tossing it over the heads of Kanjaviti and his six companions. Tall trees all around them caught fire, which is a dreadful, awe-inspiring sight. The whole plain became the arena for the wind's fury.

Kanjaviti shimmied up the tallest tree he could find close by, seeking refuge from the burning inferno getting nearer. As he climbed higher and higher the flames licked at his feet, as if teasing him. Finally, when he could climb no higher, the flames engulfed him and his scorched body fell with a terrible thud to the ground far below. That noon Kanjaviti did not even have time to heed the wise saying of his tribe, "When you see a bush fire, flee while it is still far from you."

The African evangelist Dwarf moved quickly through the blackened countryside searching for the hunters, and eventually he found seven burned bodies, one of them Kanjaviti's. Sadly he recalled seeing them that very morning in the gospel service. They had sat in front of him on the wooden benches listening to the voice of the Saviour pleading with them to receive his free offer of salvation. But their minds were too occupied with thoughts of the hunt to respond to that offer.

Dwarf carved a wooden plaque and inscribed it with the words, "*Kanjaviti, watoka, watoka* (you have perished, you have perished)".

Resurrection

Jungle Leaf:
   A river in flood should not be tested by the leg.

The Bantu-speaking people of Africa believe firmly in reincarnation. I had been in Africa quite some time when one day Little Bird and I were out on the jungle trail together hunting for meat. I was delighted when some wild pigs suddenly jumped up from the long grass and ran right across the path in front of us. I took aim with my rifle and was about to shoot when Little Bird cried out, "Ngana! Don't shoot! Don't shoot!" Astonished at this sudden outburst, I lowered my gun and the pigs ran off into the jungle to continue their lives meantime.

"What is it, Little Bird? Why did you call to me like that?"

"Ngana, do you not know that these village people we will be visiting soon believe that some of their ancestors have come back to earth in the body of a wild pig?" he said.

"What, in the body of a pig?" I repeated, astonished, "a pig?"

"Ngana, if we shoot a wild pig in this district the people will all turn against us. So do not offend them and hinder the gospel. Please do not kill a wild pig." And so I was introduced to the local belief in transmigration, a variation of reincarnation whereby people return after death in the form of an animal. Some tribes believe that fathers and mothers are reincarnated in the bodies of their grandchildren. Such a belief explains the deep-seated fear of childlessness among the Africans, as they would then have no means of reincarnation. The value of children extends beyond the present to a future life governed by ancestral spirits.

I expected that these beliefs would be somehow connected to belief in resurrection, but found nothing beyond a mythological reference to a dog or a snake coming back to life in some jungle story. And so the missionary's task of explaining the Biblical concept of resurrection to the African is very difficult, as there is no clear cultural bridge, and the idea of a person returning to life to be recognised as he or she was, is a shattering concept.

Quite a stir erupted in one district, therefore, when one year a story passed from village to village that the old chiefs of that district would be raised from the dead on a particular date. They would snatch their land from the white rulers! Now the only snag was that the people had to kill off all their white cattle, white sheep, white goats and white chickens. If all white animals were not killed, the chiefs would refuse to rise from their graves. Margaret and I visited some of these villages, and were saddened to see the mass slaughter and the widespread fear that gripped the people.

As I approached a village on one of these days, I saw a man killing a white chicken with a sharp knife. He looked up at me and said, "Ngana, this is what is going to happen to the white people when our chiefs come back to life!"

We quickly figured out that evil witchdoctors had spread this rumour throughout the area to promote the fear that helped them retain control over the people. Almost no one would listen as we pleaded with the villagers not to kill their animals, as we knew the food supply was already limited, and many would starve. In reply, villagers told of a white cow which some folks had refused to kill, and which subsequently rotted away with disease. The killing increased more and more.

Finally the day of the announced 'resurrection' arrived. The sun rose in the east and passed high overhead and set quickly in the west, but no chief arose from his grave! The old burial places remained undisturbed. Disillusionment set in, and there was widespread famine of meat because so many animals had been killed. Not only did they lack food, but now the people had few animals with which to pay the witchdoctors for favours or for appeasement of the ancestral spirits. How we longed to communicate the message of the true Resurrection of our Lord! Little could we have known, however, that not many years later (though without the resurrection of dead chiefs) there would be a terrible mass bloodbath when the rebels would rise up against the Portuguese, and whites would flee from Angola by the thousands.

The absence of belief in bodily resurrection is nowhere more evident than at a heathen funeral. There is no hope, no light, no comfort, no thought of a glorious resurrection when the Saviour returns. There is nothing but weeping and wailing and the chanting of mournful dirges. How different it was when Mrs. Wiseman passed into the presence of her Saviour and we buried her mortal remains there in the African soil, in the country where for many years she had served the Lord she loved. Yes, there was sadness, but there was also an overwhelming sense of victory and hope as we sang triumphantly around her grave.

African mythology offers no hope of resurrection to people, and various reasons are given for it being withheld. Some lay the blame on the mole, which they say God punished so that it comes out only at night when men do not see it. This represents to them a picture of fear and darkness, devoid of the light of resurrection and the hope of a life beyond the grave in an eternal body.

Both Bushmen and Tswana blame the wife of the first man on earth for causing the gift of resurrection to be lost to humanity

(Kidd). In other Angolan tribes a story is told of people building a great tower to reach God, because He had withdrawn Himself from them when they lost the gift of resurrection.

Mythology is capable of recording what is lost, but it never holds out any possibility for the future. Thus, the Bantu tribal folk tell me that what man has lost in the past, he has no hope of regaining in the future. But it was always a great joy for me to give to them the message of John 11.25, "I AM the resurrection and the life: he that believeth in Me, though he were dead, yet shall he live". This ray of light has pierced through the darkest forests and into the darkest hearts, as the life-giving message of the gospel has been heard in these remote parts of the jungle. Men and women have listened and believed and they live.

CHAPTER 19

New Fields

It took David Livingstone almost three years to cross Africa in the 1850's, starting from the east coast near the mouth of the Zambesi where it empties into the Indian Ocean, to Luanda, Angola, overlooking the Atlantic Ocean. When I landed on that west coast about eighty years later to begin my missionary travels I little thought that it would take me, not three years, but forty-three years to cross the continent. Dr. Livingstone was a pioneer trailblazer and explorer. I was a pioneer preacher of the gospel, church planter, learner of many languages, and translator of the Scriptures. I had the honour of following the Livingstone trail in reverse, from west to east, from the Atlantic coast to the Indian Ocean. I had begun in Angola, spending more than twenty fruitful years there, but I had yet to go farther east as circumstances developed under the all-wise providence of our great God.

I had to return to Scotland for two major operations, and when Margaret and I were finally able and ready to return to Angola, the Portuguese refused to give us visas. Trouble had broken out in northern Angola, and from 1965 to 1968 no foreigners were allowed into the area, especially men. What were we to do?

We spread out a map of Africa on the table in the missionary home in Prestwick, Scotland, and scanned it with prayer. We thought of returning to Africa and settling on an established mission station, and wondered if we were now of an age when we should take things a little more easily and quietly. But the more we studied that map, the more we sensed the Lord saying,

"Lift up your eyes and look on the fields."

"Fields, Lord! We had a vast field in Shinjiland, but what now, Lord?" As we continued studying the map we began to notice something rather obvious that had never really caught our attention before. Assembly missionaries had landed at Benguella on the west coast of Africa, spread through central Angola and into Zaire (Belgian Congo), then down into Zambia. We also saw that missionaries had advanced northward from Cape Town, worked in Natal, and moved on to the Transvaal. Their advance was virtually halted on the south bank of the Limpopo River. Thus between the Zambesi and the Limpopo there was a large gap where few missionaries had ventured and no major work had been established. The gap was comprised of Namibia (South West Africa), Botswana, Zimbabwe (Southern Rhodesia), Malawi and Mozambique - five relatively large countries needing the gospel. In all of these vast lands only one very small assembly had been established among the Africans in Bulawayo. There was nothing else.

"Stake all on God and move forward," said C.T. Studd. "True religion is like smallpox. If you get it, give it to others." I had got it, not religion, but Christ, and I must obey God and pass it on.

And so in 1961 Margaret and I entered the land of the Shona in Zimbabwe-Rhodesia. It meant learning another new language, one much more complicated than those in Angola. After much patient persistence I became proficient enough to begin preaching the gospel among the Shona peoples. The work began slowly as our ministry led to the planting of small assemblies, facing completely new challenges. Church planting in African townships required different approaches from those used in the wilds of Shinjiland.

The Rhodesian government had done a fine job in elementary education, producing a comparatively literate population of young folk, in contrast with the Portuguese in Angola who discouraged education and left schooling to the missions. This repressive policy was one of the sparks which ignited the explosive and bloody insurrection of the Angolans, ending with the mass exodus of the Portuguese before the wrath of the people whom they had exploited for so long. The ruling party in Rhodesia, the Rhodesian Front, had developed good elementary education, but they made little attempt to increase and develop the secondary schools.

With so many readers nearby, and a shortage of appropriate reading material, I began to write tracts in various languages, especially in Shona. The messages were illustrated with stories of my jungle life among the Shinji and the Chokwe, and were easily understood by other Africans, who were all familiar with bush life, folklore and proverbs. This work caught like a bush fire in the dry season and spread throughout Rhodesia to adjacent lands.

Although I could readily write the tracts in various languages, the difficulty of printing them often faced me. One day as I spoke with Mr. Ron McBride, an elder in the local assembly, he asked if I'd ever thought of starting a mission printing press. A mission press! But that would cost a great deal of money! However, so insistent was this a conviction about what we should do that

Answering mail from Tracts

when God sent in 500 pounds sterling we bought a second-hand Heidelberg press in Durban, South Africa. We had it shipped from Durban to the port of Beira, Mozambique, from where it was sent overland to us in Rhodesia.

The press arrived safely, but we didn't have an operator. Again Ron McBride stepped in, and with the help of his son Malcolm, began production. What a thrill it was to see thousands upon thousands of tracts coming off that press! I bought a guillotine, and later an electric folding machine, and production increased.

One of God's great surprises for me came when George and Emma Wiseman could not obtain visas to return to Angola at about this time, and they decided to join Margaret and me in Rhodesia. This was a great thrill after all our hard days of pioneering work to be able to work together again in a new endeavour. What a praise meeting we had! They settled down to learn Shona and soon mastered it also.

Since George was skilful with machinery he took on the printing work, though he had never actually operated a press before. I provided the material, and George and Ron McBride printed it. Soon hundreds of letters began to pour in from men and women who had read the tracts, begging for more spiritual help. We began a great work of correspondence with those seeking help in salvation. One of the tracts reached a young man named Manuel Chisale. The tract related the story of the antelope with the horns curving towards the front instead of the back (see chapter 14). Chisale read it and became deeply convicted concerning his sin and his life without Christ.

One Saturday afternoon Chisale entered arrived at our door, and not knowing that I spoke Shona, he said in his limited English, "Sir, is this where Jesus lives?" That rocked me back on my heels! Does Jesus live here? What a challenge!

The young man told how he was born in a village in Mozambique but had wandered across to Rhodesia. "*Ishe* (teacher)," he said, "those horns of that antelope are my sins, keeping me away from Christ." That afternoon Manuel Chisale found the Saviour and the Saviour found him. He was the firstfruits of the assembly work in Shonaland. Soon he requested baptism, and went on to become an active member in the first small assembly there. I invited him to join me in the work as a language consultant and he joyfully helped in this way for many years. He also answered thousands of letters in the correspondence ministry, and became a gifted evangelist and teacher of the Word of God. Finally he was commended to full-time service in Rhodesia, and began spending three months of his year in a teaching ministry in Malawi. His wife was brought to the Saviour in Margaret's Sunday School class, and they have three lovely children.

The freedom fighters threatened Chisale, political parties tried to force him to buy their party cards but he has stood firm against it all. He has been caught and grilled by gun-toting men, yet his clear answer has always been, "We preach Christ and only Christ." He has been called to the path of suffering but counts it all joy to suffer for the name of Christ. He is gifted in three languages, in which he can preach and teach the Word. I thank

Manuel Chisale recording

God for this precious first-fruit of the gospel in my labours among the Shona.

Another outstanding conversion was that of a young man called Joshua Zemba. "*Zemba*" means "the one who fires and never misses the mark". In his future life this man was to live up to his name. Somehow a gospel tract reached him in his village, and as it was suitably illustrated with an African bush story he read it. He wrote to me, and after Margaret and I prayed at length, we went to visit him over a hundred miles away in his bush village. We wandered from village to village, but one knew of Zemba. Then one evening we found him. We made a camp in the woods outside the village and Zemba brought with him a crowd of village people to listen to the gospel message.

At the conclusion of a very long gospel service, Joshua Zemba stood up and told his own people how God had spoken to him through a gospel tract in his own language. Then he, together with his wife, made a public confession of faith in Christ. How thrilled we were, after the long, tiring search to find the sheep who had been lost, now found by the Good Shepherd. This event was the harbinger of an assembly to be planted in that village. Was it worth it to wander one hundred miles in the bush for one soul? Yes, for from this one sheaf came a rich bundle of sheaves. Zemba and his wife were baptised and he gave himself to the preaching of the Good News that had changed him.

The assembly at Chirau where Zemba lived grew, but it was called to undergo terrible persecution. Wandering fighters rounded up Zemba and some unsaved villagers at gunpoint and made them sit in the shade of a tree. They passed around a pot of beer and each man poured some on the ground as a libation to the ancestral spirits. Zemba politely but firmly refused, saying, "If I do this, I will be denying my Saviour. I cannot drink this cup as I have trusted Christ as my Saviour. I left these things long ago." Zemba knew that to drink the beer was an outright denial of his Lord since it represented an oath and veneration of the tribal spirits. He also knew that others had been shot for a less important refusal. For a tense moment the rifles pointed directly at Zemba. Then they were lowered.

Again the pipe was passed to each man in turn. And again Zemba refused to participate. This, too, would be a denial of his Lord. And this, too, could cost him his life. Only a few weeks previously the same men had shot one of the women in the local assembly when she answered their knock at her door. Even in the face of death Zemba remained steadfast. He opened his Bible and read, "In all these things we are more than conquerors through Him that loved us" (Romans 8.37).

Another time the men rounded up the elders of the assembly and demanded money. There is never much cash circulating in remote bush areas, but the elders handed over all that they had. Toward the end of the 1970's Zemba heard shouting outside his house and rose from his bed to see what was going on. As he opened the door he was surrounded by ten heavily-armed "freedom fighters". One pushed the barrel of his Russian-made rifle against Zemba's chest shouting, "Ah, we'll shoot this *Mufundisi* (religious teacher); we don't want this man here!" Right then Zemba's wife came out and she too was grabbed. They were going to rape her. "Look, I've just given birth to a baby!" she cried. They refused to believe her until she went into the house and showed them the newborn baby. Again they focused their evil intent on Zemba.

"*Muuraye! Muuraye!* (Let's kill him)" some called.

"No, let's not kill a *Mufundisi*; let us beat him instead," the leader said. Yes, Zemba could well have written 2 Corinthians 11.25,26: "Thrice was I beaten with rods; once was I stoned...in journeyings often, in perils of waters, in perils of robbers, in perils by mine own countrymen."

The fighters then seized another elder, beat him and stabbed him because he refused to allow them to rape his daughter. Despite his efforts to protect the girl and some of her friends, the young girls were rounded up and brutally abused. Many of them had to be taken forty-five miles to get medical help.

Praise God for men and women who utter not one word of denial of their Saviour although they are abused, assaulted, beaten up, threatened by death. Surely they are to be acclaimed with those mentioned in Revelation 12.11 who are not deceived by the Evil One, but who "overcame him by the blood of the Lamb, and by the word of their testimony, for they loved not their lives unto death."

* * *

English is the official language in Zimbabwe-Rhodesia, as Portuguese was in Angola and Mozambique. But no efficient gospel work, let alone assembly planting, can be done without a working knowledge of the African languages. All services in the local assemblies are conducted in both Shona and Chewa. Some folks from the United Kingdom have come to these parts with the mistaken idea that they could work for the Lord in their spare time, using English. One competent engineer came to Malawi with this idea but soon found himself in trouble. Once when I was interpreting for him into Chewa he began to use the illustration of an electric kettle. Sitting before him on mud benches were men and women who had never seen or even heard of such a thing! An electric kettle! They did their cooking in pots on open fires! Just to make the story a little more complicated, the man began to explain about the heating element inside the kettle! I had to stop the address and give the people a story of an animal in the bush - which they understood a lot better.

As the work grew in this new and vast field, others came to join us. Mr. and Mrs. Willie Hastings from Ayrshire in Scotland (my home county) came since they, too, could not obtain visas for their return to Angola. Willie had gone to Portugal to explore the possibilities of acquiring visas there, but the door was closed. The Portuguese remained adamantly opposed to the re-entrance of male missionaries to Angola. The Shinji spiritual revolution had shown them the dynamic power of the gospel.

Willie and Betty Hastings became a great blessing to the work in Zimbabwe-Rhodesia, as Willie equipped himself very quickly with a good knowledge of Shona and carried on a valuable teaching ministry among the new converts I had reached with the gospel.

Dr. and Mrs. Sam Emerson also joined us and laboured well in Zemba's district, where their medical work was greatly appreciated. Sam learned Shona and was a gifted evangelist. He was also gifted with a trumpet voice, and had no need of a loud-speaker! I enjoyed sweet fellowship in camp life with Sam and felt the loss of it very much when the Emersons believed they should move south to the medical work at Murchison Hospital, in Natal, in 1973.

* * *

In 1968 George and I travelled to Botswana to survey possible future spheres for gospel work. In Shinjiland there are many beautiful rivers where water is never scarce, but here, further south, the desert has swallowed up the moisture from the earth, and vast miles of nothing but sand and scrub brush spread out to the horizon in every direction. This is the land of the vast Kalahari Dessert. In such a place, where lack of drinking water is of constant concern, it's easy to understand how the word for mouth is literally "the drinker", for that is a mouth's primary use.

One Saturday night, tired after travelling through this difficult terrain, we set up camp and kindled a fire. Soon we were joined by a group of bushmen, who sat silently and stared at the strange white men. We knew little of their language, and wondered how we could communicate the Good News to them. These were nomadic tribes, wandering wherever they could find food and any meagre pasture. Conventional missionary work was out of the question, as these folk never remained in the same place for two consecutive seasons. I was beginning to feel the strain of pioneer life, yet I yearned to bring the gospel to these people.

That night we brought out our transistor tape recorder and began to transcribe this most difficult bushman language with its clicks and unique grammar. I wondered if these were descendants of the people who saved the life of pioneer missionary Fred Stanley Arnot, when he was found lying weak from thirst in their desert, all alone, about eighty years before. They put long reeds down into the sand and sucked up enough water to revive him so that he could continue his journey northward to finish the work to which God had called him, that of opening up a large stretch of Central Africa for missionary work in this century. I felt a debt of gratitude toward such people who had not gone off and left Arnot as some Bantu had done to George and me many years before, leaving us injured and helpless in the bush.

Little by little we made connections between what we knew of Bantu languages and the bushman tongue, and we began to build a linguistic bridge to these people, a bridge which would be used greatly in the future development of the work in Botswana. From this experience I also gained a new appreciation for the cost of supplying a person with a cup of water in the desert. When one is dying of thirst, it is of no concern that another has sucked the water from the underground source through a hollow stick and spat it into the cup to give it to you!

To Bridge the Gap

The tract ministry which George, Ron McBride and I developed, continued to be used by the Lord not only in the salvation of specially gifted men like the evangelists Zemba and Manuel Chisale, but in the local assembly work also. Here and there in the African townships, out on farms, and away out in the deep bush, little assemblies began to form and to grow, chiefly as a result of people being saved through reading or having had read to them one of these tracts written in their own language and using illustrations from their own tribal life.

One day a tract found its way into the Gokwe area of the Zambesi Valley. A man who had been a backslider for many years read the tract, showed it to his wife and said, "Look, this is what we need!" He hastily posted a letter to me pleading with me to visit them. I could never resist the call "Come over and help us!"

What a journey that was, over two hundred and fifty miles through deep bush, over dried-up rivers, on and on until at last I reached this man and his wife. Not only were they waiting for me, but they had persuaded six African chiefs to come and hear the message I would bring. What a grand company of Shona tribesfolk gathered around the fire that evening to hear the same story of God's love that George and I had taken to the Shinji in far-off Northern Angola! It was such a familiar sight - the people sitting around the fire while I explained the Good News as best I could. And how it thrilled my soul! The people interrupted my talk by shouting, "*Ndizvozvo!*" just as the Shinji had shouted, "*Momo!* (That's it! That's the stuff!)."

The man who had received the tract had earlier fallen into a sinful lifestyle, but that night both he and his wife found a forgiving Saviour who loved them and restored them to Himself. Just one tract, but what a harvest! Crawford, was it worth that long, lonely, difficult trip in the heat of the valley for just two souls? With the poet Anne Ross Cousins who put Samuel Rutherford's writings into verse, I would readily say:

"*Oh if one soul from Anwoth (Shona, Shinji, Chewa, Sena)*
Meet me at God's right hand,
My heaven will be two heavens
In Immanuel's Land."

And that wasn't the end of the story. An assembly grew in that place, and also a school to educate the children. What a rich harvest! And stories like this were multiplied in many other places - Kariba, Gatooma, Beatrice, Marandellas, Umtali, to name but a few.

Many years before while trekking in Angola, I paused one day along the path to wait for my carriers who had lagged behind. I rested against a tree and opened my Bible at random. My eyes caught Revelation 1.11: "What thou seest, write in a book." At that point I could not foresee the day when not only the tract ministry would reach many more people with the gospel than I could reach with preaching, but also many books would be written in local languages and distributed throughout the country.

Years before this I had worked hard with missionary colleague David Boyd Long to translate the New Testament into Chokwe. We continued with some Old Testament books until my health broke down and I had to leave the completion of the task to him. Little did I know that ahead for me yet lay the work of translating Scripture into Shona, Chewa and Sena. God thus fulfilled the direction I received in so strange a manner that day as I waited for my carriers in the Angolan forest. These Scriptures have been used to build up many believers in Zimbabwe and to bring others to the Saviour.

The next question we faced was what could be done about the many folk who needed regular Bible teaching. Our solution was to translate into Shona and Chewa some of the Emmaus Bible Correspondence courses, and these were wonderfully used by the Spirit of God. George and Emma Wiseman assumed responsibility for this work and built it up to the point where it needed to be divided among many more. So Willie Hastings handled the Shona courses, Mr. and Mrs. Jack King the Chewa courses, Margaret Row the English ones and Arthur and Christine

Hallett the Portuguese ones.

In December, 1969, an expert printer and his wife, Alan and Jeanette Chambers from Australia, joined the work. Margaret and I were humbled to see how God continued to bless and provide for each branch of the work that we had pioneered under His guidance. Assembly planting, the printing press and Emmaus Bible courses continue through the work of many other missionaries who have followed us. Some of these are Archie and Virginia Ross and Tom and Ruth Wilson in Bulawayo, Gordon and Margaret Jones and Deryck and Sandra Jones at Gatooma, Marston and Betty Martin at Marandellas, and John and Eleanor Sims in Salisbury (Harare). Most of all we rejoice when we think of the many companies of native believers who gather in the bush and in the urban townships each Lord's Day to break bread and to engage in gospel preaching and ministry of the Word of God.

Another facet of the work which developed in the seventies was an audio tape cassette ministry. For a long time Margaret and I were concerned about establishing this help for assemblies in Zimbabwe, Malawi, Angola and Mozambique. As we prayed, a concern also developed among several men at C.M.M.L.(Christian Missions in Many Lands) in New Jersey. In the goodness of God two recording studios were installed within our mission compound, and equipment was very generously donated by friends in the United States. John Sims, Manuel Chisale, and another African brother, Andreas Makasi, an elder in one of the local assemblies, have developed this important ministry. Messages have been produced in three languages: Shona for Zimbabwe, Chewa for Malawi, and Chokwe for Angola and Zambia. My friend George Atmore, who is also the father of my daughter-in-law Lorraine, has stood with me as a true yokefellow in the work in Zimbabwe.

One other work that has been greatly blessed is the teaching of Scripture in the Zimbabwean schools. Missionaries have received "right of admission" from the government, and each week hundreds of African schoolchildren receive instruction in the way of salvation. Some of the African believers have also taken up this wonderful challenge.

I believe that the missionary's primary purpose is to plant assemblies, establishing them in the truth. The Holy Spirit then raises up men to take the lead in the churches which have been planted. It is a great temptation in Africa, and elsewhere, for the white man to try to retain control for too long. This is not only unwise, but unscriptural. We have seen that God the Spirit has raised up godly national leaders both in Shinjiland and in Shonaland, and the missionary must be prepared to fulfil his calling and then move on.

In the grace of God, the entire work in Zimbabwe today is a standing testimony to the power of the printed page. The pen and the press were used by the risen Lord for planting and enlarging His churches in Shonaland. It is with gratitude to the Lord and great joy in my heart that I look back over these many years and affirm with Paul,

"Their sound went into all the earth,
and their words unto the ends of the world"
(Romans 10.18).

Epilogue

On the 15th November, 1979, from Salisbury, Rhodesia (now Harare, Zimbabwe), Crawford Allison wrote the following letter:

Dear Praying Friends,

Please excuse the delay in replying to your kind letter received some time ago. This delay has been caused by another time of sickness that threatens to take me home to glory. Nevertheless, the Lord is faithful and is good and I am at perfect peace resting in Him.

There are many precious promises in the Word of Truth that flood my mind at this time. Isaiah 43.2 says, "When thou passest through the waters, I will be with thee; and through the rivers, they will not overflow thee. When thou walkest through the fire, thou shalt not be burned, neither shall the flame kindle upon thee."

Jim and Irene Legge who are both registered nurses and who labour for the Lord in Botswana are here and administer morphine injections and look after me medically.

Our sons, Kenneth and David, and daughter Helen are with me and they are a great comfort and cheer to me.

Margaret is a tower of strength to me but needs much grace to minister to me in this trial the likes of which she has not yet seen during these many years of so often being laid aside. Please pray for her.

Thank you for your prayers and interest in every way.

"Thou shalt guide me with Thy counsel, and afterward receive me to glory" (Psalm 73.24).

Yours in the Train of His Triumph,

R.C. Allison

Fourteen days later, on November 29, Crawford Allison entered that glory to meet the Saviour he had served so faithfully.

Appendix 1

Significant dates in the life of
ROBERT CRAWFORD ALLISON

1911, May 4	Born in the country village of Galston, Ayrshire, to Barbara and Robert Allison
1925, June 6	Born again - saved by grace
1930, June	Newmilns missionary conference - challenged to missionary service through Mr. T. Ernest Wilson speaking of lost tribes in Northern Angola
1934	Studied Portuguese in Portugal
1935	Sailed for Africa, settling temporarily at Peso Mission Station with Donald McLeod, to learn Songo & Chokwe
1937	Married Margaret at Boma, and travelled to Chitutu Mission Station
1938, Aug. 13	Son Kenneth born
1940	Moved to Camandambala Mission Station (near Saurimo)
1941, Dec. 25	Son David born
1946	Furlough in Scotland
1948, Jan. 2	Daughter Helen born
1948, April 6	Left for Camaxilo with George Wiseman & Donald McLeod on first trek through Shinji country
1948	Second and third trips to Shinjiland
1949	Fourth trip to Shinjiland
1950	Fifth and sixth trips to Shinjiland
1951	Seventh trip to Shinjiland

1952-57	Eighth to fifteenth trips to Shinjiland
1954-55	Furlough in Scotland
1961	New Fields based in Rhodesia (Zimbabwe)
1964	Beginnings in Malawi
1967	Furlough in Scotland
1968	Survey of Botswana
1974	Furlough in Scotland
1975-79	Further work in Salisbury, Rhodesia - mainly writing and publishing
1978	Last furlough in Scotland
1979, Nov. 29	Crawford Allison passed into the presence of God, and was buried in Salisbury.

Appendix 2

Memoirs and tributes from some of his missionary colleagues

From Willie and Betty Hastings, Fish Hoek, South Africa

The first time I set eyes on Robert Allison (as he was known in Scotland) was at the Kilmarnock Missionary Conference shortly after he and Mrs Allison returned home after their first term in Angola. It was his graphic description of the needs and triumphs of the gospel in that land that started a desire in my soul to go there in service for Christ if He so guided me. He and George Wiseman had done a great job as pioneers in the north and so he spoke and wrote with great assurance and conviction about the need and opportunities there.

Robert Allison suffered much physically for many years owing to the very primitive and disease-ridden areas into which they ventured with the soul-saving and life-reforming Evangel of Christ. He was uncomplaining in it all and spent much time in the Scriptures which he loved, resulting in ability second to none in expounding them and also in radiating from his personality the Lord whom he served.

His reputation as an accomplished linguist had spread far and near before we ever got to Angola in 1953 but we weren't long on the field until we realised and witnessed that such a reputation was completely without exaggeration. He was not only a master of Chokwe but spoke and preached in a number of other languages as well. What could God not do with a man totally yielded to Him and His service, even though his background was that of a humble brick-layer and who had no advanced education in his boyhood? His habit of rising early in the morning paid great dividends. Visiting those northern regions in the early 1960's I could only be deeply impressed with what God had done through him and a few colleagues in a region where a few years before heathen darkness ruled supreme. Even today, and in spite of over 20 years of war and trouble, hundreds of New Testament churches exist and go on for the glory of God.

During a brief visit to our area with Mrs Allison and David, one afternoon a messenger came in calling us to go and help them as their car was stuck in a roadside village. Stuck it was! right down to the running boards, as he hadn't realised that the ground was much softer and wetter in that part of the world. However, they were unperturbed as they sat under a tree with a few local folks speaking about the Saviour until help would arrive to retrieve them. He had the heart of an evangelist and found it difficult not to reach out with the message even though he was only spending a few days in that locality.

In the early 60's, having moved to Rhodesia because of conditions in Angola, the Allisons and Wisemans launched out with the same dogged zeal into the work of the gospel amongst a very different people with a very difficult language which they soon mastered, and in which they produced a lot of Emmaus literature and booklets for the help of the local Christians - this all with the precarious health which afflicted him, and also his advancing years. A number of African churches were soon established in new areas, and as the years went on more workers including ourselves arrived to help them.

Robert Allison was a pioneer at heart and tried to reach out into backward areas where the gospel was greatly needed. During a visit with him to one of these districts where a hall was in the process of being built, we arrived late at night because of the bad roads. After erecting the tent and making some food, I almost had to carry him to his bed as he was utterly weary and exhausted. I actually wondered how I'd find him in the morning. You can imagine my great surprise when about 6 a.m. my senior colleague gave my bed a shake and presented me with a lovely hot cup of tea! "Time to get up Willie, they will soon be here for a meeting!" This was the loving spirit of this man of God who was so like his Master who "came not to be served but to serve and to give His life a ransom for many".

During our years together in Zimbabwe we had a number of happy and profitable visits to Beira in Mozambique to encourage a godly Portuguese brother by the name of Nascimento Freire. The preaching over there was usually in Portuguese, but sometimes in Shona in the country districts, and Robert Allison with his great desire for the advancement of the gospel in that land gained also quite a knowledge of the Sena language to the north where brother Freire and others had done a good work in former years. Today God's work goes on in that country through the efforts of other workers in spite of the havoc wrought by over twenty years of war and destruction.

Robert Allison in spite of his many physical problems lived an exemplary missionary life to the end with the love of Christ and love for the needy burning in his soul.

W Hastings, August 1998

From Gordon and Margaret Jones, Bulawayo, Zimbabwe

Mrs Allison came out to Africa in 1937, with Mr & Mrs Rew, Margaret's parents, on the same boat to Lobito. Margaret remembers that very well - Robert was there to meet his bride-to-be. It was soon after that he sustained a nasty attack of amoebic dysentery the results of which plagued him for rest of his life. The result was that he had a "thorn" to live with through so many years. What can one say to these things? Through the years that followed, the never-failing kindness of God was at all times present with them.

It is so easy and habitual to project the image of the husband and say little of the wife behind the scenes. If ever it was true to say that "behind every good man there is a good woman", it was true of Robert and Margaret Allison. We had occasions after 1972 in Rhodesia to see this loving care so demonstrated. There have been other instances on the mission field where one might justifiably ask the question, Would the brother concerned have been able to achieve what was achieved without the support and never-failing care of the wife so often in the background? No doubt all will be made clear in a coming day. My memory of them is of a couple devoted to the Lord, and dedicated to His work wherever that might be.

There was only one occasion when Robert and I shared ministry together in English; it was at a ministry conference in the 70's at 'Restawhile', convened by the assembly in Salisbury, a real time of happy and profitable fellowship together during a few carefree days. He was a gifted linguist, and used his gifts wherever possible, no doubt at times under stress, yet the Lord continued to enable him until the end, when he was called into the presence of His Lord and Master.

Gordon Jones, August 1998

From Jim and Irene Legge, Serowe, Botswana.

He was one of the many great Scottish missionaries associated with this land of Botswana. When we came to Africa in 1968 we lived with Gran and Granpa Allison, as they were lovingly known by our two children, Judith and Crawford, in what was then Salisbury, Rhodesia. It was as we lived and worked with him that the many facets of his life would be revealed to us.

He was a man of the 'daybreak'. By this I mean, before anybody was up and moving in his household, he already had been up, pouring over the Holy Scriptures, having fellowship with the Lord he loved. He told me no matter what book of the Bible he was studying, Old or New Testament, he sought to find Christ first in the pages of the book. More than once, we were wakened by the clatter of his typewriter, as he sought to put some of his thoughts into print.

He was wholehearted in everything he did. He never walked slow. Nothing was done half, and everything was done as fast as he could do it. You see, he believed that he had only one life, and he must pack into that life all that he could while he was still able.

He was a man of untiring vision as far as the assembly work was concerned. That is what brought him to Botswana, along with George Wiseman, seeking an open door for the gospel. There were no assemblies in this country in these days. But he did not only open doors to countries, he also had a burden on his heart for the assemblies that had been planted there.

He had an unusual gift in languages. If he found an open door in a country, he set about learning the languages of that country and began producing tracts for the spread of the gospel. It was he who gave us our first lessons in Setswana, and I remember, after he listened to me preaching, he would kindly point out some grammatical mistakes that I had made.

He had a unique gift in communicating the message of the gospel which he so dearly loved. His use of African proverbs and stories all served to make the message clearer to his hearers. He came to visit us here in Serowe for the opening of our hall. One sister, after listening to him, said in her own language, "*Monna yo o itse go gama* (That man knows how to milk the cow)". She recognised in him one who could take the Holy Scriptures and make them understandable and meaningful to our daily lives.

He was a very generous man, and many a time as young missionaries when things were difficult for us, he supplied our need. He had an old Land Rover, and when we were guided of the Lord to come to Botswana, he gave it to us for the work of the Lord. But he knew as well that we would need literature for the spread of the gospel, and he contacted Dr Merriweather from Molepolole, and he was able to have tracts and Emmaus courses translated. His son, David, was a tremendous help, for it was through him that these courses were duplicated and sent to us. The same courses we use today, although we have updated the Setswana and put them into book-form.

Thus, he was our spiritual mentor, our great missionary example, and often passed on to us words of surpassing wisdom, which today we use. He said to us:

- "Always err on the side of grace."
- "Above everything else, be honest, and you will never be afraid of yesterday."
- "You look after the Lord's work, and the Lord will look after you."

We have proved these things to be true.

For many of us, we live in Africa, but it could be said truly of him, "Africa was in him." But we must also mention Granny, his wife. He could never have done all of this work if it were not for her unfailing care and devotion to him. We were with him when he died, and I remember saying to him, "Granpa, you taught us how to live and to serve the Lord, now you have taught us how to die." Such was his example, in life or death.

So, we salute the memory of a man who gave us a chance, and through his vision, the assembly work began in Botswana.

Jim and Irene Legge, August 1998

From Roy Wood, Plymouth, England

We first enjoyed happy fellowship with Mr and Mrs Allison over 42 years ago before we were married.

He was the master of colloquial Chokwe. His translation of *Jungle Doctor's Fables* still leaves people spellbound as they listen (fascinated may be a better word). We appreciate his Topical Concordance in Chokwe, and even now I see brethren using it in preparing their messages.

In 1996 I used his typed notes in Portuguese and Chokwe in preparing messages on the Holy Spirit in Ephesians. At one meeting I asked the believers if they understood what was meant by "the earnest of our inheritance", and "being sealed with the Holy Spirit of promise". They replied in the negative. Thereafter I quoted from his notes, and they said, " Now we understand!" and some doubts which had arisen about the eternal security of the believer were completely removed.

We entered into other men's labours. In 1970, a hall was built at Cafunfu (being an extension of the Camaxilo work). In 1996 we flew in with Brian Howden after it had been besieged in 1995. Over one thousand believers remembered the Lord, and we had over 1300 people at the Gospel service. We could only bow our heads in worship and praise for what God has done.

I can remember Robert Allison's illustrations and stories in Chokwe, He would linger on the ending of words. When I try to imitate him, the believers who knew him recognise it; and they still quote him. He was quick and alert, with a real sense of humour, and in his prime no one could lay bricks faster than him.

My favourite story is of the bush fires turning everything black, and then it rains, and all is green again - "beauty for ashes". To work in Angola, you need to be a born optimist to believe it will be green again, and that anything beautiful will ever appear again. We still hope that peace will be restored. The people of God have suffered so much.

Robert Allison was a sterling example of one who pressed forward to the mark whatever the pain, whatever the cost.

Roy Wood, August 1998

Poems

Farewell for Mr. Robert Allison, in Galston, December 13, 1967

What deep emotions surge within your breast
As in this sacred place you stand once more,
And call to your remembrance through the years
The men of God who sent you on your way,
Who gave to you the hand of fellowship,
And bade you speed upon your chosen path;
A path of service in the gospel cause,
To Portuguese Angola, where dense tribes
In pagan ignorance and darkness dwelt,
In terror of a wicked spirit world!

Forth with their blessing on your head you went,
A stripling from a simple Christian home,
Not from a mansion of the worldly great,
To blaze a trail where none before had gone;
And pioneer the gospel of God's grace,
And carry to the lips of dying men
A draught of living water from the Lord.

How oft from Bankhead's humble cot you came
To worship in this sacred meeting place,
With saintly men whose influence today
Still lingers in this hall of memories.
Yours was no easy Christian pathway then.
Along two miles of winding ways you walked,
On summer morns when songbirds cheered the road,

On wintry days when snow made going hard.
E'en yet the scenes are vivid in your mind:
The river Irvine gliding toward the west
To join the sea some dozen miles away,
Past Ladyton, Goatfoot and Grougar Rows.

Surrounded by a wall with iron gate
Nearby there stood the ruined tiny church
Whose time-worn stones with moss were overgrown,
Built centuries before the Hastings came
To occupy the spacious Loudoun lands,
Perhaps by followers of Kentigern,
Or missioners from Ninian's Whithorn Isle.
An eerie place by night that churchyard was.
Owls hooted from their haunts and yew trees cast
A frightening gloom, or creaked with chilling sound
On stormy night. Within the church there lie
In leaden caskets stored in narrow vault
The bodies of successive Loudoun lords.
Perhaps the shadow cast by arching trees
Was pierced by fitful gleams from oil-fed lamps
That lit the well-kept homes of Loudounkirk,
That picturesque Ferm Toun of former days.
Your way lay past the Houston's cream-washed home,
Near auld Tom Parker's tempting apple trees,
To join the railroad built to transport coal
From Loudoun Number One and Bankhead mines
To furnish cargo for the boats at Troon.
Oft have you heard the engine's strident notes
Warn of its nearer coming. Shift the points
For wee bankhead, big Bankhead and Loudoun.
Across the wooden bridge your way might tend,
Or, turning to the left 'mong leafy trees
Beside the fields the Clachan family farmed,
Along the river bank and o'er the bridge,
The Muckle Brig by locals fondly called.

High o'er the cross there stood the Parish Church,
Its four-faced clock a well-known monument;
But past its massive gates you made your way
To reach that trim and well-built meeting place,
The Glebedykes Hall, to serve and worship there.

E'er that had come that memorable day,
The day you heard the call to serve abroad.
'Twas summertime, and folks from far and near
In Ayrshire came to sit on grassy slopes
By Jacob's Ladder in the weaving town,
Newmilns, quaint village on the Irvine banks.
Among them sat three earnest Christian youths,
Houston and Templeton and Allison,
Attracted by the missionary's themes
To be discoursed upon that afternoon.
Attent, they hear, and listened while one spoke
Of words the Saviour said, "And other sheep
I have; them I must also bring." Like goads
The words were fastened in their minds,
And two responded to the Master's call
To yield their lives for service overseas.
One laboured faithfully in Trinidad,
And gathered other sheep into the flock,
His name respected still by people there.

'Tis not without significance your name
Has Crawford in it, linking you with one
Who spent his lifetime in dark Africa,
For two-and-twenty years without a break
In Portuguese Angola, "thinking black".
Others had gone before. Through jungle dense
Fred Arnot reached the Garanganze land.
There joined him Swann and Faulkner, noble men;
And when they met they clasped hands round the flag,
And sang till cruel Mushidi's kingdom rang,

Jesus shall reign wher'ere the sun
Doth his successive journeys run;
His kingdom stretch from shore to shore,
Till moons shall wax and wane no more.

What memories surround that favoured spot,
From Benguela to Lake Mweru's verge,
Where Crawford's model town, Luanza, stands,
To many known as The Beloved Strip.
Names cluster to the mind as one recalls
John Wilson, Gammon, George and Pomeroy.
The Campbells, Fishers, Arnots, Lamonds, Sims,
The godly Cobbe, the Antons and McPhies.
The jungle soil has been enriched by dust
Of sleeping Christians who await the trump
To call them on the resurrection morn.

Back to those scenes you once again set out,
Rejoicing in the triumphs you have known.
Among the Chokwes you have labored long,
The tribe that blocked the missionary's path.
Through snake-infested grasslands you have trekked,
Crossed death-trap bridges, forded swollen streams,
And rafted o'er Zambezi near its source.
The Lualaba and Lufira floods
Could not deter you as you pioneered
Among forgotten tribes who had not heard
The messages of God's redeeming grace.

What joy it must have been when darkness fell
And blazing fires lit up the forest dense
To gather native Christians, won at length
To hear the Word, and sing in native hymns
The praises of the Saviour, yours and theirs.
That sphere of service is no longer yours;
But from another centre still the Word

Goes forth in printed form to other folks,
To heathen tribes you could not reach on foot,
To door-closed Mozambique, to Zambia,
And to Malawi, once Nyasaland,
To countless others you have never seen.

Go once again. In strength divine go forth.
It is the Lord's command. He will not fail.
Slack not your tasks, for the reward is sure.
Go! labour on until the race is run.
Go! faint not till the long, long fight is won.
Go! and your rest will come at set of sun.
Go! Sweet will be your Master's praise, Well done!

Andrew Borland (12.12.67)

Farewell in Galston, December 3, 1974

His name is not inscribed on history's page;
He is not reckoned as a worldly sage;
The realm of science does not know his name;
In art and literature lies not his fame;
Yet he is known for work which he has done,
In almost every land beneath the sun;
For where men speak their native English tongue,
The name of Robert Allison is sung.
E'en in dark Africa's Beloved Strip
His name's on almost every Christian lip.
For even those who have not seen his face
Know that by sovereign and redeeming grace,
As pioneer where white foot had not trod
He took the liberating Word of God.
The forests of Angola heard his voice,
He made believing Chokwe folk rejoice.
Then in Malawi and in Mozambique
He made his business Afric's sons to seek.
He's travelled long and wide, and laid in store

An endless fund of precise native lore.
Not academic, yet few know as he
The tongues the natives speak, whate'er they be.
With scholar's pen, devotion, fertile mind,
With skill in words, he's left, for years, behind
The Book translated into native ways
Of speech and art that "Thinking Black" displays.
Dan Crawford was the author of that book;
And Crawford Allison's the name Bob took
In honour of that worthy pioneer
Who built Luanza after many a year
In Africa's long grass to spread abroad
In native tongues the wondrous works of God.

Our subject was of very humble birth
Who parents were not great ones of the earth,
A pious pair who taught the lad the road
That leads to truth and righteousness and God.
Pupil at school in Galston Higher Grade;
At fourteen left to learn bricklaying trade.
He grew to early manhood and became
A preacher of the One who bears the name
Of Saviour of the world who gave command
To carry gospel news to every land
Where men in ignorance and darkness dwell.
The apostolic band set forth to tell
In glowing terms the measure of God's love
Who sent the Son Redeemer from above,
The Son who died but triumphed o'er the grave
And lives in power the lives of men to save.

Then followed noble preachers, pioneers
Who brought to Britain in those distant years
The message of salvation, and to Kent
Came Augustine, from Rome by Greg'ry sent.
Saint Patrick came to where the shamrock grows;
To brave Columba Scotia tribute owes,

For from the Emerald Isle he boldly came
To stern Iona with the Saviour's name.
Through centuries the gospel truth has spread
Along these shores, and missioners have sped
O'er land and sea to take the saving word
To men and women who had never heard.
Carey and Hudson Taylor, Paton too,
Arnot and Hannington are but a few.
Crawford of Greenock, still a slender youth,
To Afric's forests took redeeming truth.
Some thirty years he served, then came the word
The servant had been called to his reward.

A host of others followed, noble, brave,
To tell the story of the power to save;
Among them was a slim-built Galston lad
Who answered to the vision he had had
When on a summer's Saturday he heard
The call to take to others God's own word;
And Templeton and he responded then
To take the gospel to their fellow men
Who dwelt in darkness in the chains of sin.
Thus did their missionary work begin;
The one to serve in Trinidad was sent,
While Allison to wild Angola went.

Nigh forty years have passed, and now once more
We wish him well, another furlough o'er.
With Margaret, his dear faithful partner true
Who's battled with him their long campaign through;
And as we say "good-bye", for both we pray
That God will go before them in the way
Will keep and use them till the task is done
And victory over evil forces won.

Andrew Borland (28.11.74)